Sustainability for Retail

Sustainability for Retail

How Retail Leaders Create Environmental, Social, & Cultural Innovations

Vilma Barr and Ken Nisch

BEP
BUSINESS EXPERT PRESS
Leader in applied, concise business books

Sustainability for Retail: How Retail Leaders Create Environmental, Social, & Cultural Innovations

Copyright © Business Expert Press, LLC, 2023.

Cover design by Chris Redmon

Front cover images:

Upper left: Exterior, Selfridges, London. Courtesy, Selfridges.

Upper right: Planet Earth rising over moon's horizon, taken from Apollo II spacecraft. Courtesy, NASA. Inset, Project Earth logo, courtesy, Selfridges.

Lower left: Interior, Timberland, King of Prussia Mall, suburban Philadelphia, Pennsylvania. Courtesy, VF Corporation.

Lower right: (Re)Store department, Galeries Lafayette, Paris. Courtesy, Galeries Lafayette.

Interior design by Exeter Premedia Services Private Ltd., Chennai, India

First published in 2022 by
Business Expert Press, LLC
222 East 46th Street, New York, NY 10017
www.businessexpertpress.com

ISBN-13: 978-1-95152-790-7 (paperback)
ISBN-13: 978-1-95152-791-4 (e-book)

Business Expert Press Environmental and Social Sustainability
for Business Advantage Collection

First edition: 2022

10 9 8 7 6 5 4 3 2 1

To the spirit of the Swadeshi movement and its founder Mahatma Gandhi; true to the spirit of social, cultural, and environmental sustainability.

—Ken Nisch

To my extraordinary children, Lesley and Glenn, whose thoughtfulness and sincere friendship have been prime sustaining factors in my life.

—Vilma Barr

Description

Sustainability for Retail: How Retail Leaders Create Environmental, Social, & Cultural Innovations, by Vilma Barr and Ken Nisch, AIA, is an important international overview of the role of retail in the worldwide climate crisis. The focus is on apparel and related products brought to the retail marketplace, from supply chain to selling floor displays. These classifications are quoted as responsible for 10 percent of the world's carbon emissions, one of the top three industries responsible for polluting the environment.

While it will take the combined efforts of the world's largest and most industrialized nations to control the practices that have led up to this situation affecting the global population, *Sustainability for Retail* presents the successes that have been achieved in the private sector. The book presents interviews with leaders of firms ranging from multinational operators of retail stores to owners of specialty boutiques, from widely distributed brands to purveyors of limited collections, to reports on the technologies creating fabrics from natural products and reprocessed waste.

Behind each story and report described is an example of the strong determination of an individual or the commitment of organizational management to establish and uphold practices that cut the energy used in production, support providers of raw materials with living wages and lifestyles, and mount campaigns to educate the consumer on supporting products that are part of the circular economy. Resale, reuse, and remake comprise a widespread and escalating movement that didn't exist even a decade ago to extend the life cycle of products that previously had a high potential of becoming landfill. It has become big business, sanctioned with promotions across the retail board, from mass merchandisers to small local workshops.

The combined depth of the co-author's experiences brings the reader a comprehensive guide to the forces driving the advancements in the sustainability movement and its growth, virtually daily, throughout private sectors of the retail universe. *Sustainability for Retail* offers businesses and consumers alike, an insight into making their most beneficial decisions, for themselves and for the greater good.

Keywords

sustainability; circular economy; retail design; fashion; consumerism; consumption; environment; environmentalism; transparency; accountability; technology; global economy; cultural heritage; resale; distribution; supply chain; climate change

Contents

Testimonials

"Vilma and Ken dared to go where few others have by undertaking voluminous amounts of research to create the only published work that presents the enormous issue of sustainability across the retail industry, including on an international scale, its impact from sourcing through to consumption. They brilliantly define the global problems and how both the public and private efforts are dealing with it in the present, as well as providing a vision for a hopeful future."—**Robin Lewis, CEO, The Robin Report**

"Today, managing social impact and sustainability efforts has become a business critical initiative for companies in every sector as they strive to contribute to the health and well-being of their global and local communities. Sustainability for Retail: How Retail Leaders Create Environmental, Social, & Cultural Innovations *underscores the importance of that work and provides the critical guidance needed for companies to take a holistic approach towards embedding social impact, sustainability, and innovation across their company culture."*—**William P. Lauder, Executive Chairman, The Estée Lauder Companies**

"There is a serious opportunity for policymakers to insist that once and for all kick the highly polluting, environmentally damaging, carbon-intense industries and business practices of the last century or more. This is an once-in-a-lifetime opportunity to change towards a low-carbon, sustainable future."—**Lord Greg Barker, Executive Chairman, En+ Group**

"This book contains examples of organizations which have done great work, and will help with spreading the message. Ultimately, it's up to individual companies to affect meaningful change! I spend a great deal of time talking to peers and other organizations about why it makes sense to follow green principles in doing business. As soon as an organization understands, we get them started to move forward. While the solutions are often industry and business-specific, it is very rare to not find solutions with overlap benefits to

the planet and profit for any business today."—**Anirban Ghosh, Chief Sustainability Officer, Mahindra Group**

"For over 20 years, Simons have been innovating to ensure our social responsibility and reduce our environmental footprint. Our initiatives include expanding our supply of organic and recycled fibers, multiplying our eco-social partnerships, and optimizing the energy consumption of our infrastructure. We are convinced that fashion can be a source of beauty while also being sustainable."—**Peter Simons, Chief Merchant, La Maison Simons Inc.**

"Disposable fashion is draining our wallets and wreaking havoc on the planet, and consumers are waking up to this waste. They seek products made ethically as well as for their value and variety. Retailers who don't integrate a circular component into their business models will be left behind. Clothing reuse is a big step toward a new normal in the fashion industry."—**James Reinhart, CEO and co-founder, thredUP**

"Conscientious consumerism is changing the relationship consumers have with brands. That calls for brands to take a proactive stance on environmental, social and corporate governance (ESG) issues. This groundbreaking book by Vilma Barr and Ken Nisch, Sustainability for Retail, *shows the way. It provides a comprehensive analysis of some 70 brands that have risen to the ESG challenge across a full spectrum of brands, from "mass"–Target, Walmart, Kohl's, Nestlé–to "class"–LVMH, Tiffany, Kering, Harrods. For the future, brands must build sustainability into their business model."*—**Pamela N. Danziger, President/Founder, Unity Marketing**

"Our planet Earth is under threat, and if we don't embrace sustainability in every aspect of our actions, we will do it great damage. This book creates a dialogue around creating sustainability in retail, an industry plagued with extreme consumerism and hence impacting greatly as an environment polluter. Nisch and Barr's ardent description and narrative around very useful initiatives in retail opens up a new perspective for all of now and to look ahead. It is a perfect read for people who love retail, to love it more, be guilt free, and be proud that retail can be sustainable!"—**Sanjay Agarwal, Managing Director, Future Research Design Company**

"There may be no time more exciting in the retail industry than now to be a part of such dynamic change. It's time to fully embrace the age-old phrase, "reduce, reuse, recycle," to new ways of using materials and even existing spaces and fixtures to create the new physical retail. It creates under a whole new mindset, as described throughout Sustainability for Retail.*"*—**Harry Cunningham, former Senior Vice President, Store Planning, Design and Visual Merchandising, Saks Fifth Avenue**

"This important book begins the conversation around creating sustainability in fashion. The industry has been woefully neglectful of the impact it has on the environment as the third largest polluter. Through dozens of case studies and interviews, Barr and Nisch tell the story of how individuals are leading the changes needed to make fashion more environmentally friendly. This book is inspiring and a perfect place to begin one's journey on the road to sustainability."—**David Jaffe, Chairman, SubjectToClimate**

"A key insight running through this book are the stories of individuals, brands, and companies that have decided to step up to the challenge of making human ecology one of the cornerstones of their business. These ethical pioneers bring a sense of heightened awareness to environmental sustainability, social, and cultural innovation and you'll be inspired to join them on this journey." —**J Mays, Former Group Vice President, Design, Ford Motor Company**

"Sustainability for Retail is a great work that states its strong case simply and attractively, making it easy for the reader to comprehend. We can't deny the harm to the Earth that has been created, but I, like the others in this book, are doing all that we can to contribute to improving the world's environment. Thank you for having me as a part of this project"—**Nina Lekhi, Founder, Baggit**

"The environmental problems we face today——from climate change and environmental injustice to the nature crisis——demand solutions and approaches that are unique to our time. On this Earth Day, Let us also reflect on and recommit to this simple and time-tested idea: that we can and must pursue environmental quality for the benefit of all people in this country."—**Clair Brenda Mallory, Chair of the Council on Environmental Quality, a White House agency.**

To Our Readers

There is far more relevant information on the topic of this book, *Sustainability for Retail: How Retail Leaders Create Environmental, Social, & Cultural Innovations*, than we could fit into one volume. We have profiled outstanding individuals and organizations that are doing excellent work to further move the industry needle over from "disposable" retail to circular retail, but there are more examples than we are able to mention here. We hope to continue our research, analysis, and reporting in the future.

In our involvement over the past nearly three years to assemble the text and images for this book, we have seen a fundamental shift in looking at a manufacture-sell-and-dispose model changing to a model that emphasizes the future model for products that retailers will sell to customers who are looking for liquidity, social conscience about waste, and the effect on the environment, or who see it as both an opportunity as well as a responsibility to consume in a different way.

An entire economy has been created around "previously owned," to encompass retail apparel, furniture, home furnishings, and ultimately to construction, by harvesting value. This is an outreach process to help people better use their clothes and other produces. There are examples of the dedication to sustainability as exhibited by small boutiques as well as the far-reaching efforts of the world's major conglomerates.

Retail industry leaders, in dealing with the impact of COVID-19, have still made great strides in integrating sustainability into their operations. *Sustainability for Retail* includes news of advancements ranging from applying technology to the entire system to visual communications to educating the buying public about the fast-track pace represented by sectors of the industry.

Our book serves as a guide to one of retail's most important phases in its history as one of the primary drivers of the world economy.

—Vilma Barr
Ken Nisch

Preface

Passion, Commitment, and Energy: Creating a Sustainable Retail Industry

I received a call, nearly three years ago, from my co-author Vilma Barr. Vilma and I have known each other for many years through her role as a writer and thought leader within the retail design business. Her comment, unusually somber with a great deal of gravitas, for the world of retail, fashion, and consumerism, was that there is a void in the communication of the scope of sustainability, and therefore an interest around the topic of sustainability. There is a need, she said, to educate the international market on what is being done and what should be considered for the future of the health of the planet.

Growing up in the 1960s and 1970s, environmentalism was something that was radical, involved marches, and a tearing down of the establishment. Conversely, it was about escape, nature, a place away from everyday life. Neither of these roles, one angry and the other in denial, fit well with the business world as a platform for change. Yes, as an architect, various organizations, structures, and rating systems, were brought into place with "awards" (sounding much like a bank or frequent traveler programs) assuring gold, silver, or platinum status, for your efforts. A plaque would ensue, fees would be paid to the organization, and the "check box" of sustainability would be achieved.

In talking about how society was changing, elements such as transparency, accountability, from investment banks to concerned individuals, was growing, the time seemed right to think about a book that looked at sustainability more as an ecosystem, bringing together science, culture, technology, and even art. Together, they evolve into sustainability—environmental, social, and cultural.

My career as a design and brand consultant to retail organizations, with its "privilege" of traveling throughout the United States, and the world, including Europe, India, Brazil, the Middle East, put me in a position to see what lack of sustainability, excess consumption, and waste can build and destroy. On the other hand, how often, in small and timeless ways, societies make and make do with the lack of resources that they have had for generations, yet succeed in creating beautiful craft and art, while respecting the environment in simple and integrated ways.

It prompted the question: How do industries and brands, in the context of culture, live and learn from elements inherent in who they are and where they are from that influence their response in today's global economy? These influences might range from cultural heritage, values that grow from families, beliefs, and are a key part of who these brands and companies become. How do they both give to and responsibly take from the world? Some brands take on massive goals: water quality, fair trade, and renewable energy. Others have much more day-to-day and granular goals, with businesses that help make lives and places better, one village, one family, and one person at a time.

We found great examples of companies worldwide, in every continent, that understand that to change "things," first, you have to change "hearts." These companies use their economic "pulpit" in some ways subtly, others more through economic power and coercion, to bring those businesses that they influence into a better place, and effectively demonstrate the ultimate win/win: that sustainability delivers to all touch points along the retail supply and distribution chain.

What became clear, reflected in the examples included in this book, is that **people, and people with passion, commitment, and energy, ultimately can change things for the better.** While governments can legislate, industries can mandate; ultimately, it is individuals, we as individual business leaders, educators, and most importantly as consumers, that through our personal choices and our willingness to influence those across all segments of consumers, that real, sustainable, and equitable change will take place.

—Ken Nisch

June, 2022

Acknowledgments

To Chris Redmon, for keeping the text and the images current throughout the book's development and handling the myriad details of organizing the final manuscript. To MaryBeth Turmel at JGA, for assisting in obtaining needed approvals for text and images. To the many helpful contacts at the firms that participated in supplying information, photos, and graphics. Particular appreciation to Molly Cuffe at VF Corporation; Sophie Lyndon at Selfridges; Natalie Tomlin at thredUp; and Chiara Cortesano at Tiffany & Co.

Introduction

Retail Sustainability Leadership,
A Private/Public Effort

The private sector has invested in sustainable programs of all sizes for their markets, and for the greater good. Now, the United States should lead an international regulatory effort to make retail a zero-sum contributor to the climate crisis.

In our research for this book, it became clear that the damage to the climate by the apparel and accessories industries ranks as the third worst perpetrator, following energy and agricultural. Rolled into one category, fashion, whether classic or trendy, generates $2.5 trillion annually worldwide and employs more than 75 million people working from sourcing to retailing. It has been identified as responsible for polluting the Earth and oceans at virtually every step of the process. The fashion industry is a big time polluter, responsible for 10 percent of the world's carbon emissions.

The heroes of fashion industry remission can be found in the private sector: huge multinationals like Nestlé, icons of retailing like Selfridges and Simons, and dedicated manufacturers and retailers of all sizes, from Patagonia to Tentree. They operate in every populated continent on the planet. We are pleased with the response from the companies profiled in this book.

The advancement on achieving sustainable goals by individual entrepreneurs and corporate leaders have been remarkable. Their stories do not make the headlines in the pages of business journals or segments of the nightly news reports. They are the real movers-and-shakers in the advancements made in the retail industry's efforts to affect the negative influence of climate change, by applying such factors as the conservation of raw materials, and the equatable treatment of all who work in the many sectors of the retail manufacturing, distribution, and selling products to the ultimate user.

That's why the authors undertook the preparation of this book. It has taken three years to contact, talk to, and report on our findings.

Private industry's efforts can go only so far to halt the onrush of warming temperatures, rampant forest fires, and devastating floods. Multination advisory councils formed by the United Nations, such as the Climate Accord, are wide-reaching but are voluntarily in their structure. The United States is still ranked as the richest country in the world. Total retail sales for 2020, even with the negative effect of the pandemic, will reach $5.506 trillion, an increase of 0.8 percent over 2019.

It's up to the United States to offer meaningful suggestions for a large-scale oversight and regulation. President Biden has brought the country back into the Paris Agreement, and has expressed a desire to make the United States a leader in the climate fight at home and abroad. As part of this effort, he can set the agenda on how to clean up the global fashion industry, paving the way for other nations to do their part.

A Private/Public Partnership

Other countries are beginning to realize that governments can play a meaningful role in supporting the fashion industry as a by-product of overall sustainability goals. France, in 2016, adopted a strategy, "Let's Innovate Together," to prompt businesses to take corporate social responsibility (CSR) to the next level and encourage social and cooperative economic initiatives, but none have yet created a Ministry of Fashion. Barbara Pompili in July 2020 was named by Prime Minister Emmanuel Macron as Minister of Ecological Transition, cited as the No. 2 post in the French Government. Part of her mission, which is to guide sustainable development, climate effects, energy transition, and biodiversity, is also to focus on the fashion industry's footprint, championing policies such as banning brands from destroying unsold products, and making microplastic filters mandatory in industrial washing machines.

In the February 9, 2021 issue of *Fast Company*, columnist Elizabeth Segran headlined her feature, "President Biden, appoint a fashion czar!" The fashion czar could advocate for the Congress to pass laws that would hold brands accountable for labor violations that take place across their supply chains and incentivize companies to come up with creative technologies that would tackle pollution. This individual could transform America into a global hub of sustainable and humane fashion, ensuring it stays a thriving part of the economy.

Two weeks later, on February 23, *Fast Company* published a follow-up by Ms. Segran, "Pressure mounts on President Biden to appoint a fashion czar," reporting that more than 80 brands, experts, and organizations signed on to a letter asking President Biden to help make the fashion industry more sustainable and humane. It was delivered to the White House and members of the Congress. Two signatories to the letter—Lynda Grose, chair of the fashion department at the California College of the Arts, and Caroline Priebe, founder of the Center for the Advancement of Garment Making—are creating a working group to continue campaigning for a fashion czar and identifying top priorities for such an appointee.

A multifaceted approach can be considered, not unlike the Civilian Conservation Corps established by President Franklin Roosevelt in 1933, which employed three million workers to create public-related environmental projects around the country. Supporters of the concept today point out that the U.S. Government could help create green-type jobs in the fashion industry, leading to the country's economic recovery and help to alleviate the pandemic's economic blow to the many suppliers and retailers throughout the United States, from major metropolises to small towns.

In the meantime, we have "America is All In," a coalition headed by Michael R. Bloomberg, the United Nations Secretary-General's Special Envoy for Climate Ambition and Solutions, to drive a societywide mobilization that upholds the country's commitment to domestic and international climate action. Fashion's contribution should be at the top of their list.

SECTION 1

Environmental/Operational

Introduction

You can be fighting for the planet and dress sustainably without having to sacrifice being stylish, fashionable, and professional.

—Tan France

Retail researchers have determined that paying a bit more that goes toward funding ethical and responsible consumption—be it social, cultural, or environmental—is a price that consumers are likely willing to pay. The who, what, when, where, and how we buy—with accessible, transparent, and credible information to make these decisions, whether it be B2B or B2C—are germain to the decision to purchase in this environment of heightened awareness and accountability in today's world.

The Real Cost of Fashion

- The $2.5 trillion fashion industry is one of the biggest polluters, accounting for roughly 10 percent of global greenhouse gas emissions—more than all international flights and shipping in total, according to the United Nations Environment Program, and the second biggest consumer of water, enough to meet the needs of five million people every year.
- Most of the fabrics in cheap garments are synthetics and polyesters, which are derived from oil and petroleum production.
- Unlike wool or cotton, synthetic particles don't biodegrade. So, when clothes are dumped into a landfill, toxic synthetic fibers pollute water sources.
- A new tank top has already emitted 6 pounds of CO_2 and used 700 gallons of H_2O in the process of manufacturing

through Sustainability For Retail delivery, representing CO_2 emissions equivalent to charging 385 smartphones and water usage of 17 standard bathtubs filled to capacity.

- Production of a pair of jeans emits 7.3 pounds of CO_2, the equivalent of driving a standard car for as long as 85 miles.
- Manufacturing sneakers results in 31 pounds of CO_2 emitted and 23,000 gallons of H_2O, comparable to the amount of water used in 23,850 cups of Starbucks.

Overproduction Leads to Waste

Between 2000 and 2015, the fashion industry doubled its production. The average shopper bought 60 percent more clothing, too, but kept each product for about half as long, according to research from consulting firm McKinsey & Co.

The production of synthetic textiles is accelerating as the demand for cheap clothes continues to rise. In turn, the amount of textiles filling landfills is skyrocketing. In the United States, people on average produce about 75 pounds of textile waste each year, according to the EPA data.

Garment waste is not only a sustainability issue but an economic problem, too. The Ellen MacArthur Foundation estimates that about $500 billion is lost every year as a result of clothing being thrown out instead of being reused or recycled.

Adapting to Full Transparency

"Every T-shirt, every garment should have transparency to see where it's made, who it's made by and the credentials of the company making it. We need to build a model so companies that share information about themselves are recognized and rewarded. You need incentives for the data providers, not just the data recipients," says Vivek Ramachandran, CEO of Serai and Ramachandran.

A transparent supply chain contributes to a more sustainable industry by requiring brands and companies to fully annotate the details of what is happening upstream and to be willing to communicate this knowledge both internally and externally. This is even more critical as discerning consumers are demanding information detailing product ingredients and materials, the source of these materials, and the working conditions in which they were produced.

"Sustainability isn't separate from a business strategy. Sustainability is integral to creating value for all stakeholders through innovation, operational excellence, and highly disciplined capital allocation," says Ramachandran.

The Consumer's Role in Retail Sustainability

According to a recent study, sixty-two percent of Gen Z consumers, those who were born after 1995, prefer to buy from sustainable brands. Researchers at the MIT Sloan School of Management found that consumers may be willing to pay 2–10 percent more for products from companies that provide greater supply chain transparency.

Larger retailers are getting into used clothing as the second-hand market booms. Consumers can help to lower their clothing footprint by reading clothing labels and researching how products were made before purchasing them, as well as buying used clothing on shopping apps or in thrift stores.

The stigma around previously worn garb is a vanishing one, and millennials and subsequent generations are embracing it. More people are becoming consignors and participating in the growth of the circular economy.

CHAPTER 1-1

Selfridges

Reinventing Retail Through Project Earth

Creating a Profitable Business that Respects the World, Builds Trust, and Embodies Creativity and Innovation

Project Earth is about us taking radical action in response to the climate crisis. Our commitments to science-based targets and a net-zero future include ensuring the use of environmentally impactful materials coming from certified sustainable sources.

— Commitment to Sustainability Selfridges

Selfridges' Project Earth initiative defines the companywide commitment to change the way shopping is practiced in its stores and beyond, serving as an industry guideline. Released in mid-August, 2020, the commitment details the deep scope of the programs currently in place and for the foreseeable future. "For a multi-brand retailer to set targets as significant as these is a considerable undertaking, and we are absolutely focused on meeting them," said Daniella Vega.

Selfridges takes justifiable pride in the fact that it has instituted sustainability in its operations for the past 18 years. Citations for their success include the World's Best Sustainability Campaign by a Department Store at a Global Department Store Summit, and the first department store (Figure 1-1.1) to achieve the Carbon Trust Triple Standard for a significant reduction of carbon, water, and waste.

Figure 1-1.1 Project Earth store banners

Photo courtesy: Selfridges & Co.

Project Earth is a roadmap to demonstrate how Selfridges believes it can lead the way to changing the way retail shopping is carried out by 2025. As stated in their media announcement, "We believe that by driving a transition to more sustainable materials, exploring new business models, and challenging the mindsets of our partners and customers as well as our own teams, we can offer an alternative perspective on retail and create a sustainable future."

Style and Sustainability

Project Earth encompasses new shopping alternatives described as having circularity at their heart, programs that put style and sustainability hand-in-hand, to be incorporated into the future of Selfridges' business. Project Earth is underpinned by three commitments: changing the materials, models, and mindsets within retail (Figure 1-1.2). Partnering with charities such as Woodland Trust and WWF (World Wildlife Fund), Selfridges' new fashion services also include:

- ReSellfridges. A collection of archive and pre-loved clothing and accessories from leading designers.
- Rent With Us. Collaboration with fashion rental service HURR Collectives to create The Selfridges Rental Collection.
- Repair With Us. The Repairs Concierge will handle repairs ranging from luxury handbags to footwear.

Figure 1-1.2 The Accessories Hall for Selfridges' Project Earth

Photo courtesy: Selfridges & Co.

Selfridges has established a Diversity Board, created to be accountable to all team members and supported by an Executive sponsor. "I will ensure that, together, we have robust discussions and take up Selfridges' invitation to 'do better', ... to experience that euphoric sense of belonging in the place we clearly love," said Melissa Clottey, Head of Food Technical and Chair of Selfridges Diversity Board, in the Selfridges publication, *Science-Based Targets: Driving Ambitious Corporate Climate Action.*

Selfridges' Ethical Trading Requirements is closely monitored for adherence to the legal regulations and the terms and conditions for doing business with the company. They state "Standards" to ensure that products sold by Selfridges are produced under humane working conditions involving respect for workers and human rights, that animals are treated and transported humanly, and that suppliers minimize their impact on the environment.

Doing the Right Thing

An internal team implements Selfridges' far-reaching sustainable programs.

Selfridges has banned the use of single-use plastic water or drink bottles, straws, carrier bags, microbeads, and packaging. In Selfridges dining facilities, foie gras is banned along with endangered fish or seafood. Selfridges published a *Good Food Guide* that helps diners make sustainable choices by selecting fish of a species that comes from sustainably managed stocks and is caught or farmed in a way that causes minimal damage to the marine environment or other wildlife.

"Green Warriors" are over 100 Selfridge employees who take part in beach cleans and tree plantings. They volunteer at retail outlets operated by Age UK. Selfridges publishes a Vegan guide that informs customers of products made with animal-derived ingredients for beauty products.

Project Earth Labeling (previously Buying Better, Inspiring Change) is a set of guidelines applied to cotton, denim, and British Makers that Selfridges developed in collaboration with the Center for Sustainable Fashion, a program under the direction of the London College of Fashion. Both institutions set their goal to reach both retailing professionals and the customers to make more informed, sustainable choices. Professor Dilys Williams, Director of the Center for Sustainable Fashion, in describing the collaboration, stated: "Selfridges is a world leader. We have to change things, what people see and what is in fashion. Selfridges has the opportunity to show the positive contribution fashion can make."

Since 2011, Selfridges **Project Ocean** represents a long-term partnership with the Zoological Society of London, seeking to protect the oceans. Activities range from funding a maritime reserve in the Philippines to the fighting of plastic pollution. They refer to a survey that said that there had been observed a patch of floating plastic estimated to be larger than the state of Texas.

A set of **fashionable reuse vessels**, commissioned by Selfridges to carry water and other liquids, is for sale in the store.

Bright New Things promotes emerging designers who emphasize sustainability in their collections, utilizing innovative new production methods. Womenswear designer Katie Jones was the recipient of a £50,000 ($62,700) award to develop her practice.

Material World was a campaign funded by Selfridges that examined sustainable textile development by pioneering designers, with a focus on the impact fabrics have on the world's environment.

Recycled coffee cups and timber. Via a process called Cupcycling, coffee cups are treated to be turned into the store's yellow carrier bags. Timber for construction is either reused from previous projects or certified from the Forestry Stewardship Council.

Communicating Sustainability

Selfridges Hot Air Webcasts

Selfridges engaged Jasmine Hemsley, London-based food, lifestyle, and wellness commentator and author, to host a six-part, SELF-Sustainable Podcast series. The theme was based on narrating examples of where luxury and good taste meet with sustainability, to make the consumer aware of steps they can take to follow the examples set by Selfridges.

Inspiring Change

The Project Earth announcement recognized that "business as usual" is not an option in a world where uncertainty is the new normal. Selfridges' rationale in investing time and energy into the launch of Project Earth is stated: "… to position itself to set the agenda for sustainable luxury retail and inspire customers to buy better and to discover the brands that are doing better."

Project Earth (Figure 1-1.3) will be supported by a program of events and activities to engage with issues, amplify conversations, and challenge mind sets by exploring the most exciting ideas in sustainability with some of the most influential thinkers in the space. A series of 13 talks, and screenings such as "Intelligence Squared," and with more than 20 events engaging with stories, brands, and services to engage customers with the future of shopping.

Let's Change the Way We Shop

As part of Selfridges' Planet Earth ongoing storewide program, RESELL-FRIDGES (Figure 1-1.4) is a curated section in the Oxford Street flagship specializing in high-quality previously owned apparel and accessories.

Figure 1-1.3 Project Earth window, Selfridges, London

Source: Theme Banners

Figure 1-1.4 Resellfridges

Photo courtesy: Selfridges & Co.

Selfridges initiated RESELLFRIDGES to offer customers a shopping initiative as a part of its sustainable Project Earth program. RESELL-FRIDGES showcases pre-loved, archival, and vintage pieces, presenting planet-friendly ways to shop and contribute to closing the loop on fabric-generated waste that is harmful to the environment.

Several expert resale vendors have taken up residency in The Corner Shop at Selfridges as part of RESELLFRIDGES; whereas on selfridges.com, customers can shop Selfridges-curated collection of previously owned pieces. For the United Kingdom and the European Union customers, directions are given to sell their own items through the site.

To counter the throw-away image of fast fashion, Selfridges urges customer support for retail models such as RESELLFRIDGES that are crucial to reducing the amount of discarded garments clogging landfills and contributing to global warming. Preowned pieces of apparel and accessories accepted for sale by Selfridges are selected for their high quality design and condition, and are priced from mid to upper

Figure 1-1.5 *Resellfridges: The Wedding*

Photo courtesy: Selfridges & Co.

range. RESELLFRIDGES: THE WEDDING (Figure 1-1.5) offers one-of-a kind pre-loved and vintage wedding outfits and accessories for brides, grooms, and best-dressed guests as part of its Project Earth sustainability commitments.

Selfridges: The Wedding

During August, 2021, THE WEDDING concept took the center stage at the Corner Shop destination on Selfridges Flagship store in London. The RESELLFRIDGES: THE WEDDING platform offers new ways to shop, giving customers access to a curation of pre-loved products from iconic brands in-store and online.

The collection includes everything needed to complete a wedding wardrobe, from designer dresses, to upcycled menswear suits, to vintage wedding rings and accessories, as well as upcycling services and a rental offering for the entire wedding party. Sebastian Manes, Executive Buying & Merchandising Director, said: "Our customers are considering how they live and shop and weddings are no exception. From vintage bridal dresses, to upcycled suits, to services that help to reimagine special pieces, RESELLFRIDGES: THE WEDDING is the destination for planet positive weddings."

RESELLFRIDGES: THE WEDDING follows the launch of Weddings at Selfridges, as Selfridges looks to become a destination for all things wedding. Couples looking for a nontraditional wedding ceremony can say "I do" in its iconic Oxford Street building with wedding packages centered around extraordinary experiences—including the Earth Lovers Wedding package, curated for the earth-conscious.

Nestlé

Focusing on Regenerative Agriculture and Environmentally Friendly Products

Redoubling Efforts to Combat Climate Change

Tackling climate change can't wait and neither can we. We have a unique opportunity to address climate change, as we operate in nearly every country in the world and have the size, scale and reach to make a difference. We will work together with farmers, industry partners, governments, non-governmental organizations and our consumers to reduce our environmental footprint.

—Mark Schneider, CEO, Nestlé S.A.

Nestlé CEO Mark Schneider leaves no doubt about his position to thwart the advancing effects of climate change. Nestlé S.A., based in Vevey, Switzerland, is the world's largest food and beverage company. Underway are measures to halve its emissions by 2030 and achieve net zero by 2050. Planned funding of $3.6 billion over the next five years is marked to accelerate its programs, and $1.33 billion for regenerative agriculture and across the supply chain.

"A company like Nestlé has been able to thrive for more than 150 years by always looking around the corner and anticipating the world's needs. This foresight is a key ingredient of our success," Schneider states. "As a good steward of the planet, Nestlé feels a moral obligation to make these changes and believes that the work we are doing is critical to the survival of supply chains and our business."

Three Main Areas Being Implemented

Regenerative agriculture. A far-reaching multination program in place has Nestlé working with over 500,000 farmers and 150,000 suppliers to support them in improving soil health and maintaining and restoring diverse ecosystems. In return, Nestlé is offering to reward farmers by purchasing their goods at a premium, buying larger quantities, and co-investing in necessary capital expenditures.

Figure 1-2.1 Nestlé's Nescafé Gold Blend Coffee ad

Reforestation program. Nestlé is scaling up its reforestation program to plant 20 million trees every year for the next 10 years in the areas where it sources ingredients. More trees mean more shade for crops, more carbon removed from the atmosphere, higher yields, and improved biodiversity and soil health. The goal of the company's primary supply chains of key commodities is to be deforestation-free by 2022, providing farming communities with greater certainty and higher incomes.

Benjamin Ware, Global Head of Responsible Sourcing for Nestlé S.A., follows the premise that reforesting is critical to reversing the loss of biodiversity and the resultant climate change. "Trees represent the benefits of providing habitat for numerous species, store water, absorb carbon dioxide, and release oxygen," he points out. Ware is part of the Nestlé team that manages the extensive planting schedule to place trees on the farms or in the immediate surroundings where the raw materials are grown that go into the Nestlé products. Planting of three million trees for the Americas start in Brazil and Mexico, and another three million to be planted in Malaysia by 2023.

Operations. The transition of its 800 sites in the 187 countries where it operates to 100 percent renewable electricity is expected within the next five years. Switching its global fleet of vehicles to lower-emission options is underway, along with implementing water protection and regeneration measures and tackling food waste.

Figure 1-2.2 Nestlé powdered milk plant in Lagos De Moreno in Mexico. This factory uses waters from the milk it processes instead of drawing on an outside supply

Environmentally Friendly Products

Expansion of its product lines of plant-based food and beverages reformulating products to make them more environmentally friendly is an ongoing program throughout the Nestlé organization. Nestlé has had its emissions reduction targets approved by the Science Based Targets initiative (SBTi), as consistent with levels required to meet the goals of the Paris Agreement.

These include *Garden Gourmet* plant-based food and supplements as well as Garden of Life supplements; *Sweet Earth* plant-based food, plus brands in the Nestlé Waters category such as *Nespresso, S.Pelblegrino, Perrier,* and *Acqua Panna*'s. Commitment to carbon neutrality by 2022, through to 2025, is in place. Annual progress updates are provided.

Nestlé, the leading international coffee roaster, is boosting sustainability spending on its flagship Nestlé coffee brand, responding to its market observation that consumers increasingly want to know where their food and drink comes from and how it is produced. This and related programs at the firm are built on more than a decade of work in environmental sustainability.

The company's long-range program aimed at its coffee labels is an estimated $787 million effort that involves responsible sourcing of all its coffee, tracing supplies back to groups of farmers, and reaching net zero carbon emissions by 2050.

The Private Sector as Sustainability Driver

Schneider is a strong proponent that private industry prioritize the implementation of broad-sustainability practices. "We should not expect comprehensive public policy and unanimity to do the job for us," he has stated. He urges his leadership peers to support, as does Nestlé, the stable and consistent government policies established as the targets of the Paris Agreement.

"Consumers care deeply about these issues as well, and if we don't listen to them, they understandably won't do business with us," Schneider implies. Regular issuance of reports will keep the public aware of Nestlé's contribution to stemming climate change. Such communications adopted by other companies will lend credence to the support of sustainability by participants at all economic levels.

Photos courtesy: Nestlé

CHAPTER 1-3

VF Corporation

Stewards of Corporate Sustainability and Responsibility

"Made for Change"

Questions posed by Ken Nisch to Sean Cady: Vice President, Global Sustainability & Responsibility, VF Corporation

KN: What is your company's overall general sustainability message?

SC: "Made for Change" is the VF Corporation's commitment to a more sustainable future. There are three main issues:

- People–Our associates are a force for good in the world, sparking global movements that genuinely make a difference.
- Planet–The well-being of people and the planet is inextricably connected. We're taking bold and urgent action on climate across our value chain.
- Products–VF Corporation uses circular economics to keep materials and products in circulation for as long as possible. This includes: re-commerce (sell as-worn, regenerated, or renewed products); or as rented products; or designed in circularity from the beginning so they can be taken and create something new.

"Made for Change" is the overall general sustainability message, but each brand uses it differently; sustainability measures are in alignment with each brand's strategy/company/consumer base/brand purpose. The results are similar from brand to brand. One of the primary reasons more products aren't kept in circulation is that they weren't designed to be circular. VF Corporation's "Made for Change" circular strategy is building the systems to introduce more circular design.

"Made for Change" covers VF Corporation's objectives relating to water conservation and materials used, but isn't necessarily around manufacturing and supply chain. The brands are also intentional when it comes to supporting their workers and the communities they come from and live in.

KN: Where is the consumer's concerned initiative going to come from in order to affect climate change and the health of the planet?

SC: We believe that consumers today, and in the future, will integrate social and environmental performance of the brand into their purchases, and that this will become more and more prevalent as companies become more transparent about their activities relating to sustainability. For example, Kipling rents products for travel; people live in smaller spaces today and can't store much luggage.

Rented apparel continues to grow in popularity. This growth—combined with significantly lower environmental impact versus purchasing new ones—makes delivering high-quality products through a rental experience, which has become an important component of circular vision.

We can't do this alone, so we participate in many stakeholder industry initiatives and signed onto the United Nations Fashion Charter for Climate Change. We have taken leadership roles in the Sustainable Apparel Coalition, for example, to get consumers to have objective data in front of them to influence purchasing.

KN: What political or advocacy measures do you as a company take in order to influence sustainability at a global level?

Acquisitive and Inquisitive: Acquisitive——some parts of the world are still acquiring and engaging consumers, while others are in the Inquisitive stage——they have their consumer base and are ready to pass around topics like sustainability

SC: We advocate for international trade agreements, free trade, AND fair trade; and use VF Corporation to enable businesses to fulfill their whole potential.

KN: Do you have to connect with consumers differently depending on where they're coming from?

SC: In general, people are more alike globally than they are different. Sustainability resonates no matter where you're coming from. Younger generations, in some countries, have grown up in bad pollution their whole lives, so they're the target base for environmental and sustainability measures and for making purchases that can have a positive impact on where you live.

It's not just marketing to those who have the money to be sustainable, as price points for sustainably produced products can be higher than those made from practices lacking these controls. The widespread intake of more sustainable products should not be only for those who can afford them—all consumers should have the ability to purchase more sustainable products.

KN: A lot of sustainability also refers to buildings as well as clothing— what are you doing as a company to ensure that your buildings are also environmentally sustainable?

SC: We're committed to our buildings being environmentally sustainable and LEED (Leadership in Energy and Environmental Design) certified. In addition, we have a goal to utilize 100 percent renewable energy across our owned-and-operated facilities by 2025.

CHAPTER 1-4

Ecoalf

Because There Is No Planet B

Transforming Waste Into Fashion Products and Fabrics

Ecoalf is much more than just a fashion brand; it's a sustainable lifestyle experience.

—Javier Goyeneche, president, Ecoalf

Figure 1-4.1 Ecoalf bag

Javier Goyeneche, president and founder of Madrid-based Ecoalf, realized in 2009, the year that his sons Alfredo and Alvaro were born, that the next generation would have to deal with a continuing reduction of natural resources. He decided to do something about it, and established Ecoalf as a sustainable fashion brand. He chose the memorable tagline, "Because There Is No Planet B" to represent the company's mission.

Ecoalf utilizes innovative technology to develop collections of clothing and accessories (Figure 1-4.1) made primarily from recycled materials and the balance from low-impact fibers. Ecoalf retail stores operate in three Spanish cities—Madrid, Barcelona, and Malaga—plus in Berlin and Tokyo. Sales in 2020 grew by 74 percent.

From Waste to Fabric

Ecoalf takes a strong participatory role in activating its core sustainable values. Their menu of accomplishments includes recycling over 200 million plastic bottles; recycling over 100 tons of discarded fishing nets; and working with over 3,000 fishermen in 40 ports whose trawlers removed over 700 tons of waste from the bottom of the Mediterranean Sea. From these different types of raw waste, Ecoalf has developed more than 400 fabrics used to make quality garments.

To make discarded tires a source for reuse, Ecoalf invested in a two-year-long R&D project to remove metals, antioxidants, and fabric pieces to produce a clean powder that is turned into its line of flip-flops. By using recycled cotton, Ecoalf estimates that it saves 660 gallons of water per T-shirt.

Ten percent of all branded "Because There Is No Planet B" merchandise is donated to Ecoalf Foundation to support the expansion of its Upcycling the Oceans project to the Mediterranean. They focus on the state of the world's oceans and to finding solutions by supporting over 300 institutions worldwide to emphasize prevention through environmental education.

Figure 1-4.2 Ecoalf yoga legging and bra

Collaborations with Viccarbe, Michelin

The collaboration with Valencia-based Viccarbe's Maarten collection is a new upholstered line made with Ecoalf fabrics (Figure 1-4.2), produced from recycled wasted resources (plastic bottles, fishing nets, and post-consumer coffee grounds). Availability for the new collection was Summer 2021.

Both brands are already working on new furniture pieces (Figure 1-4.3). To develop these new designs, the two firms are launching an R&D project to ensure not only that all materials are recycled, but also that, at the end of their useful life, they can be easily separated for subsequent reuse and recycling, thus generating a perfect ecosystem of circular economy.

Figure 1-4.3 Ecoalf Viccarbe silla chair

Figure 1-4.4 Ecoalf shoe

B-Corp fashion brand Ecoalf has teamed up with multinational tire and footwear soles manufacturer Michelin for a recycled loafer collection. The two companies worked together to develop a shoe sole (Figure 1-4.4), made from rubber that would otherwise be wasted, in the production of soles by Michelin. The footwear's knitted fabric upper is then made from a mix of 30 percent polyester and 70 percent "Ocean Yarn," a material developed by Ecoalf using plastic bottles collected from the ocean as part of their Foundation's Upcycling the Oceans project. Shoes are shipped in Ecoalf's packaging made from 100 percent recycled cardboard.

Each pair of the unisex loafers contains five plastic bottles, with Ecoalf estimating the entire unit of shoes created will reduce CO_2 equivalent emissions by 14,773 tons and save 102,000 gallons of water when compared with the same number of traditional, non-recycled loafers.

Photos courtesy: Ecoalf

CHAPTER 1-5

Architectural Systems

Bringing Sustainable Products to the Marketplace

"We Are Watching a Big Revolution in All Segments, Including Workplace, Retail, and Wellness."

Interview with Nancy Jackson, co-founder of New York-based Architectural Systems with Ken Nisch.

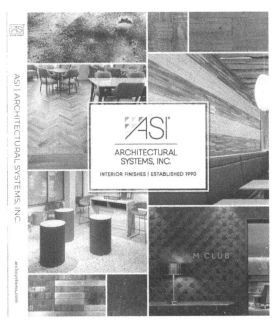

Figure 1-5.1 Architectural Systems, Inc., workbook cover

KN: How does sustainability and Architectural Systems fit in to the industry?

NJ: The company was founded in 1990 by me and my husband, Ron. Our business model was to introduce innovative materials to architects and designers who actually select materials and generate specifications. Originally, we were importers of trend-setting proprietary materials, able to anticipate what the market was looking for, and deliver these distinctive products.

KN: You have worked across building types lines: retail, hospitality, restaurants, and corporate, correct?

NJ: Yes, because we never wanted to be reliant on each market's cycle. We found that innovative materials could be used in different markets. Designers could customize products and we could deliver an order that met the design intent and budget requirement. Our objective was to become the source where designers could find products that augment their project in one place.

We were pioneers in man-made materials. Porcelain tiles were introduced when most of the architectural community was purist, only wanting real stone, even though they complained about the variations. When hardwoods became an industry disrupter, we began marketing engineered hardwoods when the awareness of ecological products started to surface. That was the real challenge because there were very few materials with any real sustainable sensibility and were not attractive. There was recycled rubber, but it was not aesthetically pleasing.

This trend probably began around 1999. We were one of the first distributors in the country to establish an Eco Projects division. One of our early commissions to source out for a national retail chain was a problem with Australian Cyprus hardwood. It was coming in too varied and the designers wanted a solution. We located a production facility in the Redwood Forest area that had closed because of the endangered spotted owl, which we learned could be reactivated. Ron and I flew across the country for a meeting with this retailer and its head of sustainability and a representative from the Redwood Forest. The designer said it was fabulous, but wouldn't pay a nickel more per square foot. At that time, nobody wanted to pay for anything that was environmentally friendly.

KN: How did you overcome that?

NJ: Thankfully, we are able to value-engineer our materials, and still capture some of the product's opportunities. So, in this case, the option was selected.

KN: You have to be creative in win-win situations.

NJ: It became more apparent with the acceptance of LEED (Leadership in Energy and Environmental Design) certification, the ecology-oriented building certification program run under the auspices of the U.S. Green Building Council (USGBC). Financial incentives offered to the corporate and design worlds result in the use of sustainable materials which may carry a somewhat higher purchase price. Manufacturers began to rethink their production process to become more sustainable.

Designers caught on very quickly and all levels of the process began to adapt. To explain how materials contributed to LEED, we prepared a workbook (Figure 1-5.1) to be used a reference by designers.

KN: How do you identify repurposed materials? How do they fit into the marketplace?

NJ: We've always been able to identify artisan manufacturers. We visit factories around the world, qualify them, make sure they can support an architectural sample program, and that they can produce a quality material.

In some cases, like with the use of reclaimed wine barrels, it's never going to look exactly like the control sample. So, it's all about articulating this to the designer and their relaying it to the client for their approval.

KN: How are you promoting new materials?

NJ: The big concern today expressed by professionals is that the product is made in America. It's about the ecological well-being of the world, not only in our country. They want domestically made products; but, they also want high design.

An example is Italian porcelain producers who use their advance technology to simulate marble and wood. To encourage designers to specify their Italian-designed porcelain and to satisfy the made-in-America criteria, they built and operate plants in Tennessee.

Today, designers, and their decision-making clients, assume that we wouldn't be marketing products that do not have environmentally friendly, sustainable qualities. They don't even ask anymore; they just expect this level of compliance.

KN: How do you make available materials that are unique and one-of-a-kind, and that are environmentally friendly?

NJ: It's keeping your hand on the pulse of the market. A recent flooring product is a luxury vinyl made of recycled content that can be installed directly over stone or hardwood. The existing floor need not be ripped out, minimizing waste and extra labor costs. It was used in a restaurant in Boston that had an original terrazzo floor. The wood grain vinyl product was safely installed over the existing terrazzo to update the contemporary concept in minimal time while preserving the facility's landmark status.

Sustainability's initial awareness phase has passed. It's now a sustainable sensibility in all segments, including workplace, retail, and wellness.

CHAPTER 1-6

Aldo Group

The Customer, The Store, and Retail Education

Fashion and Social Responsibility

Montreal-based ALDO Group owns and operates a worldwide chain of shoe and accessories stores. Founded by Executive Chairman Aldo Bensadoun in 1972, it has grown to become an international corporation, with nearly 3,000 stores visited by an estimated 200 million customers annually in over 100 countries. It operates three major retail banners: ALDO, Call It Spring/Spring and GLOBO. Stores in Canada (Figure 1-6.1), the United States, the United Kingdom, and Ireland are owned by the Group, whereas other international stores are franchised.

CEO David Bensadoun believes the company's stores are prime assets to drive brand equity, customer experience, and data collection. "We are streamlining decision-making and supply chains so we can reach the customer with a compelling proposition. What I believe in is exciting product, consumer insights, and data analytics," he stated.

The ALDO Group controls every stage of production with attention to detail. Through direct sourcing, the company's in-house designers and line builders are able to customize products. "In that way, the company is able to put the customer directly in touch with manufacturers from around the globe," Bensadoun points out. All franchise store plans are provided by the ALDO Group and undergo the same design and development process as the company's corporate stores. The ALDO Group supplies fixtures for approximately 90 percent of its franchisees.

Although the ALDO Group's model specifies a single design concept for each banner, the company takes local needs and cultural differences

Figure 1-6.1 ALDO, Queen Street, Toronto, Canada, interior displays

Photos courtesy: ALDO Group

into consideration and adapts concepts to better fit their location. "Our partners are provided with regional visual planning that has been developed through analysis of regional buys and availability in the market," Bensadoun indicates. "We stress a flexible approach towards region-specific needs. To remain competitive on a global scale, we make sure we deliver tailored strategies and content," he states (Figure 1-6.2).

Influencing Both Fashion and Social Responsibility

Guided by a strong set of values, founder Aldo Bensadoun built a company founded on compassion and ethics, to influence society in both fashion and social responsibility. "We've extended our climate neutral commitment to include all ecommerce and product transportation carbon emissions, from production to the end customer. In addition, our bagless program encourages customers to use an eco-designed shoebox, which saves an estimated 11,000 trees per year," says David Bensadoun.

ALDO is a member of the Leather Working Group and the Sustainable Apparel Coalition and is a signatory of the G7 Fashion Pact and the

United Nations Fashion Industry Charter for Climate Action. In 2019, the company was named Best Canadian Retailer of the Year by Connex FM for their sustainable store initiative.

Bensadoun School of Retail Management

Through the Bensadoun Family Foundation's $25 million contribution, McGill University opened the Bensadoun School of Retail Management. Established as an interdisciplinary educational institution dedicated to all facets of the retail industry, its research and course programs focus on fostering sustainable consumption, healthy societies, and bringing retailers into the 21st century.

Comments by Caroline Poirier, Senior Director, Store Design, and Brand Environments for ALDO Group, at EuroShop 2020 panel discussion, led by Ken Nisch

"In everything we do as a company, whether it be with customers, their communities, our suppliers and their products, we always are striving to find ways to be more thoughtful, sensitive, and smart.

Figure 1-6.2 ALDO, Singapore

Photos courtesy: ALDO Group

We have a team in our company that is focused on sustainability assessments and rates of various initiatives on an ongoing basis, looking for continuous improvement. We were able to increase our sustainability rating by up to 50 percent by implementing such changes as transitioning to zero-VOC paints, and using recycled materials. More localized suppliers are working on our projects, and we are using fixturing to deliver much of the lighting in the store rather than creating redundant lighting.

"By simplifying our procedures, we can have fewer shop types and therefore less redundancy and waste to repurpose elements within the space. We are always looking for ways to do less more effectively. An example is a renovated store in Toronto where we invited local artists to create an original work of art for the storefront. It built community interest and engaged local resources. Rather than retrofitting the storefront with a typical design, a local artist incorporated the storefront into the neighborhood. It's an example of doing something simply, minimally, and effectively to achieve our results."

CHAPTER 1-7

Everlane

Building the Next-Gen Clothing Brand

Selling Customers on Sustainable Fashion

"We've realized that there is much more to do to spread the Everlane story," says Michael Preysman, Everlane founder and CEO.

Since launching the company in 2011 with a $1.1 million investment as a direct-to-consumer clothing brand committed to "radical transparency," Preysman and his team have been strategically expanding its scope. Current estimated valuation is up to $200 million for Everlane, a private company. Everlane has used its website and social media to offer customers a glimpse into its factories around the world, give voice to the workers making its garments, and share a price breakdown of each product it sells.

At an Everlane retail store (Figure 1-7.1), on display are the firm's signature, sustainable high-quality basics—cashmere sweaters, pima cotton T-shirts, and denim jeans.

Diversifying with Sustainability

Everlane is ramping up production, making everything with transparency and environmental responsibilities in mind. They use denim made in one of the world's cleanest denim factories, produce products ranging from lower-impact sneakers to puffer coats made from recycled plastic bottles. The company has shipped products to more than two million customers. Everlane valuation is estimated up to $200 million by industry ranking sources.

Everlane's messaging, coupled with its spare, fashion-forward aesthetic, has turned customers into emissaries. Preysman is also pioneering new approaches to retailing, making use of steady product launches, waiting lists, and limited inventory to both predict and drive demand. "Everlane created a sense of urgency and exclusivity [around its products]," says Marshal Cohen, a retail analyst at NPD Group, Inc.

Creating Demand

Although denim is a more than $40 billion global market, Everlane delayed coming out with jeans until it could locate a factory that met the

Figure 1-7.1 For its 4,400-sq-ft Everlane store in the Williamsburg section of Brooklyn, the upper-level selling floor is dedicated to sustainable men's apparel and accessories

Photo courtesy: Guillermo Cano, Everlane

company's sustainability standards. They found one in Vietnam that recycles 98 percent of the water used in denim manufacturing and turns the leftover sludge, filtered of chemicals, into bricks that are used to construct affordable housing.

When items sell out, Everlane can restock quickly, thanks to close relationships with more than dozens of factories worldwide. This generates the specter of scarcity, which Preysman leverages. Customers sign up for early access to new clothes and to be notified when popular styles are back. When Everlane's new ballet-inspired shoes sold out, thousands of customers added their names to the waiting list.

To avoid the appearance of discounting, Preysman developed a Choose What You Pay model for overstocked items, where customers can purchase, for example, a dress shirt for one of three different prices. The website explains that the lowest level lets Everlane recoup its costs, while paying more allows the company to invest in future product development. The latter option has gained customer support.

Storefronts are free of mannequins so passersby see customers and staff milling about inside. "The people are the important component of the store, not product," he says. Preysman says he is intent on building Everlane. His focus is on finding new ways to sell customers on his vision for sustainable fashion that can withstand the test of time.

CHAPTER 1-8

The Tiffany & Co. Foundation

A Responsibility to the Greater Community

TIFFANY & CO.

Figure 1-8.1 Tiffany & Co., founded in 1837, now operates over 300 stores worldwide

"For the past 20 years, The Tiffany & Co. Foundation has been proud to support organizations that protect the natural world," says Anisa Kamadoli Costa, chairman and president of The Tiffany & Co. (Figure 1-8.1). "People need nature to thrive, and in order to protect nature, we must look to local communities as the stewards of these precious places," she says.

Since its inception, the Foundation has awarded over $85 million in grants, with $4–$6 million in average annual grant making over the past several years. Through its programs, The Tiffany & Co. Foundation seeks to preserve the world's seascapes and landscapes.

The Foundation supports organizations dedicated to the stewardship of natural resources in the areas of responsible mining and coral and marine conservation. Specifically, the Foundation promotes responsible mining through remediation and land preservation, and coral and marine conservation through key research and targeted educational outreach.

Coral Conservation

The Tiffany & Co. Foundation values healthy oceans and the important role that corals play in these ecosystems. The Foundation believes that

Figure 1-8.2 Coral Reef, Raja Ampat, Indonesia

precious corals (Figure 1-8.2) cannot be sustainably removed from the oceans for use in jewelry or home décor. Support is offered to organizations that work to improve the health of oceans through research, preservation, and management of coral reefs.

It promotes the preservation of healthy marine ecosystems through outreach to targeted constituencies such as consumers, ocean enthusiasts, and select marine-tourism providers.

Responsible Mining

The Foundation believes that the manner in which precious metals and gemstones are extracted is of the utmost importance. Its program supports organizations that promote responsible mining of precious metals, diamonds, and gemstones as well as organizations that assist communities where mining occurs, particularly in the American West and Sub-Saharan Africa.

Funds are applied to developing models of reclamation and restoration work that bring together local communities, government, business, and civil society in an effort to reclaim and remediate land and watersheds in which mining has occurred.

Figure 1-8.3 Tiffany Save the Wild lion brooch in 18-k gold with diamonds; Tiffany Save the Wild elephant brooch in 18-k white gold with diamonds; Tiffany Save the Wild rhino brooch in 18-k rose gold with diamonds

COVID-19 Relief

The Tiffany & Co. Foundation in April, 2020, committed $1 million to COVID-19 RELIEF to support the UN Foundation and New York Community Trust. Of the total, $750,000 was allocated to the COVID-19 Solidarity Response Fund for the World Health Organization, powered by the UN Foundation, and $250,000 to The New York Community Trust's NYC COVID-19 Response & Impact Fund.

Tiffany Save the Wild

Since its launching in 2017, funds donated by Tiffany & Co. to the Network have been distributed to support more than 450 on-the-ground conservation efforts to protect the three identified endangered species: lions, elephants, and rhinos (Figure 1-8.3).

CHAPTER 1-9

Walmart

Shaping a More Equitable and Sustainable Future

Committed to Do Right by Their Communities

In the shadow of these tough months, we're more motivated than ever to make meaningful environmental, social and economic progress— and we're eager for other to join us. Our world depends on it.
—Doug McMillon, President and Chief Executive Officer, Walmart, Inc.

In his message that appeared in Walmart's 2020 Environmental, Social, Governance Report, CEO Doug McMillon stressed that the issues of sustainability and opportunity didn't take a back seat during the period when the world was in the throes of the pandemic. As the world's largest retail with combined sales in fiscal year 2021 of $559 billion, McMillon pointed out that Walmart has, for many years, used its scale to create positive change.

"It's time for business to take the lead working together with government and NGOs on serious issues like workforce opportunity, racial equity, climate, and sustainable, responsible supply chains. Consumers are keeping score. They no longer look the other way, and we are committed to do right by our communities," said McMillon.

Chief Sustainability Officer Kathleen McLaughlin supported McMillon's statements by pointing out that Walmart, in addition to serving more than 265 million customers per week, and providing jobs to more than 2.2 million people, donated more than $1.4 billion in cash and in-kind donations. Starting wages were raised by more than 50 percent, benefits were expanded, the Walmart Academy was launched, conducting

trainings for more than 1.8 million associates, and the company launched
Live Better U, a pathway to earning a $1-a-day college degree.

Walmart and the Walmart Foundation's reach extended to an investment of $130 million in Retail Opportunity grants, which included
establishing more than 50 nonprofit organizations to share learnings and
insight in investing in frontline workforce.

Walmart operates 11,500 stores in 27 countries. Formats include
neighborhood stores (Figure 1-9.1) of approximately 42,000 square feet.

Walmart's Sustainable Packaging Playbook

Walmart has issued for the use of its 2,800 suppliers its *Sustainable Packaging
Playbook*, a 94-page guide focused on the most common packaging formats
found in Walmart stores (Figure 1-9.2). It presents information designed to
capture recyclability information with a focus on North America.

The document provides perspectives on feasible recycled contents
levels based on current industry practice. Walmart encourages all suppliers
to take a lifecycle perspective when planning to optimize package design.
Benefits of the application of the Playbook's detailed instructions to
improve packaging sustainability include the conservation of natural
resources, improved product protection, support of human health, increase
use of recycled content, and minimization of greenhousegas omission.

Figure 1-19.1 Walmart neighborhood store

Figure 1-9.2 Walmart's Sustainable Packing Playbook

Target Corporation

"Future at Heart," A Multimillion-Dollar Agenda for Operating Sustainably

I am proud of all that our team and partners accomplished in this past year, yet humbled by all still left to do. The challenges we face as a company and a society will continue to evolve, but we will keep moving, making progress, every step of the way.

—Brian Cornell, Chairman and CEO

(Excerpts, comments by Brian Cornell, *Target 2019* and *Target 2020 Corporate Responsibility Report*)

Target is committed to addressing the environmental impacts of our business within our operations and across our value chain. Operating a sustainable business and using resources responsibly allow us to serve our guests for generations to come. By using our size and influence, we are tackling two of the planet's biggest issues: climate change and waste, including plastics.

Concurrently, a new philosophy shifts corporate responsibility to the core of our overall business, called "Future at Heart." It was designed to fuel growth and create lasting value for our guests, team members, stakeholders, and our planet. Four key themes connect to our company's overall strategic priorities.

- **Empower our teams**. They are our brand's greatest ambassadors and advocates. Our supporting programs include wage commitment, investments in training and career development, and enhancements to our benefits. Investment in our team members provides a place where they can grow their skills and careers, take care of themselves and their families, and make a difference for our communities.
- **Serve our guests**. More than 30 new brands have been introduced, offering value without compromise on quality, safety, raw materials, or great design.
- **Foster communities**. As we open dozens of new stores in cities and on college campuses around the country, it is important to let these communities know Target will be a good neighbor. More than one million hours are volunteered each year by Target team members. Target gives $200 million annually to community programs, including in-kind donations and aid in-crisis situations.
- **Design tomorrow**. Chainwide, aggressive climate, and energy goals have been established, along with new operational policies relating to managing water consumption, recycling, and waste reduction.

Countering COVID-19

As COVID-19 hit the United States this spring, we faced a lot of challenges simply to run our business, and we did more than just keep our doors open. We overhauled how we operate to make Target easier and safer to shop, as guests turned to us for food and essentials, as well as for supplies to create home offices and home classrooms. We invested in our team by increasing pay and expanding well-being benefits so team members would have everything they need to care for themselves and their families.

And we quickly invested $10 million toward pandemic response efforts, with an emphasis on supporting organizations that reach vulnerable populations and underserved communities. Then, the murder of George Floyd by a police officer just a few miles from our downtown

Minneapolis headquarters forced us to take a hard look at what Target stands for.

We've been on a 15-year journey to build and refine Target's diversity and inclusion strategy. Many team members and guests made it clear to me that we needed to use the full power of the Target brand to support a broad-based movement against systemic racism in all of its forms. We began by committing to rebuild our stores damaged in the protests and listening to our communities to help ensure these stores don't just reopen, but are a force for lasting good in the neighborhoods they serve (Figure 1-10.1).

We also invested $10 million to help communities rebuild from this summer's protests and support groups fighting for social justice and racial equity. We launched the Racial Equity Action and Change (REACH) Committee. This group of Target leaders is tasked with guiding us as we work to help Black team members grow and advance in their careers at Target, to welcome Black guests into our stores, combat racial inequities in our communities, and advocate for civic engagement and public policy that addresses systemic racism, safety and police reform, economic and educational opportunity, and access to fair and safe voting.

Our country faces unprecedented challenges that have fundamentally changed what it means to be a "good corporate citizen." Our value is defined by more than just the earnings we report to Wall Street or the money we donate top philanthropic causes.

Ultimately, we will be judged by the actions we take for our guests, our team, and our community—every day. The Target team knows we can make a difference. With partners in our communities, we can meet this moment and help build a stronger, more prosperous, and more equitable future for all.

—Brian Cornell

Target's Sustainability Reach

(Described by Amanda Nusz, Target Corp. vice president of corporate responsibility)

Target is engaging its entire supply chain to help achieve 2030 goals to reduce carbon emissions. A circular economy is one of our biggest opportunities to design a sustainable future.

Figure 1-10.1 Façade of a Target store, Richmond, Virginia

Photo courtesy: Target Corp.

With our heritage in democratizing design, we bring the greatest number of sustainable choices to the sales floor so that our guests can feel great about their Target shopping experience every time they visit us. We will build, remodel, and operate efficient buildings and spaces that are designed for sustainable operations. Upgrades have already been completed to over 1,800 stores.

- **Resource-efficient buildings with LED lights**. By replacing old fluorescent light fixtures with LEDs, more than two million smart LED ceiling fixtures are in place across nearly all 1,800-plus Target stores nationwide, and will be added to new stores. Electricity required to power our stores has been reduced by 10 percent annually, an average of 470 million kilowatts (kWh) of energy each year, enough to power nearly 40,000 homes or to reduce our greenhouse gases emissions, an amount equal to removing 70,000 cars from the road annually.
- **Renewable energy**. By 2030, our goal is to source 100 percent renewable electricity for our domestic operations

and 60 percent by 2025. We are committed to increasing the use of renewables in communities where we operate our facilities, distribution centers, and supply chains.

- **Solar and wind power**. More than 500 Target stores and distribution centers have rooftop solar. Each installation has the capacity to offset between 15 percent and 40 percent of its energy needs. Target joined other customers to construct 50 MW of solar panels in Colorado, which started producing energy in 2019. Target has installed more solar systems than any other company, according to the Solar Energy Industry Association, and have been cited as helping to create a cultural shift in how top companies power their operations.

- **100 percent of our domestic electricity from renewable sources by 2030**. By pooling our energy demand with other companies in the Renewable Energy Buyers Alliance (REBA) and partnering with electric utilities in the World Resources Institute's Clean Power Council, we are advancing clean energy beyond our own operations and into the communities we serve.

We are committed to designing solar installations as an important part of the future. Our work is aligned to the UN Sustainable Development Goals (SDGs) in which we have identified where we can make the greatest impact. UN SDGs call on governments, businesses, and civil society organizations to take action to address the urgent problems facing our world today. Target values the important role these goals play in equitable, sustainable development. We have explored how our Future at Heart strategy can support the UN SDGs.

- **Six goals**. Target's six goals are those we believe we can have the greatest impact: Gender Equality; Clean Water and Sanitation; Decent Work and Economic Growth; Sustainable Cities and Communities; Responsible Consumption and Production; and for worldwide Climate Action, to take urgent action to combat climate change and its impact.

Figure 1-10.2 Center isle of current Target store

Photo courtesy: Target Corp.

A major renovation and modernizing program has been undertaken. Merchandise is displayed in "shops" throughout the store on elevated product fixtures. LED lighting has significantly reduced the amount of energy needed to illuminate retail and support spaces (Figure 1-10.2). Founded in 1902 with headquarters in Minneapolis, 2021 reported revenue was $106 billion. Target Operates 1,931 stores in every state in the United States

CHAPTER 1-11

Amazon

A Global Approach to Worldwide Sustainability

The $100 Million Right Now Climate Fund

"While we worked hard to safely deliver products to consumers during the COVID-19 outbreak, sustainability remains a top priority at Amazon," wrote Kara Hurst, director of worldwide sustainability for Amazon, in *The Amazon Blog*. Hurst's teams focus on supply chain management and social responsibility in Amazon operations, involving packaging standards, renewable energy and energy efficiency, hazardous waste, and social and environmental policy setting.

At the corporate level, Amazon Inc., is investing in a $2 billion venture capital fund with the advocacy group, Global Optimism, to create sustainable and decarbonizing technologies to eliminate its carbon footprint. Directed by the company's corporate development group in collaboration with Amazon's internal sustainability team, its mandate is to back technologies being developed to reduce greenhouse gas emissions, a major contributor to climate warming.

Amazon's $10 million commitment in collaboration with The Nature Conservancy is part of Amazon's $100 Million The Right Now Climate Fund, to support family forest owners in the Appalachian Mountains by creating a new income source to restore and conserve forest lands and protect wildlife, while removing millions of metric tons of carbon from the atmosphere.

Amazon, which had total 2021 revenues of $470 billion, has placed orders for 100,000 electric delivery vehicles from Rivian, an electric vehicle maker and automotive technology maker. The first group of 10,000 vehicles is expected to be operating in 2022.

The Climate Pledge

The Climate Pledge was co-founded by Amazon in 2019 in partnership with the United Nations Sustainable Development for Climate. By 2025, the goal is 100 percent of Amazon operations are powered by renewable energy. As of April 2021, Amazon has 206 renewable energy projects across the globe that have the capacity to generate over 8,500 megawatts (MW) and deliver more than 23 million megawatt hours (MWh) of energy annually—enough to power more than 2 million U.S. homes (Figure 1-11.1).

Figure 1-11.1 A major Amazon wind farm in Texas contributes 1 million megawatt hours to the energy grid

Photo courtesy: Amazon Media Library

Installation of solar rooftops is underway at 50 Amazon facilities. Solar farms in the United States are providing electricity for Whole Foods Markets (owned by Amazon) and Amazon fulfillment centers. Other renewable wind and solar energy projects operate or are planned for Australia, Spain, France, Germany, Italy, South Africa, the United Kingdom, as well as the United States. With the addition of more than two dozen 26 utility-scale wind and solar energy projects, energy output will rise to an estimated 4 GW, making Amazon one of the world's largest corporate users of renewable energy.

Amazon's Packaging Lab developed a fully recyclable padded paper mailer for customer orders. Manufacturers, through the Frustration-Free Packaging program, have been encouraged to package their products in easily opened 100 percent recyclable containers that are ready to ship to customers without additional Amazon boxes.

Sourcing and Manufacturing

Hurst and her team are investigating opportunities in the company's sourcing and manufacturing of its products. Included are ways to communicate directly with workers in factories, and share that information with the factory owners and managers so they can make improvements, part of the company's objective to create an overall circular operation.

CHAPTER 1-12

Adidas

Game-Changers for Sustainability

Ultraboost Made To Be Remade Can Be Ground Up and Melted Back Into Materials for a New Shoe With Zero Waste

Adidas is the world's second largest sports apparel and accessory company, with 2021 sales of $22.1 billion. Headquartered in Herzogenauah, Germany, where it was founded in 1949, the company's production can top 900 million products a year. It operates 2,184 retail stores in 50 countries.

Adidas is exploring new ways to minimize waste and recycle products. Companywide ambitions include using less water, cutting back energy consumption, and helping to keep plastic trash out of the ocean.

A Sign of Things to Come

In 2021, Adidas launched a new series of Ultraboost drops to coincide with Earth Week 2021, as part of the company's continued commitment to help end plastic waste and address the devastating levels of plastic pollution in the oceans. The four Ultraboost drops each feature their own innovation and encompass the idea of creating a product "for the future" with sustainability at the forefront.

First in the series is the Ultraboost Made To Be Remade, which dropped on April 22 as a Creators Club exclusive. Designed within the framework of Adidas's circular loop with materials and technology the shoes can be run down and then returned to Adidas to be remade into something new. The shoes feature a prominent QR code which can be

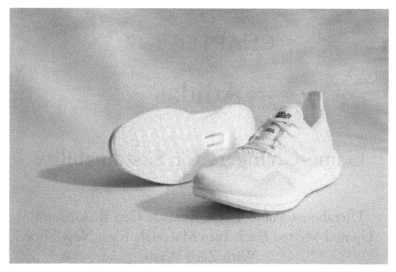

Figure 1-12.1 Ultraboost Made To Be Remade sneaker, containing a high-performance recycled yarn made from ocean plastic

scanned with a smartphone to open a digital series where the returns process can be easily accessed (Figure 1-12.1).

According to an Adidas spokesperson, the company's intention is to develop further Made To Be Remade products which invite the wearer into the experience and drive a circular relationship. The next drops made in collaboration with Parley for the Oceans were the Ultraboost 21 x Parley and Ultraboost 6.0 DNA x Parley editions. The Ultraboost 21 x Parley is a performance running shoe with sustainability at its core. Designed to bring energy to people to drive positive change and self-betterment, the Ultraboost 21 x Parley are shoes made for comfort and the future of the oceans.

Featured are Ultraboost 21's key technological innovations such as optimized BOOST for support and comfort and the new "Linear Energy Push" system, which increases forefoot bending stiffness. The shoe also features a Forged Primeknit upper made in part with Primeblue, a high-performance recycled yarn containing 50 percent Parley Ocean Plastic, upcycled plastic waste intercepted on beaches and coastal communities, preventing it from polluting the oceans.

The Ultraboost 6.0 DNA x Parley features the iconic Ultraboost silhouette with an upper made of Adidas Primeknit, created in part with Primeblue, while the cage and heel counter are made of a layered material consisting of recycled plastics, 20 percent of which comes from reprocessed end-of-life fishing nets. Precision-made, seamless zones combine strength and performance with smooth comfort to ensure distraction-free movement.

The last Earth Week drop in 2021 was the Ultraboost 6.0 DNA which has two new classic designs for women and men. Adidas believes that the Ultraboosts of Tomorrow represent a bold statement from Adidas to drive innovation around materials, products, and new ways of using them with the goal of helping to end plastic waste.

"These Ultraboost alone won't save our oceans," Adidas states, "but they will get us one step closer."

Supply Chain

Adidas is working with suppliers to continuously improve their environmental footprint, providing them with policies and best-practice guidance for environmental management, and training sessions tailored to their needs.

Suppliers receive the Adidas "Environmental Good Practice Guide and Toolkit," a manual to recommend good industry practices for reducing environmental impacts of manufacturing facility operations. It outlines the implementation of Environmental Management Systems, data management, wastewater management, and Green Building Management, and provides over 60 saving opportunities on energy, water, and waste management and renewable energy.

Adidas initiated a system of multi-level and cross-functional training sessions with its global supplier network. The "Energy and Water Investment Plan" project works with facilities located in main sourcing locations including Cambodia, China, Indonesia, Vietnam, and Taiwan. These facilities conduct on-site assessments and develop an investment plan enabling them to deliver on their energy and water reduction targets, to identify potential efficiency measures and achieve actual savings by implementing these opportunities on-site.

Plastic bags have phased-out of Adidas retail stores globally. The company supported the global innovation platform Fashion for Good with a donation of $1.69 million to support the foundation's development of durable and reusable materials for the fashion industry.

Integrating Technologies

Parley Ocean Plastic™ is in the Terrex Parley 3-Layer jacket, a lightweight waterproof jacket that uses layers of breathable Climaproof fabric to keep consumers dry and comfortable, and an outer shell made with plastic from the Parley collaboration (Figure 1-12.2). Parley Ocean Plastic is derived from upcycled plastic waste gathered on remote islands, beaches, coastal communities, and shorelines.

Figure 1-12.2 Terrex SS21 PARLEY MISSION Jacket

Photos courtesy: Adidas

Primeblue/Primegreen: Primeblue is a recycled technical material made in part with Parley Ocean Plastic, now included in some of Adidas' most iconic and visible performance franchises, like Ultraboost, and in the jerseys of some big league and sports teams in the world. Primegreen, also made from recycled virgin plastics ingredients, is used for high-performance apparel. Both materials played a significant role in Adidas reaching more than 70 percent total volume of recycled polyester.

CHAPTER 1-13

IKEA

Achieve Big Positive Changes in the World, and the Entire IKEA Ecosystem

What Sustainability Means to IKEA

Adopted from IKEA Sustainability Strategy, August 2020, and media references.
The IKEA People & Planet Positive strategy describes the sustainability agenda and ambition for everyone in the IKEA franchise system and value chain. We want to have a positive impact on people, society, and the planet. For us, it's about balancing economic growth and positive social impact with environmental protection and regeneration. We always think long term—to be able to meet the needs of people today without compromising the needs of future generations.

Doing this requires rethinking and inspiring changes in lifestyles and consumption, and to adopt new ways of working. We are committed to leading the way forward together with our co-workers, customers, and partners, and to using our size to make a positive difference. This is both a responsibility and a business opportunity.

The more people we reach, the bigger the impact we can have together, and the more people we can enable to live a better everyday life. It will stimulate action across IKEA in the coming years. We don't have all the answers and cannot achieve our goals alone. We will rely on our culture of entrepreneurship, always moving forward and not waiting for perfection. Our sustainability ambitions and commitments are set for 2030 in line with the UN Sustainable Development Goals (SDGs).

Investments for the Future

Climate change. It is one of the biggest challenges that humanity faces. Temperatures are rising; the six years between 2014 and 2019 were the hottest years on record. The urgency to act now is clear. The signing of the Paris Climate Agreement was an important step toward coordinated global action to limit the global temperature increase to well below 2°C, aiming toward 1.5°C, by the end of the century. By 2050, at the latest, this combined effect must reach net zero emissions.

Unsustainable consumption. By 2030, the global population is expected to reach nearly 8.6 billion. More people will look for a chance for a better life. In a world that already uses resources requiring more than one planet, billions of new consumers put an even greater pressure on the planet. In many parts of the world, consumption is growing at an unsustainable rate. Today, it's estimated that the world must produce 70 percent more food by 2050 due to population growth, but also due to trends in rising consumption of meat and dairy, and the current loss or wastage of one-third of all food produced. The calls for action are described in the UN SDGs.

Enabling as many people as possible to generate and use renewable energy and to reduce their home energy and water consumption would have a great impact. Water, food, and air quality are major concerns for people around the world.

Resource scarcity. Air, water, and land pollution are very visible due, in part, to unsustainable consumption and wastefulness. For IKEA, unsustainable consumption is one of our biggest challenges. How can we continue to grow and enable more people to live better everyday lives within the boundaries of the planet?

As one of the large food companies in the world, we also have a responsibility to provide healthy and nutritious food. We strive to not only offer more sustainable home furnishing and food products, solutions, and services, but also to inspire and support people to make positive changes in their lifestyles and to consume in more sustainable ways.

By 2030, our ambition is to inspire and enable more than 1 billion people to live a better everyday life within the boundaries of the planet.

Toward a Circular Economy

- Creating a movement in society that is sustainable, supports safety, health and well-being, and is within the means of the many people.
- Offering better, more affordable, smart products and solutions that enable people to live safer, healthier, and more sustainable lives.
- Offering a food range that is more sustainable, healthier, tastier and affordable.
- Seeing IKEA products as raw materials for the future and ensuring that all products have circular capabilities: designed from the very beginning to be repurposed, repaired, reused, resold, and recycled.
- Inviting and enabling customers and other partners to be part of the solution by making it easy to buy, fix, sell, share, and give away products.

Figure 1-13.1 Creating a business model for the refurbishment and resale of products is an important piece of IKEA's circular business. The first full test took place in late FY19 when sofas were collected from customers (as claims and takebacks), refurbished, and resold

Photo courtesy: IKEA

- All IKEA products and solutions are designed with quality, form, function, low price, and sustainability based on the IKEA democratic design dimensions.

Sustainability That Is Affordable, Attractive, and Accessible

We will make healthy and sustainable living a desirable choice that is affordable, attractive, and accessible for as many people as possible. The IKEA business will enable people to generate renewable energy, to purify the water and air in their homes, eliminate waste, and contribute to adapting their homes to cope with the impact of climate change. We will come together and work to improve health and well-being (Figure 1-13.1).

(*Sources*: IKEA Sustainability Strategy, June 2018. Updated: August 2020; *Interior Design*, October 23, 2020; Reuters, October 30, 2020)

IKEA Opens Pilot Secondhand Store in Sweden

IKEA, opened a pilot secondhand store for IKEA furniture in Sweden as part of its efforts to reach its 2030 climate targets (Figure 1-13.2).

"The store in Eskilstuna west of Stockholm will, after the used furniture is repaired in an adjacent shop, sell the items at below their initial price," IKEA Sweden's head of sustainability Jonas Carlehed said. The goods come from municipal recycling centers in the area, where people can donate furniture.

IKEA has a target to be circular, which includes using renewable or recycled material, and helping customers prolong the life of their products, by 2030. It aims to reduce more greenhouse gas emissions than its value chain emits, from the production of raw materials through to customers' use and disposal, by the same year.

"We are making a huge readjustment, maybe the biggest IKEA has ever made, and one of the keys to reaching (the targets) is to manage to help our customers prolong the life of their products," Carlehed told Reuters. He said, "The store, which is located in a shopping mall focused on recycling and reuse, would be a learning experience for IKEA about the secondhand business and how to attract shoppers."

Figure 1-13.2 In the fall of 2020, IKEA opened a secondhand shop in Retuna shopping center, in the Swedish town Eskilstuna, known for having stores offering upcycled and recycled products. In the secondhand IKEA shop, tables, chairs, utensils, and bookshelves that have been repaired and made ready for resale

Photo courtesy: IKEA

"IKEA will evaluate the project after six months and thereafter decide whether to roll it out to more markets," he said. Ingka Group, earlier this month, said, "It was rolling out a buy-back scheme to many of its stores under which people get vouchers in return for their old. IKEA furniture which IKEA then recycles, resells in the store, or donates."

The store is owned by Ingka Group which owns most IKEA stores and is a strategic partner as well as franchisee to brand owner Inter IKEA.

(*Sources*: IKEA Sustainability Strategy, June 2018. Updated: August 2020, and others)

CHAPTER 1-14

UN Alliance for Sustainable Fashion

Launched in 2019, it is composed of 10 member organizations to harness the reach and creativity of fashion to helps achieve the UN Sustainable Development Goals, for meaningful action on both the labor side and the consumer side of the industry.

The Clothing and Textile Industry today is estimated as one of the top three most polluting industries, following energy, and agricultural due to the following reasons:

- Contributes US $2.4 trillion to global manufacturing
- Employs 300 million people worldwide across the value chain (many of them women)
- Is responsible for an estimated up to 10 percent of the world's greenhouse gas emissions
- Around 215 trillion liters of water per year are consumed by the industry
- Annual material loss of US $100 billion due to underutilization
- Textiles account for approximately 9 percent of annual microplastic losses to the oceans

Statements from the UN indicate that the scale of the industry is only expected to grow over the coming years. Given its size and global reach, unsustainable practices within the fashion sector have important impacts on social and environmental development indicators. Without major change to production processes and consumption patterns in fashion, the social and environmental costs of the sector will continue to mount.

On July 07, 2021, a "Sustainable Fashion Hard Talk" was livestreamed to explore policies to recommend shift from the current model of wasteful fast fashion to one of sustainable "slow fashion" and emphasize the dual need for healthy working conditions and low environmental impact within the sector.

The session featured of speakers with experience in disparate facets of fashion.

They agreed that "sustainability" in the context of the fashion world is defined as prioritizing the health of the environment over runaway profits and corporate growth. Attractive, commercially successful apparel, they stated, needn't be sacrificed so long as designs have long lifespans and are as widely accessible to consumers as possible.

Among their suggestions:

- Fashion industry journalists to treat environmental impact and economic performance as equally important metrics of fashion houses' success.
- Public-private partnerships and increased investment in the Global South.
- Improved distribution, robust recycling pipelines, and a cultural shift toward higher prices for more slowly developed but higher-quality clothes.
- Legislation-backed requirements that companies disclose the environmental consequences of their products, emphasizing the need to raise the legislative bar to hold the industry accountable.
- A needed cultural shift, to be driven by the ascendance of a new generation comprised of young people who stand up for sustainability and do due diligence when shopping to spur the changes needed in the business of fashion worldwide.
- Stop buying what we don't need.

CHAPTER 1-15

National Retail Federation

Retailers Are Making Sustainable Shopping Easier

Responding To Consumer Demand

The National Retail Federation (NRF) is the largest association of retailers in the world with members from all phases of the retail industry. Retail is the largest private-sector employer in the United States. Approximately 52 million Americans work in retail. It represents a wide variety of retail segments in the United States and over 45 countries. Based in Washington, DC, the NRF created the NRF Foundation, a nonprofit, to provide resources and experiences for those interested in jobs or long-term careers in retail. Its main goal is to support the next generation of potential retail leaders. The NRF Foundation's offerings include a career center, job boards, and training. It also provides scholarship programs for retail employees and students.

An NRF and IBM survey from 2020 found that nearly 80 percent of consumers report that sustainability is important for them. Nearly 60 percent are willing to change their shopping habits to be more sustainable. More than 70 percent of consumers who report that sustainability is very or extremely important are willing to pay a 35 percent premium for more sustainable and environmentally responsible products.

The challenge for both retailers and consumers is to know when a product is more sustainable than alternatives. Some definitions focus on the materials used to make or package the product. Do they contain recycled-content or renewable materials? Are they compostable, recyclable, or biodegradable?

Some sustainability definitions focus on product production. Is it more energy- or water-efficient, healthier, or safer than alternative products? Who makes the products and how those workers are treated? Are they treated fairly and working under safe labor conditions?

Retailers are demanding a lot of additional sustainability information from their suppliers. They then use it to select appropriate products and to identify those products in-store or online.

Some of the many retailers highlighting their more sustainable product offerings include:

Amazon's "Compact by Design" and "Climate Pledge Friendly" designations identify products that meet the criteria of 30 independent certification programs.

Best Buy identifies energy-efficient products meeting the U.S. government's Energy Star program. It also highlights available government and utility company rebates for buying energy-efficient products.

Rite-Aid identifies "eco-friendly" products online and places shelf tags throughout its stores identifying products with "Proud Planet," "Free From," "Smart Choice," and "Well Being" labels that provide additional information.

Sephora's "Clean Beauty" program places visible badges throughout stores and online. They highlight products that exclude specific chemicals of concern along with products with more sustainable packaging or other environmental or social benefits, including identifying Black-owned brands.

Staples and **Office Depot** both promote more sustainable products in-store and make them easy to find online. This is particularly important for business and government customers with public sustainability goals.

Target's "Target Clean" symbol places products meeting its sustainable products criteria throughout its stores with prominent messaging explaining the benefits, and has a designation for Black-owned brands.

Walmart's "Built for Better" program uses icons to identify products that are built better "for you" and "for the planet."

Ultimately, retailers exist to meet the demands of consumers. Consumers want more sustainable products, and retailers will find a way to provide them, the NRF has stated.

CHAPTER 1-16

Richemont

Movement for Better Luxury

An All-Inclusive Sustainability Commitment

The 177-page *Richemont Sustainability Report 2021* provides an in-depth examination of how the company currently manages and implements its corporate sustainability program for its four groups of luxury products—People, Communities, Sourcing, and Environments. Richemont's portfolio includes Maisons in four business areas: Jewelry with Cartier, Van Cleef & Arpels, and Buccellati; Specialist Watchmakers, with Jaeger-LeCoulture, Piaget, and Baume & Mercier; Online Distributors, with Net-A-Porter and The Outnet; and Other, encompassing Chloé, Montblanc, Alfred Dunhill, Serapian, and Alaïa. Founded in 1988, it is based in Bellevue, Geneva, Switzerland (Figure 1-16.1).

Figure 1-16.1 Headquarters of Richemont in Bellevue, Geneva, Switzerland

Photo courtesy: Richemont

By joining the International Reference Center for Life Cycle of Products, Services and Systems (CIRAIG), Richemont Research and Innovation is supporting the expertise of two universities in Montreal, Canada—Polytechnique Montreal and L'Université du Québec à Montréal, and two universities in Sion, Switzerland: the University of Applied Sciences and Arts of Western Switzerland, and École Polytechnique Fédérale de Lausanne. Analysis of the studies being conducted at these institutions will allow Richemont to assess the environmental impacts of their Maisons' creations throughout their life cycle.

Recent Initiatives

Several major launches were carried out by Richemont Maisons to reduce their environmental footprint.

- Animal-free alternatives to leather were announced by three brands. Chloé introduced the "pot de confiture mini bag" produced by using apple waste.
- Serapian's Grape Eco Craft capsule collection is made using grape leftovers.
- The Specialist Watchmakers groups is integrating such materials as TimberTex, a paper-like material using natural plant fibers.

A design of Cartier Tank Must has a solar-powered movement and a strap made of upcycled apple waste.

As part of its Plastic Shift Initative, Richemont published an internal, 50-page handbook, the "*Branded Packaging Material Handbook*" containing guidelines for packaging designers and procurement specialists. The "*Zero Single-use Plastics in Catering Activities*" handbook for Richemont's Facilities Managers provides the practices to be followed by staff restaurants, offices, and external events, as well as recycling systems.

Eliminating single-use plastics is also being pursued for such products as tape and to significantly reduce the use of PU foam. Circular Logistics concepts are focused on transporting goods with reusable packaging.

Lighting and Energy Use

Energy audits are undertaken across Richemont businesses to establish environmental standards when building new facilities or refurbishing its Masons' retail network of approximately 1,200 boutiques. The firm's Real Estate Department undertook the researching and issuance of a series of booklets on lower energy solutions for better workspaces. Topics covered include: "*The Green Handbook*" for construction projects; "*The Lighting Guide*" for LED illumination for workspaces and display cases; and "*The Energy Monitoring & CO$_2$ Reduction Guide.*"

Since its inception, Campus Genevois de Haute Horlogerie runs on 100 percent renewable electricity. An adiabatic-free cooling system that uses 40 geothermal sensors meets an estimated 80 percent of annual cooling requirements. On the buildings are mounted 2,600 photovoltaic solar panels.

CHAPTER 1-17

Gabriela Hearst

A Personal Expression of Sustainability

Combining Fabric Technology with Handcraft Details

Gabriela Hearst's line of elegant women's and men's apparel and accessories attracts a fashion-aware clientele as well as a number of international awards. Born and educated in Uruguay, she moved to New York and started her label for Fall 2015, with designs characterized by quality craftsmanship and innovative materials.

She presented her first runway show in 2017, staged with a no-plastic policy. Cashmere pillows for guests were knitted by the nonprofit organization Manos del Uruguay from excess yarn from her previous collection; seven sets of clothes were made with existing fabrics and materials. In the Resort 2018 collection, a group of styles was made of a fabric that is infused in aloe vera which softens linen, giving it the property to moisturize the skin.

All Hearst production systems relate to the environment and sustainability, including the use of wool coming from Hearst's sheep farm, part of her ranch in Uruguay, that help to minimize environmental impact. Hearst also makes use of Tipa, compostable bioplastics for all their packaging, developed by an Israeli startup for a flexible alternative to plastic that can be added to compost to decompose in 24 weeks.

LVMH Luxury Ventures, that supports emerging brands, invested in Gabriela Hearst in January 2019. French brand Chloé, in December 2020, named Hearst as its creative director.

Carrying Sustainability to the Next Level

For Spring/Summer 2020, Gabriela Hearst staged the first carbon-neutral fashion show, using local models and local catering services. She participates in a program to offset emissions by donating the energy costs associated with production to the Hifadhi-Livelihoods Project in Kenya, a country where Hearst has traveled in the past with Save the Children. Offset funds will be used to provide modern, efficient cookstoves to families in Kenya's Embu and Tharaka Nithi counties, cutting down on wood usage and the noxious fumes that accompany it, which primarily impact women and children.

New products have been made from repurposed Turkish kilim remnants to make outerwear, old pieces from Hearst stock disassembled and reconstructed, and 30 percent of the collection has been made with recycled cashmere, hand-knitted by the Manos del Uruguay collective.

With the SS20 collection, Hearst introduced the digital identity for the collection in partnership with Eon. The digital identity connects all products with a QR Code providing each garment's origin, material, production process, and carbon footprint. This technology provides customers transparency about the clothes and an understanding about how to recycle the products to support a circular fashion economy. Hearst sets a goal to use 80 percent dead stock and plans to phase out virgin materials.

Jill Biden's Inaugural Ensemble

Gabriela Hearst designed the ivory coat and dress ensemble worn by First Lady Dr. Jill Biden (Figure 1-17.1) for the 2022 presidential inauguration evening events. The message of "Unity" was the main inspiration for the ensemble, made in New York City from fabrics available at Hearst studio. The flowers from every U.S. state and territory were embroidered on the hem of the cashmere coat, the silk organza arms, and neckline of the coordinating dress.

Figure 1-17.1 Dr. Jill Biden's coat from her inaugural ensemble, January, 2022

Designed by Gabriela Hearst

SECTION 2

Ethical Consumption

Introduction

UN: Shopping for a Better World

The United Nations Environment Program (UNEP) is the leading global environmental authority that sets the global environmental agenda, promotes the coherent implementation of the environmental dimension of sustainable development within the United Nations system, and serves as an authoritative advocate for the global environment.

Modern consumption patterns are putting severe stresses on the limited available resources' base, on the one hand, and, on the other hand, are resulting in mounting waste discharges to the environment. The retail sector's shift to sustainable consumption and production (SCP) would not only be beneficial for society at large, it would also make a valuable business case for the sector itself. By promoting new, safer, value-added, and environment-friendly products to customers, retailers can tap into a fast-growing market segment of sustainability aware consumers.

The UNEP (United Nations Environment Program) assists the retail sector by:

- providing relevant information and training to help the sector control its own environmental and social impacts
- highlighting key measures to green the supply chain and favoring the development of sustainable products/services
- prompting the purchase of eco-friendly products by customers and introducing such programs as take-back systems, reusable bags, and repurposing old clothing.

Shifting to more SCP patterns is a standard for future international improvement of the industry's role in effecting a change to harmful environmental practices.

- **Cleaner Production and Environmental Management Systems**
  Implementing environmental management systems for energy/water conservation, waste management, logistics, and recycling programs.
- **Supply Chain Management**
  Retailers can cooperate with their suppliers to develop products featuring enhanced environmental and/or social attributes that encourage consumer acceptance, and to provide information on the sustainability aspects of their products to contribute to product transparency.
- **Education and Information of Customers**
  Retailers can mount storewide programs that encourage consumers to purchase eco-friendly products such as those staged by Selfridges in London, and Galeries Lafayette and Printemps in Paris.
    The UNEP is preparing a Guidance Manual/Training Kit/Resource CD-ROM to facilitate sustainability initiatives across the retail sector.

CHAPTER 2-1

Communicating B Corps Certification

Increase Consumer Support of Sustainability

The ultimate success of sustainability for the retail industry lies with the consumer, industry observers indicate. Are consumers beginning to expect more from retailers with regard to environmental and social support? Are they making more of an effort to shop at stores that align with their beliefs and carry these products?

Retail consulting firm, McMillan Doolittle, conducted a proprietary survey of 1,920 consumers in 2020. Initial findings show that more than two in five American adults agree that identifying a retailer whose values align with their own is critical to choosing where they shop. This has been especially evident lately as social media users have been identifying companies to boycott. "Many corporations have thus started marketing their green practices and charitable donations," says researcher Rachel Stern.

Unfortunately, some companies do not practice what they preach or are participating in greenwashing, in which companies use green marketing to deceive the customer. Protection is offered to consumers by a variety of certifications that validate these claims, including the prominent B Corp Certification (Figure 2-1.1).

B Lab, a nonprofit that certifies businesses, was founded in 2006 to enable companies to use their power to solve problems like wealth inequality, climate change, and social unrest. But without a sustained public information campaign, there is a gap in the consumer grasp of the validity of Certified B Corporation (B Corp) operations and their importance to the products they produce. A B Corp is a for-profit company

Certified

Corporation

This company meets the highest standards of social and environmental impact

Figure 2-1.1 Logo with tagline

that has met the rigorous standards of social and environmental performance, accountability, and transparency, according to B Lab. According to co-founder Bart Houlahan, to become certified, the company
must undergo a thorough process in which they are evaluated on their
impact on their workers, community, customers, and the environment,
and provide documentation to support these claims and recertify every
three years.

Defining Shopping Preferences

McMillan Doolittle's research indicates that people want to shop at
stores that are socially and environmentally responsible but have not yet
connected those ideas to B Corps. In their survey, 64 percent of those
questioned agreed that brands have a responsibility to serve the local
communities in which they operate. During the certification process,
companies are evaluated on their contribution to the economic and social
well-being of the communities they operate in by answering questions on
diversity and inclusion, job creation, civic engagement and philanthropy,
supply chain management, and more. B Corps are also evaluated on
how they manage their environmental impact in areas such as climate,
water use, sustainability, and effects on land and life, and 62 percent of
respondents agreed that retailers need to address the negative impact they

have on the planet. Three-quarters of those queried agreed that retailers should ensure a positive and safe working environment for all qualified people regardless of age or disability, gender, race, religion, or sexual orientation. The B Impact Assessment evaluates companies based on how well they treat their employees, including their compensation practices, benefits, training, worker ownership, and work environment.

However, only 54 percent of consumers indicated that attaining certification made a brand more appealing in their eyes. The disconnect between consumer shopping preferences and the appeal of B Corps lies in the lack of awareness and understanding of them. Despite the fact that there are over 3,500 Certified B Corps in 740 countries across 150 industries, many consumers are not aware of their existence. When customers buy Ben & Jerry's ice cream, for example, they may know they are supporting a socially responsible company with flavors that highlight important causes like Pecan Resist, which celebrates activists who resist oppression, harmful environmental practices, and injustice. They are unaware, however, that they are buying from a B Corp because this logo is not displayed on their products.

Respondents who demonstrated greater receptivity toward Certified B Corps include women, those living on the West Coast, urban residents, and those with a college or advanced degree. The study showed that 64 percent of younger consumers, ages 18–24, felt that a B Corp Certification made a retail brand more appealing.

Certified B Corp firms that publicly market their status include Athleta, a women's athleisure company that uses window space to explain their B Corp certification, and New Seasons Market, a Pacific Northwest grocery chain that places a large sign outside each store demonstrating their achievement. Even if a customer sees that a company is a Certified B Corp, many of those we surveyed reported that they found the concept confusing and did not know why they should trust the certification. Customers may also shy away from Certified B Corps' products in the belief that they are more expensive, which may be true depending on the product. But the challenge is to communicate that the markup ensures employees are being paid well, products are being sourced responsibly, and the community is being supported.

Other Certifications

Along with the B Corp Certification, there are other environmental and social certifications for companies and products, including Fair Trade, Leaping Bunny, and EWG. Fair Trade is commonly used to certify coffee and chocolate products that are made according to rigorous social, environmental, and economic standards. The Leaping Bunny Certification is used for cosmetics, personal care, household, and cleaning products and guarantees they are not tested on animals. EWG-verified products are certified by toxicologists, chemists, and epidemiologists not to contain any ingredients that are harmful to people or the planet, to list all ingredients on the label, and to be safely manufactured.

An important difference is that the B Corp Certification certifies the entire company as opposed to a product.

By increasing the awareness of B Corps, customers can feel confident in their support of businesses. B Corps are a nascent trend with increased recognition among the younger, urban, and highly educated population. An effective communications campaign would increase the number of consumers interested in supporting businesses that align with their values and the support of B Corps and their environmental and social benefits.

Certification From B Lab

B Lab, the nonprofit that certifies B Corps headquartered in Berwyn, PA, was founded in 2006 by Jay Coen Gilbert, Bart Houlahan, and Andrew Kassoy after Coen Gilbert and Houlahan sold AND1, a basketball apparel company they started. The co-founders felt that charitable initiatives within companies did not go far enough, and created the B Corp Certification to publicly hold businesses accountable for how they treat their workers, customers, communities, and the environment.

In addition to the certification, B Lab developed a way for companies to retain their social mission after selling or going public by establishing the Benefit Corporation, a legal structure similar to an LLC that requires the consideration of all stakeholders. Companies can incorporate as a Benefit Corporation in 38 jurisdictions in the United States including the District of Columbia and Puerto Rico, but B Lab continues to advocate for its adoption everywhere. A common misconception is that B Corps are the same as Benefit Corporations when in reality Certified B Corps do not have to be Benefit Corporations as long as they meet the legal requirements of the certification.

To receive certification from B Lab, a company must take the B Impact Assessment, a free tool that measures their impact on their workers, community, customers, and the environment, and achieve a minimum verified score. Next, the company must review their results with a member of B Lab to ensure the answers are accurate by providing documents to support six to fifteen elected questions related to company operations.

They also must fill out a Disclosure Questionnaire about the company's litigation history and other areas of potential concern. After the evaluation, the company must publish their B Impact Report on bcorporation.net, meet the legal requirement of their jurisdiction, sign the B Corp Declaration of Interdependence and the B Corp Agreement, and pay the annual certification fee, which varies by region. In the United States and Canada, the certification is dependent on a company's annual sales, and begins as low as $1,000 for companies with sales less than $150,000.

The company must maintain a public profile on B Lab's website, pay an annual fee, and recertify every three years by retaking the B Impact Assessment and keeping a score above 80.

CHAPTER 2-2

Ellen MacArthur Foundation

Energizing a Circular Economy

Launching *Circulytics*, a Digital Measuring Tool

Launched in 2010, the Ellen MacArthur Foundation works to accelerate the transition to a circular economy and has emerged as a global thought leader. It has established the circular economy for clothes and related consumer end products on the agenda of decision makers across business, government, and academia through Make Fashion Circular.

Founded by former professional racing sailor, Dame Ellen MacArthur, the organization is headquartered on the Isle of Wight. It has released more than 20 reports and books, defining global initiatives on plastics, fashion, and food, and developed worldwide innovation networks.

Make Fashion Circular

Make Fashion Circular is based on the Foundation's belief that for fashion to thrive in the future, there must be a cohesive effort to design a circular economy for clothes.

The Foundation estimates that $500 billion is lost every year due to discording clothing barely worn but rarely recycled. If nothing changes, by 2050 the fashion industry will use up a quarter of the world's carbon budget. Washing clothes releases half a million tons of plastic microfibers into the ocean every year, equivalent to more than 50 billion plastic bottles.

Make Fashion Circular is aimed to create a textiles economy fit for the 21 century. Its goal is to ensure clothes are made from safe and renewable materials, new business models increase their use, and old clothes are turned into new.

Circulytics, a Digital Measuring Tool

In 2020, the Foundation introduced *Circulytics*, a digital measuring tool which gives companies a fully comprehensive picture of their circularity across all operations. The appeal is to companies around the globe that are adopting the circular economy as an opportunity to create thriving businesses that meet the challenges of climate change and pollution. It is a freely available resource.

Using company-level data, with applied insights and analysis from their Data and Metrics team, *Circulytics* highlights and inspires opportunities for innovation, while allowing companies to track their progress. Developed and tested by more than 30 companies from the Ellen MacArthur Foundation's network, *Circulytics* informs strategy, allows users to see where they lie in relation to their industry, and provides a quick understanding for those actively moving away from the current "take, make, waste" linear economy.

Circulytics provides the option to have informed interactions about circular economy adoption should businesses wish to do so with investors and customers. The Foundation plans to engage with companies that generate outstanding scores to create inspirational case studies.

The Jeans Redesign

The MacArthur Foundation sponsored The Jeans Redesign which brought together 40 denim experts from brands, retailers, manufacturers, collectors, sorters, and NGOs. Resulting guidelines set out minimum requirements on garment durability, material health, recyclability, and traceability, based on economy principles.

Their aim is for companies to make jeans that last longer, can be easily recycled, and are made in a way that's better for the environment and for garment workers' health. "We're starting with jeans because we felt there was a very positive reaction from the sector to contributing to the circular economy," said Francois Souchet, lead of MacArthur's "Make Fashion Circular" initiative.

"The way jeans are produced is causing huge problems with waste and pollution, but it doesn't have to be this way," Souchet said. "By working together, we can create jeans that last longer, can be remade into new jeans at the end of their use, and are made in ways which are better for the environment and the people who make them. Over time, we will continue to drive momentum toward a thriving fashion industry based on the principles of a circular economy."

CHAPTER 2-3

Patagonia

Growing With Sustainability and Social Mission

In its Fight for a Healthier Planet, Patagonia Boosts its Power

Patagonia (Figure 2-3.1) has become a standard-bearer for companies who practice the operational model that doing good work for the planet creates new markets and strengthens their financial position. It has a

Figure 2-3.1 Patagonia, Brattle Street, Cambridge, Massachusetts

Photo courtesy: Patagonia

manufacturing capability, retail distribution, a solid one billion dollars in annual revenue, and a cadre of devoted followers, and is an active supporter of world-benefiting causes. It applies considerable corporate energy and enlightened leadership to practice and promote corporate sustainability and related enterprises.

Founded nearly a half-century ago by outdoor enthusiast Yvon Chouiard, Patagonia adopted the name of the rugged tip of South America, shared by Argentina and Chile, and the logo depicting the area's 11,000-ft-high Mt. Fitz Roy. Based in Ventura, California, the firm has intensified its efforts to support the basic requirements upon which the company was founded and prospered. It has upped its commitment to environmental activism, making an unprecedented bet on corporate social responsibility. Product innovation and marketing have grown the company's brand awareness and sales.

The company was led for a dozen years by president Rose Marcario, who announced her resignation in June, 2020. During that time, Patagonia's revenue quadrupled. A program was initiated to pursue investments in sustainable design and manufacturing, and in startups allied with Patagonia's mission. In late September, Ryan Gellert was named as new CEO. Gellert, who oversaw Patagonia's Europe, Middle East, and Africa businesses since 2014, was cited for his international experience and dedication to product and activism as factors in his appointment.

"That's The Patagonia Way"

During Marcario's tenure at Patagonia, she never lost sight of the operating model that the more they invest in their beliefs and products, the better Patagonia performs, develops creative solutions, and maps out a blueprint for other businesses, big and small, to follow. She advocated that doing good work for the planet creates new markets and strengthens their financial position.

She reviewed supply chains and streamlined production, and helped the company eliminate waste and excess packaging. She helped shepherd new technologies, working with supplier Primaloft to develop a recycled insulation which ultimately transformed not only Patagonia's products but lines by Adidas, Nike, Helly Hansen, and North Face (Figure 2-3.2).

Figure 2-3.2 Children's reversible jacket with 100 percent recycled polyester fleece on one side and a 100 percent polyester shell on the other side insulated with 100 grams of Thermogreen® polyester (92 percent recycled)

Photo courtesy: Patagonia

The company's funding of small, environmentally responsible ventures has led to Patagonia's achieving major strides in materials science as well as regenerative agriculture, leading to selling food under the banner of Patagonia Provisions (Figure 2-3.3). Its focus on reducing waste and extending the life of its gear has led to its blooming new market for used goods. More than 80 percent of Patagonia's collections are Fair Trade Certified.

Regenerative Farming

Patagonia is way ahead of the movement of regenerative farming. The company spearheaded organic cotton in the early 1990s and has just released its first collection of T-shirts made from regenerative organic cotton from farms in India. "When we realized the power of soil sequestering

Figure 2-3.3 Patagonia Provisions. Organic spicy dry chili mix

Photo courtesy: Patagonia

carbon from the atmosphere, it was a real *aha*! moment," Helena Barbour, the head of Patagonia's sportswear, explains. "It's very dramatic to find something that doesn't just mitigate a problem, or reduce the impact of a problem, but it actually does something good."

Patagonia has partnered with hundreds of farmers, many of whom are in India, where the debt cycle of agriculture can be especially harsh. "We traveled to India to see these regenerative farms, and they're little paradises," she says. "They're very biodiverse, they use beneficial insects, they have animals living on the farm … Just standing there and looking around at the birds and insects and dozens and dozens of varieties of crops was deeply moving," Barbour related.

The techniques are steeped in tradition. "Many of the farmers in India said this was like going back to their traditional practices, which is very exciting," she says. "They said their great-grandfathers used to farm like this, but then they just got approached by all the chemical companies [selling] synthetic fertilizers."

"I do believe fashion is where we can mainstream regenerative agriculture. In some ways, it's more poised than the food industry to lead [the conversation], because fashion is more permanent."

The Recommerce Initiative

On the outskirts of Reno, Nevada, four dozen technicians at sewing machines work inside the largest garment-repair facility in the United States. Nearby are racks of Patagonia's vintage Snap-T fleeces and Fitz Roy down parkas. This repair center reflects a significant leap forward from the company's first major move into recommerce.

Patagonia encourages customers to repair and reuse as much of their clothing as possible. Patagonia created a market with eBay for customers to trade items they no longer needed, generating tens of thousands of items. The more Patagonia campaigned on this anti-consumerist message, the more people have bought its products.

Deploying Investment Capital

Patagonia deploys both its investment capital and corporate clout. They sell buffalo jerky because Wild Idea Buffalo, a South Dakota startup that Patagonia backs, uses regenerative practices to raise its bison and helps restore threatened prairie grasslands.

Patagonia lists beer on its investment menu. The company wanted to prove the commercial viability of a wild grain called kernza that improves rather than depletes topsoil. Its supply comes from another of Patagonia's Tin Shed portfolio companies, Cairnspring Mills. "When we find ideas in tune with our goals, we invest in infrastructure, we build a path," according to Birgit Cameron, senior director of Patagonia Provisions. Thanks to the early success of its Long Root Ale, Patagonia has introduced kernza to Nestlé and General Mills. It is working with Stanford University and U.C. Berkeley, among others, to develop courses on scaling regenerative organics.

Action Works

Patagonia Action Works is a digital platform that's part social network, part activist recruiting tool. It allows everyone, from Patagonia's customers to 1,200+ grant organizations, to collaborate around causes, solicit donations, post calendar events, and seek out volunteers to contribute skills, attend city council meetings, run for office, and start their own NGO.

"Being able to leverage Patagonia's base and resources has put our voice up a whole other level," said a not-for-profit's executive director. John Goodwin, Patagonia's brand creative director, is integrating Action Works into the company's ecommerce site, so customers can buy into causes at the same time they're buying products. "This is a digital tool that facilitates meaningful human connection," he indicates.

Five Projects in Patagonia's Future

Patagonia believes these practices they have instituted will influence other businesses to follow.

1. Worn Wear "recommerce" platform, which incentivizes customers to trade in old gear while also attracting a younger consumer for more affordable, repurposed goods.
2. Patagonia Provisions, the company's burgeoning food line, promotes healthy food systems and regenerative agriculture that produces less carbon emissions. Its next product is canned mussels, "one of the most sustainable forms of animal protein," says founder Yvon Chouinard.
3. Tin Shed Ventures, the company's strategic VC firm, invests in food, energy, water, waste, and apparel innovations. Beyond Surface Technologies has developed the environmentally friendly textile treatments that use natural solutions to make fabrics water-repellent and moisture-wicking that are used in Patagonia's yoga and trail-running styles.
4. Patagonia has grown its stable of fair-trade products from 10 to 480, sewn in eight countries, including India, Thailand, Columbia, Vietnam, Nicaragua, and Mexico. Factory workers receive collective

bonus payments that can be distributed as cash or used for a social investment like daycare.

5. Patagonia's Action Works connects customers with the grassroots organizations the company supports. They connect individuals with their grantees, to institute action on world issues.

Since 1985, Patagonia has pledged one percent of all sales to nonprofit environmental groups as a member of the 1 percent for the Planet®, adding up to over $110 million.

CHAPTER 2-4

Cacau Show

A Chocolate Star Is Born

From 2 Thousand Chocolate Eggs, Up To 20 Thousand Tons

From his first order for $500 to the current estimated sales of $909 million, Alexandre Costa, founder and president of Cacau Show, has paid close attention to giving customers what they want.

Cacau Show began on Easter 1988, in São Paulo, Brazil, when Alexandre, aged 17, decided to experiment making chocolates to resell and earn some extra money. His original recipe was a success, and he soon got an order for two thousand 50 gram chocolate eggs. When the young entrepreneur arrived with the factory he had selected to fill his order, he met with bad news. He was informed that it was not possible for this company to produce the products for which had had agreed to supply his customer with this small amount of weight.

Costa decided the only way to fill the order was to produce them on his own. He researched a source of supply, and bought the raw materials himself. Luckily, he found an experienced candy maker who made homemade chocolate to help him with the manufacturing challenge, and retained her to help him. After both spent three 18-hour work days, the order was completed and delivered as promised, and Alexandre collected the contracted payment.

The profit from this first order, approximately $500, was the initial capital for the entrepreneur to create a new company. Cacau Show's first store was opened in late 2001, and business grew rapidly. The following year, news of the product's quality spread quickly, and the number jumped to 18 sales outlets, standardized with the company's brand. Soon, there were 46 and then scaled up to 130. Another year and the total topped 230.

Cacau Show has become the world's largest chain of fine chocolate shops, with 2,000 franchises throughout Brazil alone (Figure 2-4.1). The company's three factories—two in Itapevi, and one in Campos do Jordão, yield a production of over 20 thousand tons of chocolate per year.

Cacau Show: Sustainability Throughout Their Operations

From the Plantation to Employee Benefits

Interview conducted by Ken Nisch with Cacau Show founder and president, Alexandre Costa.

Figure 2-4.1 One of 2,000 Cacau Show retail stores

KN: Various companies approach the issue of environmental, social, and cultural sustainability in different ways. Some companies are heavily focused on vertical integration and sourcing, and see this role more legal or operational. For you, is this more of a marketing and corporate culture initiative, with credibility and criteria to address issues such as transparency?

AC: Cacau Show has been concerned with the theme for a long time. Since 2013, we have published sustainability reports that bring information about our history, guidelines, socioeconomic data, training programs for employees, results with franchisees, celebration rituals, and social actions, with all the clarity and transparency that we always have with our stakeholders.

KN: In your organization, how does the issue of sustainability—environmental, cultural, and social—come up with a single point of leadership; with the involvement of all stakeholders; an overall organizational and cultural statement?

AC: We always start our reports with the "Letter from the President," where the formal statement on the topic and the discussion about the year is made. In addition to having the sustainability themes present in our values, for example, we do "More with Less" to always grow above average, generating impact and value for all, with ethics, respect, discipline, and simplicity. We fulfill our agreements and deliver the best cost-benefit ratio.

KN: Given all the issues facing brands and retailers today: cyber security, consumer migration and digital, be it transaction and/or primarily communication, or are consumer expectations with sustainability more a price of entry vs. a way to differentiation, do you see the role of sustainability changing within the company?

AC: Yes! We follow all the steps of the cocoa plantation and its connection to the environment. Besides, in the office, we encourage our employees to use fewer plastic cups, so we distribute for each one of them a returnable bottle for everyday use.

KN: What are your suggestions to others outside of your particular business or industry? What will help their organizations think about ways to make sustainability a higher focus within their business, or do you have an ethos that already is highly sustainability focused? How might they expand and spread the impact of those views? For businesses that either do not feel challenged or are disinterested in this topic, how might you induce them to raise the visibility and engagement of their company on this topic?

AC: Brazil is going through an effort to enhance the quality, productivity, and sustainability related to its cultivation to Cacau. As the leading chocolatier in Brazil, Cacau Show is contributing to the overall national effort, and also has its own program and activities. This enhancement affects everything from agricultural practices, to enhancing the quality of life for workers and growers within their communities, their families. This includes ways in which there is more efficient use of resources be they natural, or additional ways to enhance the usefulness of the cacao product from the essential product itself through other by-products that can be created from the cacao plant.

KN: You've mentioned nibs and shells, the "honey," all being put to good use vs. wasted. How is Cacau Show contributing to this national effort and other ways in which it might be unique to Cacau Show (thinking of conditions and support of local communities)?

AC: We have three farms in Linhares, in the state of Espírito Santo. We care about the entire production chain, so we closely follow every step from seed planting, harvesting, cocoa drying, until it arrives at our factory. We also care about all the people involved in this network.

KN: You have created a foundation that works with disadvantaged children across educational, music, and sports. How they impact the communities in which your foundation is engaged?

AC: The Cacau Show Institute is responsible for serving over 3,000 children residing around the Cacau Show and surrounding neighborhoods. There we offer tutoring in music, dance, computers, English, and sports. For us, it is essential to return to the citizens some of the benefits we receive through Cacau Show. It's amazing to see the effort evolving with the children.

KN: In your new office, nothing went to waste. There are beautiful art installations, sculptures, many of which were made by local artists using materials that otherwise would have been discarded during the construction process.

AC: We have a very nice partnership with a plastics artist, Lucio Bittencourt. He was the one who transformed all the "left-overs" of our office building in the most amazing pieces of art.

KN: On your campus, there is a biosphere that brings a bit of the rainforest for your visitors and associates to enjoy every day. Does having a "piece" of the rainforest help increase everyone's appreciation for the unique and diverse biosystem that your sustainable approach to agriculture helps to preserve?

AC: Sure! Because they can observe closely what happens in a cacao harvest, beyond seeing how important it is to preserve our environment.

CHAPTER 2-5

A Flair for Resale

Printemps Supports Stylish Pre-Owned Merchandise

Printemps, the iconic Paris department store, sponsored "(Re)Créez, (ReInventez)" (or "Recreate, Reinvent") in 2019 to spotlight its commitment to support apparel sustainability. The store dedicated a bank of its show windows to dramatize reuse and recycling, and generate interest in the five-week spring event. The promotion gave dimension to Printemps retail initiative to garner consumer interest in environmental and ethical issues. It could not be held during the COVID-19 lockdown.

Printemps, one of the five great fashion-oriented major retail destinations in the city, installed a pop-up showcase of merchandising used garments by presenting a secondhand vintage clothing boutique, Tilt Vintage, on the first floor of its landmark Haussmann flagship. Styles featured were selected for timeliness with current trends.

Printemps commissioned artists to interpret extending the life of apparel and accessories by designing the displays for its store windows (Figures 2-5.1–2-5.3). "We put the spotlight on recycling, marking the latest initiative aimed at tapping into what we believe is growing consumer interest in environmental and ethical issues," said Adrien Marcant, marketing and services manager for Printemps, at the kick-off of the event.

Background scenery, props, and mannequins carried out the selected themes. Shown here are three of the windows.

Figure 2-5.1 Printemps commissioned artists to interpret extending the life of apparel and accessories by designing the displays for its store windows

Photo courtesy: Printemps

Figure 2-5.2 Plastic from discarded bottles were use to create a garden-like environment

Photo courtesy: Printemps

Customers were invited to donate used garments to all Printemps stores for the aid of the French Red Cross. The collection was distributed to people in need, or resold in Red Cross charity stores.

A 157 year Legacy

Founded on November 3, 1865, by Jules Jaluzot and Jean-Alfred Duclos (former employees of Le Bon Marché), the galleries are named after one

Figure 2-5.3 For the home, a Printemps window showed a collection of classic mid-century modern residential and commercial case pieces and seating

Photo courtesy: Printemps

season, Printemps or Spring. Architect Paul Sédille designed the new headquarters of Printemps built in 1883, becoming the first commercial building to be lit entirely by electricity in 1883, six years before the city of Paris adopted the electric lighting in the streets. It was also one of the first department stores directly connected to the subway, through a specific entry built in 1904. Printemps Haussmann is recognized one of the most beautiful Parisian buildings dedicated to retail.

How ThredUP Is Changing Secondhand Fashion

Applying Logistical Technology to Manage a Mega-Inventory

Secondhand clothing site thredUp, now a publicly traded company, to build a resale technology solution for brands alongside its customer marketplace. Competition in resale has surged in the past year, with heightened industry attention on the secondhand market, due to its relevance among younger customer. Estimated annual sales are $36 billion, expected to do while in the next years (Figure 2-6.1). It is expected to develop in the next five years.

ThredUp raised $168 million at a market value of $1.3 billion in its initial public offering (IPO). It claims $1.24 million active buyers, 428,000 active sellers, and $251.8 million in revenue in 2021. But San Francisco-based ThredUP, which holds inventory from sellers, is betting its white-label technology can help not only brands but also its own profitability.

Figure 2-6.1 thredUP warehouse

Photo courtesy: thredUP

With 1,000 new arrivals hourly to the site, thredUP is a major operation. At the beginning, the company handled inventory by hand, taking photos with cellphones and uploading them to the website (Figure 2-6.2). Now they are automating the processes with software and hardware. The company's distribution facilities have conveyor systems that can handle more than three million items on hangers and process and fulfill orders within 60 seconds. Hundreds of millions of photographs are taken every year across 45,000 brands.

The thredUP experience isn't confined to digital; "thredUP IRL" locations offer services including returns of online purchases, styling appointments, and special events. The company has three stores in California and pop-up stores in department stores throughout the United States. "A lot of retailers have a different mindset today than they had five years ago," according to Reinhart. "Offering secondhand brands a store might not normally carry adds value, to attract a younger customer," he affirmed.

Figure 2-6.2 Identifying a thredUP product

Photo courtesy: thredUP

COVID's Challenges

In the thredUP 2020 Resale Report, Anthony S. Marino, president of thredUP, stated: "For all the challenges COVID 19 posed to our assumptions about consumer behavior, one thing is clear: consumers everywhere are prioritizing value and accelerating the shift to thrift. Brands whose core proposition delivers value and convenience have the opportunity to gain share.

"The youth of the world are more switched on than ever about the health of the planet. With their words, deeds, and dollars, the younger generation is demonstrating a genuine desire to be part of the long-term solution to fashion waste. This should inspire much optimism in all of us. The consciousness of the next generation of consumers is a tailwind for businesses that deliver customer value in a sustainable way.

"This year's Resale Report, unlike any we've published, captures insights from two different consumer worlds: pre- and post-COVID. We hope it sparks rich dialogue about the enduring shifts underway and the forces fueling the future of resale."

A $64 Billion Market in five years

"ThredUP's research shows that people would buy more from their favorite retailers if they also sold secondhand. People who shop secondhand cut across all age groups," Reinhart says. "It's people who love brands, love deals, and love to have fun. That's part of our product strategy," he adds. A recent program encourages customers to exchange old clothes for another brand's credit. A primary cause that the clothing industry is the third-largest polluter in the world is its water-heavy production cycle, but responsibility also lies with the consumer. ThredUP's *2020 Resale Report* states that 64 percent of garments produced each year end up in landfill. It says that one in two people throw their unwanted clothing straight to the trash. Buying a used clothing item extends its life by an average of 2.2 years and reduces its environmental impact by 73 percent says Reinhart.

If everyone in the United States bought one used item instead of a new item this year, it would save 5.7 billion pounds of CO_2, equivalent to 66,000 trees planted, he points out.

To do more to reduce fashion-related waste, thredUP launched Retail-as-a-Service (RAAS), inviting outside retailers to get involved with the circular fashion industry. When customers send their used clothes to thredUP for resale, they'll have the option for a gift card to a partnered brand. Some of thredUP's RAAS partnerships allow customers to send their used clothes for resale in exchange for shopping credit to be used at one of their partner brands. Cooperating firms include Gap, Reebok, Amour Vet, and Abercrombie & Fitch.

"We're living in somewhat of a throwaway culture, and textile waste is accelerating," said Karen Clark, thredUP's vice president of communications and partnerships. Sustainable woman's brand Reformation is an initial participant. Customers can order a co-branded "thredUP × Reformation RAAS kit" in which to send their clothes, then they get a Reformation gift card worth the value of their clothes, plus an extra 15 percent—a bonus encouraging participation in the UPcycle program.

Clean Out Kits

Other retailers are creating the operational infrastructure to participate. With RAAS, thredUP handles all the resale responsibilities: the intake of clothes, pricing, photographing, and marketing. The co-brand distributes the "Clean Out Kits" consumers use to send clothes to thredUP.

"Retailers are realizing that two things—the good for the planet and the good for the business—don't actually have to be mutually exclusive," says Clark. "They can, through a program like this—an apparel recycling program that's essentially a sustainable loyalty program for their customers—accomplish both."

According to thredUP, consumers are becoming more environmentally conscious, and are more likely to return to stores they know participate in a "circular economy." "The modern consumer is becoming more environmentally conscious," says Clark, stating that 75 percent of consumers say they're more likely to buy from an environmentally conscious brand.

Oakland, Calif.-based thredUP, with U.S. offices in Scottsdale and New York City thredUP plans to move the partnerships offline as well, including its branded used products in stores. "Our program is not just an apparel recycling program with retailers," says Clark, "but also a shopping experience where used products and new products live alongside each other." She believes that these efforts will encourage customers to consume outside the primary market, reducing textile waste and increasing the already-booming resale industry.

ThredUP: Paving the Way for the Future Of Fashion

CEO & Co-Founder James Reinhart Inspires a New Generation of Consumers to Think Secondhand First

Questions posed by Ken Nisch

KN: In your organization, how is sustainability—environmental, cultural, and social—approached?

- **With a single point of leadership?**
- **An overall organizational and cultural statement?**
- **How you are individually engaged and connected with this focus?**

JR: As the world's largest fashion resale platform, with a mission to inspire a new generation of consumers to think secondhand first, thredUP's business model is inherently sustainable. We estimate the equivalent of one garbage truck of textiles is landfilled or incinerated every second. Shopping secondhand extends the life of clothing, keeping it in use and out of landfills.

Company values come from the top down, and by remaining committed to our mission since Day 1, we've hired a team of over 1,000 people who are inspired by our commitment to reinvent resale and pave the way for the future of fashion.

KN: Given all the issues that face brands and retailers today—cyber security, consumer migration and digital, transaction monitoring, public communication—what are consumer expectations with sustainability, more a price of entry vs. a way to differentiation?

JR: Consumers will always want value, variety, and a fun shopping experience, but sustainability is increasingly becoming a priority. At thredUP, we believe that when faced with the choice between two identical dresses—the same price, the same type of style—shoppers will choose the option that is more sustainable, because it's a choice they can feel good about.

Driven by GenZ's and millennials, secondhand is on track to surpass fast fashion in the next 10 years. Resale sites like thredUP provide all the fun of fast fashion—without the waste to your wallet and the planet. Today, 74 percent of young consumers prefer to buy from sustainably conscious brands as they become more aware of the impact of our fashion choices.

Sustainability is rooted in thredUP's DNA and will remain a priority as we expand our platform to help both consumers and retailers go circular.

KN: With social media and 24/7 access and news cycles, news of companies and their activities are increasingly under the spotlight. Highly visible and important gestures: paper or plastic, reusable, recyclable containers, and disposable plastic, are where companies are making a statement. What are your firm's policies regarding their sustainability practices?

JR: At thredUP, we see it as our responsibility to educate consumers on the impact of their fashion choices and to remain transparent with our customers. We also work hard to make it easy for consumers to make smart, sustainable choices. ThredUP customers can filter the site to only view product that is located in the distribution center closest to them to minimize shipping distances.

Additionally, our "Bundle & Buy" feature that holds purchases until a customer reaches the free shipping threshold to reduce one-off shipments. We are not only influencing consumer behavior; we are encouraging traditional retailers to go circular, produce less, and consider the end life of their garments.

KN: Applying "soft" and sometimes politicized issues such as inclusivity, workforce, and education and training, companies are enhancing not only the communities they operate in, but how they impact those they source from. Has your organization shifted its priorities into new areas of sustainability?

JR: ThredUP is committed to hiring a diverse pool of talent across all ages, races, and backgrounds. We employ over 1,000 employees at our four distribution centers, most of whom are women, and we are proud to offer these employees corporate benefits such as equity and leadership training.

KN: People are becoming an increasing part of the conversation around sustainability. What are examples your company is doing both internally and individually, as well as externally and organizationally, to advocate to others, even if they are not necessarily part of your own supply chain, customer base, or workforce?

JR: At thredUP, we aim to educate consumers on the impact of their clothing choices, and provide actionable solutions to help them do better. Together with the Ellen MacArthur Foundation, we share data with consumers about how extending the life of their clothes can combat textile waste. ThredUP also worked with the research firm, GreenStory, to create a Fashion Footprint Calculator, a tool built to educate consumers on how their clothing habits contribute to climate change across the entire lifecycle of their closet, how you buy, wear and care for your clothing.

We also started our own 501(c)(3), the Circular Fashion Fund, to support other organizations dedicated to creating a circular fashion future. We identify, vet, and distribute funds to organizations such as Queen of Raw and Fabscrap who share thredUP's mission of keeping textiles in use and out of landfills.

KN: As a company that impacts as well as is impacted by consumerism, how do you balance the shareholder and the business demands of growth with the challenges of increasing the consumption of your products?

JR: I believe being a for-profit business and doing good do not have to be mutually exclusive. *In the near future, sustainability will be non-negotiable for brands as companies embrace the triple-bottom line: people, planet, and profit.*

As thredUP has scaled in the past 10 years, we've transformed the way millions of consumers shop. It's important for us to continue to make the greatest possible impact on the future of retail. The bigger we are, the more good we can do. In 2019, we upcycled our hundredth millionth item, effectively displacing 870K tons of CO_2—the equivalent of 74K road trips around the world. Thanks to the operational technology and logistics we've built, the rate at which we can receive and process garments is only accelerating.

ThredUP has launched RAAS. By allowing brands and retailers to plug into what we've built, we are powering circularity for the broader fashion industry. As a result of our apparel recycling program with clothing brand Reformation, for example, we have upcycled hundreds of thousands clothing items. Creating in-store, secondhand shopping experiences with retailers like Macy's, JC Penney, and Madewell have increased awareness among new waves of consumers, opening the door to a more sustainable fashion future.

KN: How do you balance environmental return, ROI? How do you as a consumer think about the role of cultural, social, and environmental sustainability?

JR: *There are already enough clothes to dress everyone in the world! The single best thing individuals can do for the planet is consume less and reuse more.*

By choosing used over new, you reduce your carbon footprint by 60–70 percent. As important as sustainability is to today's consumer, they don't want to sacrifice value, variety, and style. Shopping secondhand offers all the fun of fast fashion while making the most of our natural resources. We have a wide range of consumers at thredUP who come for different reasons, whether it's the fun of the hunt or the tremendous value, but they stay because it's a way of shopping they can feel good about too.

KN: What are your suggestions to others outside of your particular business or industry?

JR: For any entrepreneur, thinking about sustainability needs to start on Day 1. Sustainability can't just be tacked on at the end—it should be woven into every aspect of your business.

To start, figure out what problem your business is trying to solve. From there, make sure that your solution will build a brighter future for your customer **and** for the planet.

The same goes for creating a culture of sustainability within your organization. You must decide your core values on Day 1, and as you build teams the culture will continue to grow.

However, it's not enough to *only* be sustainable, or *only* offer a good product. To win in today's market, you need both. Sustainability isn't necessarily the reason customers come to thredUP—they come for value, fun, trends—but it *is* the reason they feel good shopping with us and keep coming back.

KN: If ultimate sustainability is about using less, what you've done is capture a consumer sensibility, made it desirable and aspirational, added value to the process, and made a successful startup, well-funded, growing business out of what before was "last stop."

JR: The average American doesn't wear 70 percent of the clothes in their closet, and much of the clothing that's discarded ends up in the trash. Before thredUP, there was no easy, responsible way to sell all that unworn clothing. We built the backbone of resale on the Internet, and invented the Clean Out bag to allow anyone to sell any brand without even leaving their home. We've put money back in consumer pockets and upcycled hundreds of thousands of unique items that would otherwise wound up in a landfill.

Traditional thrift stores are often constrained by limited square footage, and as a result they cannot hold or redistribute the majority of the items they receive. Thanks to the technology we've built, thredUP is able to use our scale for good, returning twice as many garments back to the circular economy. ThredUP's facilities are the largest garment-on-hanger facilities in the world, and we receive 100,000 items every day and process more than one item every second.

The biggest hurdle we've faced over the past 10 years has been breaking down the stigma of secondhand. In order to convert the skeptics, we set out to make buying used clothing online just as easy and fun as buying new clothing. We've learned that customers want it all: amazing prices, their favorite brands, and endless variety.

With 45,000 brands across 100-plus product categories, we are giving customers the value and variety they crave without the waste. We've also focused on making it easy and convenient for our customers to refresh their wardrobe responsibly. To date, we've saved shoppers $2 billion in retail value. Across thredUP.com, our mobile app, thredUP stores and retail partner shop-in-shops, we are meeting the customer where they are (Figure 2-6.3).

Figure 2-6.3 The thredUP employee is measuring the garment to make sure that it is the right size that was ordered by our customer

Photo courtesy: thredUP

KN: Features have been written about the demise of "fast fashion." How do consumers relate to value, and feel smart and empowered? What motivates them to upcycle: sustainability, saving money, being more creative, or combinations of the above?

JR: The closet of the future will look a lot different than the fast fashion-filled closets of yesterday.

Disposable fashion is draining our wallets and wreaking havoc on the planet, and consumers are waking up to this waste.

In the past three years, resale has grown 21 times faster than the retail apparel market and is projected to be larger than fast fashion within the next 10 years. By 2029, secondhand is expected to claim the second largest share of market after off-price.

Consumers are increasingly seeking products made ethically and sustainably, and are thinking about the end-of-life of the garments they buy. Nearly three quarters of consumers today prefer to buy from environmentally friendly brands. The number of consumers buying with the intent to resell has doubled in five years.

Today, 40 percent of consumers are considering the resale value of an item before buying it. As consumers increasingly demand sustainability, value, and variety, retailers who don't integrate a circular component into their business models will be left behind.

CHAPTER 2-7

JEM

A Voice of New Luxury

JEM Jewellery Ethically Minded Is Based on Change, Sustainability, and Enhancing Communities and Lives

Figure 2-7.1 The bracelet collection in Fairmined gold

Photo courtesy: JEM Jewellery Ethically Minded

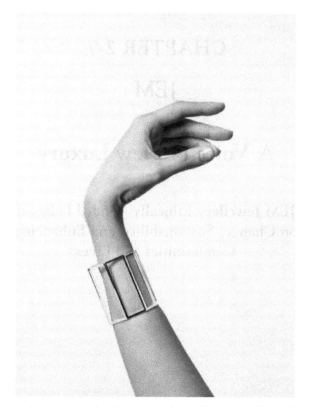

Figure 2-7.2 An example of the bracelet collection in Fairmined gold

Photo courtesy: JEM Jewellery Ethically Minded

Questions by Ken Nisch; responses from Dorothée Contour, Founder and CEO of JEM Jewellery Ethically Minded, Paris.

KN: Please describe JEM's positioning in the contemporary retail jewelry market.

DC: Our society is in constant motion, and a new kind of luxury is emerging within it. Luxury can definitely represent both the past and the future.

JEM is headquartered near Place Vendome, Paris, where the focus is on traditional luxury. Our brand represents a new version of luxury in jewelry (Figure 2-7.2), founded on our interpretation of change in the industry, the importance of sustainability in all aspects of the designs we sell, and our role in enhancing communities and the lives of those around us.

For JEM, our production methods are based on traditional know-how. We look to the future with innovation at every step of the manufacturing of our jewels. Since our creation in 2010, our jewels are 100 percent made in an ethical gold: the Fairmined gold. The Fairmined label is a positive and innovative alternative that transforms the gold mining activity by ensuring the human and social development of mining communities and the protection of the environment, through certification processes and rigorous controls.

We also use only lab-grown diamonds in our collections. We consider the lab-grown diamond as a major innovation for the jewelry sector. It has very low environmental impact, compared to the dangers inherent in the mining process of natural diamonds. Our traceable marketing chain guarantees that with lab-grown diamonds all forms of trafficking and corruption are avoided.

We adhere to a "360 Degrees" approach regarding sustainable development in all of our operations, including production methods. Our model is to be totally open to new technologies and new innovations. This extends to seeking a new more sustainable material for our jewelry cases.

KN: How does your clientele respond to JEM's "luxury for good" positioning? Is it becoming the new benchmark of true luxury?

DC: Yes, our clientele is really sensitive to our positioning. Our goal is to show that it's possible to create beautiful jewels by respecting both people and the environment.

Luxury brands now understand that their consumer base is looking for increasingly more information about the products they consider for purchase. On the one hand, there are the emerging luxury brands that take into account the social and environmental impact of their industry's merchandise, from the creation of their product lines through distribution and delivery to the customer. Older luxury brands may be unable to adapt to the evolving society. An example is the non-use of real fur.

Because of continuous pressure from the public and animal protection associations, many manufacturers decided to stop producing garments using real fur.

KN: JEM's shop design can be considered as an extension of the design esthetic of your brand. Is there a customer shift away from an "acquisitive" customer to one who is more inquisitive and responsible?

DC: We wanted to offer a different approach to what already existed in the jewelry market in terms of design. Our inspirations come from the universal applied arts of architecture and expressive design, in a refined style that is a completely new approach in jewelry.

Our collections are timeless: the same jewel can be worn for years without being considered out-of-style. A new collection will not replace the last one. On the contrary, a new collection will augment our brand, which makes complete sense with our ethical approach. Our customers want to enjoy their JEM pieces and then pass them on to future generations.

KN: How does the consumer learn about brands with JEM's ethical standards, and does it influence their decision to purchase?

DC: We are a jewelry brand and it is most important that the person who receives the jewel or buys it for herself relates to it as a personal symbol. Then we will tell them the story of our brand: our mission and values. It definitely contributes to the uniqueness of owning a JEM article. The "Made in France" attribution adds to its value characteristics.

JEM, founded in 2010, has made its ethical commitments a pioneer in the jewelry sector. Thanks to the Internet, consumers are made aware of JEM's complete approach to jewelry sustainability, from the traceability of the materials, to the manufacturing facilities, through to the composition of its jewelry boxes.

CHAPTER 2-8

Baggit

Building Customer Loyalty and Community Employment Opportunities

A People-Centered Approach for Baggit, an Indian Fashion Brand

Interview with Nina Lekhi, Founder and CEO, Baggit, with Ken Nisch

KN: What is the personal mission that encouraged you to recognize that other people might want bags and similar products that are not made of leather?

NL: Beauty without cruelty is a phrase we use a lot at Baggit. Years ago, I went to the market with my mom and would buy pieces of different leathers to bring home and experiment with. Then, I'd sit on my balcony in the sun, oil them, and watch how the colors changed. But, I came from a predominantly vegetarian household, and eventually moved away from leather because of the origin aspect.

It was a personal choice. That's how we run Baggit now. I do what I feel is good and nothing else. Our products are made in India from design to manufacturing. Baggit demonstrates that you can really succeed in the fashion industry in India and get to understand the customers better, deliver what they are looking for, and make a profit.

The Baggit brand (Figure 2-8.1) has 52 exclusive stores and is carried in more than 1,000 retail outlets through large format stores as well as multi-brand outlets across India.

Figure 2-8.1 A Baggit brand store

Photo courtesy: Baggit

KN: You also have unique programs and benefits set up for your employees, right?

NL: We provide a unique opportunity for all our employees. For examples, we give them time for meditation. We give them opportunities for internal benefit and growth.

KN: When customers pick Baggit as a brand, are they picking it for intrinsic value of the bag itself? Or, do they select Baggit because of your emphasis on beauty without cruelty, employee benefits, and community importance?

NL: There's a percentage who understand, but also those who are not as well read or informed. They do, however, have a sense of loyalty because we have been there for many years and they know we deliver a product that lasts a long time, typically up to seven years,

KN: Have you influenced other brands to operate with higher business values? Do you see yourself as a business person as well as an advocate for what you believe?

NL: I don't think I've been an inspiration for others. Rather, I'm probably looked at as a crazy person. Not many women in India run a factory employing a 1,000 people.

When I started making bags, I did not want to produce the same bags as everyone else. I really wanted to do things my way, using all kinds of cloth, corduroy, Indian embroidery, beads, and more.

Currently, we are producing a big line based on sustainability and recycling, bringing back canvas, and adding a material made from recycled tires.

KN: Do you see yourself as a pioneer in helping to open doors for other people, whether it be women or other types of workers?

NL: We work with artisans and contractors who come from impoverished backgrounds and connect them with suppliers. In this way, we can make a positive impact, not just those directly under Baggit's employment, but also in surrounding communities.

Educational classes are held by us to teach skills so people can find employment with us and grow within Baggit (Figure 2-8.2).

Figure 2-8.2 Baggit practices sustainable production methods and leverages local talent

Photo courtesy: Baggit

KN: Do you see yourself in the role of promoting and growing the cultural aspect of India? How do you make your product uniquely connected with India?

NL: The color palette in India is very unique; we wear a lot of warm colors. Shoppers here favor products that will give longer use and offer higher value out of the products they purchase, like our bags.

KN: Less fast fashion?

NL: Yes. In our factory, we put waste material through a machine that turns it into pellets that are recycled into rubber soles for shoes.

A program underway is repurposing of old Baggit products from customers. Several apparel and footwear brands are doing this. Pickup centers collect these Baggit donations in our stores and we either give them to the poor in India, or they are recycled into rubber soles.

CHAPTER 2-9

Eileen Fisher's Plan for a Sustainable Future

"We're Very Much About Sustainability"

Before sustainable became a multi-language word to denote ethical production and consumption, it was the operational model for apparel designer Eileen Fisher. Starting out in 1984 with four basic classic designs made with quality sourced fabrics, the company now employs 700 in several countries. She has become an international standard bearer for sustainability.

"We must leave the places we touch better than we found them," Fisher states. "The climate crisis demands urgent action. If not now, when?"

She believes that one of the most important ways to achieve industry sustainability is to reduce the amount of products offered for retail sale: "Just buy less, consume less, and produce less. That's a really hard line to walk when you're trying to run a business, and you're measuring your success by how much you sell," Fisher points out.

"Why are we making more, more all the time? This is a great opportunity to stop and think about how we flow product into the store, how to create product that is more timeless, and find ways to refresh it and make it new so it doesn't get stale or boring, so that enough of the product can stay for a much longer period. It makes no sense to mark down black pants and bring in more new black pants. We hope this is an invitation to the whole industry."

Systemic Change

Fisher's vision is to move away from the linear take-make-waste model to a circular one that reuses or replenishes the resources involved. The company is involved in:

- Working with farmers who are regenerating damaged landscapes.
- Adopting a manufacturing process that eliminates waste by using old clothes as the raw material for new ones.
- Doing business in a way that improves the lives of the people who make the clothes.
- Using conscious business practices to achieve fair wages, gender equity, and a culture of caring in the communities throughout our supply chain, where their actions have a positive impact on the planet.

Nearly 100 percent of the firm's cotton and linen is organic. Fisher points out that a vast majority of their wool they call "responsible wool," a certified wool, and a vast majority of that is now regenerative. A significant percent of their current product dyeing is accomplished with Bluesign chemistry.

Fisher supports the concept that the earth can actually be revived through the process of making clothes. "The sheep of our partnering farmers are grazing on farms using regenerative agricultural practices. They are rotated through the farm to allow the grass to regenerate, that their droppings are being used to fertilize the earth, that there might be other crops grown on that farm ... the whole thing works as an ecosystem. With regenerative agricultural practices, the carbon is drawn down from the atmosphere, sequestered in the soil, and trapped—meaning we are contributing to actually lower carbon emissions, increasing soil health, and increasing biodiversity," Fisher explains.

The Renew Program

The Renew program takes back old garments and remakes them into new ones, a technique to not only close the loop of a product's life cycle but to continue to produce items from older styles.

A staff of about 17 people is devoted to Renew which has become a profitable piece of the business. Products in wearable condition are brought to designated drop-off stations and sent to Fisher's main Renew facility where they are sorted, cleaned, and undergo restyling to make into salable products.

Social, Fiber, and Climate Initiatives

Empowering Women

The firm is working to help ensure women have the tools they need to advocate, are brought into decision making, and can pursue work that creates environmental solutions. "While there are established, science-based metrics for setting carbon targets, there's not yet a unified strategy for worker well-being. We're leading the way with this work," she indicates. In partnership with two Los Angeles factories, Fisher is conducting a three-year research project with Harvard SHINE to shift purchasing practices for positive impact on worker well-being.

Women Together CONNECT, made possible by the Eileen Fisher Foundation, is an interactive live-stream designed for participants to share experiences. Free sessions are offered twice weekly.

Future Fibers, New and Recycled

Selecting natural fibers from farms that make the land more resilient and increase biodiversity, helping regenerate their ecosystems, is a company policy. Some long-range objectives include building transparent supply chains based on strong relationships with partners, ensuring traceability by working with NGOs, and other brands and suppliers rather than relying solely on certification, and finding techniques to make upcycled products at a greater scale, including synthetic blends.

Climate Correction

Fisher's approach to the climate crisis focuses on people as well as products, emphasizing partnering in collective action for a large-scale change.

- Support wind power by purchasing renewable energy credits for 100 percent of the electricity consumption in all Eileen Fisher stores and corporate spaces.
- Advocate for stronger climate legislation in partnership with the nonprofit Ceres.
- Work with Renewable Energy Buyers Alliance and Native Energy to increase the number of supply chain partners supporting renewable energy.
- Reduce greenhouse gas emissions created during the production and shipping garments 25 percent by 2025, using 2017 levels as the baseline.

"We're a B Corporation, employee-owned. Our social and environmental impact meets standards to be a B Corp. The fashion industry needs to find a way for all businesses to be responsible for their environmental and social impacts. We hope to spread the word and get more fashion and clothing companies to regenerate the land, grow organic cotton, and support the application of sustainable industry standards," says Fisher.

The North Face

Waste Less. Explore More

Every year, 85 percent of textiles produced ends up in landfills. But it doesn't have to be this way. We can shift from a traditional, linear model to a circular model where people share, resell, repair and recycle clothing to keep them out of landfills and in the value chain.

—Steve Murray, president, The North Face

The North Face Renewed's REMADE collection is a line of creatively repaired, one-of-a-kind styles created by upcycling The North Face products and fabrics in new ways. Designers who participated in the 2019 Residency were responsible for the initial group of designs for men, women, and children.

The women's Thermoball Triclimate jacket (Figure 2-10.1) was hand-repaired and factory certified to meet The North Face standards for refurbished apparel.

REMADE garments are repaired based on design standards created by The North Face design team, conceived, tested, and formalized during The North Face Design Residency workshops. Each REMADE garment is individually assessed and creatively repaired, making each piece unique, one-of-a kind, and backed by a one-year renewed warranty.

The North Face Design Residency is a program to educate designers on the principles of circular design. In the classroom and on the factory floor, designers learn purposeful solutions that consider the complete lifecycle of garments. They apply techniques of hands-on repair and redesign to make future products that are more repairable, reusable, or recyclable.

Figure 2-10.1 REMADE: Women's Thermoball Triclimate jacket

Photo courtesy: The North Face

One output of The Design Residency is the creation of new standards to repair and up-cycle product. Design-led repair tech-packs allow the planning team to standardize processes and forecast future production. The eight-step process is comprised of: Pre-sort; Sort; Identify; Clean; Inspect; Repair; Finishing; and Quality Assurance. Newly repaired products are for sale in the REMADE collection.

The North Face design team partnered with The North Face Renewed and its athlete team to create a collection of REMADE upcycled chalk bags. Each bag is made entirely of pieces of unrepairable North Face products, cut and hand-sewn at The Renewal Workshop and signed by a North Face athlete. All proceeds from these chalk bags will go to support programs that lower barriers to entry into climbing through the Walls Are Meant for Climbing campaign.

CHAPTER 2-11

Timberland

Ambassadors of Sustainability

Creating a Culture of Transformation

(Adapted from Timberland Fourth Quarter 2020, CSR Corporate Social Responsibility Reporting)

Figure 2-11.1 The Timberland® brand brings the outdoors in and uses nature as the backdrop for product presentations through living plants, rocks, and natural and transparent textures, inviting shoppers to step inside and view it at close hand. Shown is the King of Prussia Mall store

Photo courtesy: Timberland

Timberland (Figure 2-11.1) believes, along with others in our industry, that factory disclosure and collaboration can create common standards and shared solutions—helping to advance global human rights in all our factories. Although our supply chain sources may change from time to time, our quarterly factory disclosure represents our best attempt to disclose all of Timberland's active factories as of that date.

VF Corporation, the parent company for the *Timberland* brand, has published full supply chain transparency footprint maps of the most iconic products from its family of brands that includes *The North Face®*, *Vans®*, and *Dickies®*. The interactive source maps, available on VF's sustainability website, help ensure every step in the production of VF's apparel and footwear meets the corporation's standards of quality, sustainability, and social responsibility—from raw material extraction to VF distribution centers.

A core Timberland belief is that a greener future is a better future. From 2001 through 2019, Timberland planted a total of 10,785,743 trees, achieving our 2020 goal to plant 10 million trees two years early. In 2020, we planted 179,337 trees. The current goal is to plant an additional 50 million trees in five years. In addition to our partners in the Dominican Republic, Haiti, and the Horqin desert in China, we also worked with Tree Aid and Trees for the Future, planting over 1,000,000 trees in Senegal and Mali. One of the projects we are supporting is the Great Green Wall, a 5,000-mile-wide swath of trees being planted across Africa. Our key partners for this project are the UN Convention to Combat Desertification and the World Bank Group's Climate4Change.

(*Details available on the Plant the Change page on Timberland's CSR website.*)

A Purpose-Driven Organization

Timberland has helped suppliers build strong management systems. That was a cultural shift for our suppliers, requiring them to spend much more time with us, engaging on a deeper level. They recognized that by doing this, it benefits their business, their employees, and the supply chain at large.

A lot of what we are doing today, and have been doing for a long time, is very topical and current. Our creative vision is that nature needs heroes. We use the energy of fashion to make it better, to engage the market around the notion that a greener future is a better future. It communicates the deeper message behind the product that visitors to the store will appreciate, creating a culture of transformation. The consumer learns not only about Timberland's approach and choices, but also choices that they can make as individuals, by supporting brands that are committed to making the world a better place.

Timberland's *Nature Needs Heroes* campaign recognizes those making a difference while encouraging others to participate in the movement. A movement can change the world. When people see the connection of how their personal actions can play a part, it turns the topic from climate change and devastation to optimism and hope.

We also have a program for our employee community called the Global Stewards. It is a formalized group of "CSR Ambassadors" who opt to take on more, above, and beyond their day job, to learn about and extend our initiatives. They bring program information back to their locations to encourage local community engagement and advance Timberland's mission toward a more equitable and green future. "Path of Service" offers all employees worldwide up to 40 hours of paid time off each year for community service.

We emphasize that we can't do this alone. Our global community needs to be a part of this process with us to make it as impactful as it can be.

CHAPTER 2-12

United By Blue

A Diverse Brand That Does Serious Conservation Work

A Certified B Corp, Philadelphia-based United By Blue practices what it preaches—including eliminating plastics from all business operations and the supply chain. The brand has curated a handful of proprietary sustainable materials that utilize bison coat fibers (harvested from live buffalos), soft hemp (which is four times more durable than cotton), and knits that are manufactured in a GOTS- and OCS-certified factory from sustainably-sourced materials. United By Blue incorporates wool, Tencel, recycled poly, and other eco-friendly fabrics into all of their designs.

Millions of Pounds of Trash Removed

For every product purchased, United By Blue removes one pound of trash from oceans and waterways.

They identify sites heavily infested with trash, organize teams to travel to the location, gather it in containers, and have them transported to professional recyclers. In 2021, 765,000 pounds of trash was collected, bringing the total since the inception of the program to 4.1 million pounds.

"In addition to removing as much ocean-bound trash from the environment as possible, our goal is to become a one-stop sustainable marketplace," says founder and CEO Brian Linton. "To curate a wide variety of sustainably-made essentials, we turn to partner brands whose products and missions we believe in just as much as our own. This year, unitedbyblue.com became home to 49 additional brand partners," Linton reported.

United by Blue created The Impact Collection, a line of responsibly-made clothing and accessories for Target. "Everything in The Impact Collection counts towards our one-for-one trash removal mission. It is produced in the same ethical facilities as our main line, and is crafted with planet-friendly materials like hemp, organic cotton, and recycled polyester," Linton states.

Some United By Blue Products From Sustainable Materials (Figures 2-12.1–2-12.3)

Figure 2-12.1 Soft hemp smocked jumpsuit

Photo courtesy: United By Blue

Figure 2-12.2 Back pack

Photo courtesy: United By Blue

Figure 2-12.3 Citronella candle

Photo courtesy: United By Blue

Business for Good

"At United By Blue, we believe business not only has the ability to be a part of environmental solutions, but also a moral responsibility to address them," says Linton. "It is the motivation behind our B Corp status, a certification we gained in 2011."

"We create our products to last, because the best way to be a conscious consumer is to ultimately consume *less*. This is attainable by designing products that facilitate new ways to generate less waste," he stresses. The company publishes an impact report at the end of each year.

"Ocean pollution is undeniably one of the most pressing issues of our time," Linton points out. "The overwhelming amount of plastic in our waterways is polluting our beaches, choking our wildlife and contaminating our drinking water. We are committed to making a tangible impact, so we confront ocean trash in the most direct way we know how: by getting our hands dirty and removing it from the waterways. By mobilizing the community to join us, we aim to not only rid our shorelines of litter, but also to inspire individuals to live less wasteful lives."

Our Philosophy: Change Comes in Waves

United By Blue organized its first community cleanup the week they sold their first tee shirt. Through community waterway cleanups, United By Blue spreads the idea that if one business can make a difference, so can one person.

Burlington Island

In early 2019, the New Jersey Department of Environmental Protection asked United By Blue to direct a tricky cleanup project on Burlington Island in the Delaware River. The historical infrastructure had broken down into piles of rusted trash and was presenting a serious threat to the health of the Delaware River. Old trash was sinking into the river after heavy rains and also leaching chemicals into the soil and riverbeds.

United By Blue partnered with the City of Burlington and the Board of Island Managers, as well as a number of private sector businesses like

Sea Tow Delaware, Allied Recycling, and River Services, to execute this complicated cleanup. Using a barge to make trips back and forth, it took weeks of transporting machinery to the island and bringing trash back to the mainland to be disposed of and recycled. A total of 96,100 pounds of trash, from tires to plastic straws, was collected. Reopening of the island to the public is underway.

Illegal Dump Sites in Oklahoma

United By Blue launched several national cleanup partnerships with for-profit businesses, showing that significant progress can happen in the private sector when companies take a stand for clean water.

United By Blue joined forces with Environmental Crimes Units in Oklahoma to target illegal dumpsites along tributaries and ponds throughout the state, using heavy machinery, paid manpower, and professional trash trucking services, 628,200 pounds of trash were removed along waterways in Geary, Tribby, and Asher, Oklahoma.

Community Involvement

"We always try to involve our community in events that rally around sustainability and conservation," Linton emphasized. The company continues to participate in worthy causes around the globe.

The company operates four retail stores, two in Philadelphia, and one each in Chicago and Scottsdale.

CHAPTER 2-13

LVMH

Managing the Lighting Program for Nearly 5,000 Stores

Making Retail Areas More Energy Efficient Worldwide

LVMH Group (Louis Vuitton Moët Hennessy) encompasses 75 "Maisons" divided into five business sectors representing over 5,300 retail stores. The company is no newcomer to sustainability. Bernard Arnault, Chairman and CEO, initiated in 1992 the company's Group Environmental Department. It was the first major retail group to take environmental issues into account.

The fact that more than 80 percent of the Group's emissions in 2016 were due to the stores, spurred the insertion of Key Performance Indicators for the stores, within the LIFE, or LVMH Initiatives for the Environment, to be a part of each of the Group's strategic plan. Half of a store's energy consumption comes from lighting (the other 50 percent is mainly from air-conditioning and heating), so less energy-hungry technologies are essential for LVMH, which aims to reduce CO_2 emissions from energy consumption by 25 percent. The luxury group has to date achieved a reduction of 36 percent.

- In April 2021, the Group revealed the LIFE360 goals during their General Assembly, defining clear objectives on the stores' power consumption.
- 100 percent of the lighting will be LED at the end of 2026.
- CO_2 emissions will be reduced by half, also in 2026, due to the procurement of green energy.

To take full advantage of new LED solutions, the Group created the LVMH lighting program in 2013. LED lighting decreases electricity consumption by an average of 30 percent compared to traditional lighting. LVMH Lighting supports architectural teams at the Maisons to install LED lighting massively to enhance retail spaces and highlight the beauty of the products.

An LVMH training program is designed specifically for architects and store planners to help them maximize the environmental performance of stores, including a module dedicated to lighting. Life Influencers Agency, the training program has been developed in conjunction with neuroscience experts and consists of short 10-minute online sessions over a six-month period, coupled with two one-day workshops.

Since 2018, LVMH created with TEMELOY, a lighting design agency, a program called "Lighting for Good," that works on solutions for a better Circular Economy model for lighting.

To better understand how lighting affects the quality of the customer experience, LVMH Lighting examines ways to match store lighting to the local culture while continuing the distinctive light signature of each Maison (Figure 2-13.1), such as the upgraded La Samaritaine department store in Paris.

The newly renovated and restored Samaritaine facility showcases an eclectic and richly historical heritage, from Art Nouveau to Art Deco. LVMH's new vision of sustainable luxury that is championed through its LIFE 360 environmental program is evidenced throughout. The building has been certified to the most demanding environmental standards that included its achievements in instituting limited energy consumption through the use of cutting-edge engineered materials and employing low-consumption lighting. These include LEED (Leadership in Energy and Environmental Design) rated "Gold" applicable to retail spaces, and BREEAM (Building Research Establishment Environmental Assessment Method) and achieving given the "Excellent" rating that covers the evaluation of retail spaces that meet its performance specifications.

LVMH established six "LIFE in STORES" Awards, since 2016, to raise awareness of the responsibility and efforts required by all levels of the Group.

Figure 2-13.1 Interior of the new renovation of La Samaritaine, Paris, part of the LVMH group, with groups of custom white circular fixtures suspended over the main atrium space. The glass-roofed grand atrium, built between 1906 and 1910, has been fully restored for retail

Photo courtesy: La Samaritaine

CHAPTER 2-14

Allbirds

A Footwear Brand Takes Off

Aiming For Zero Carbon Emissions

In an economy where 90 percent of startups fail within the first three years, Allbirds, the San Francisco-based footwear and apparel company launched in March 2016, has defeated those odds by a high margin: it racked up an estimated valuation of $1.6 billion by 2021.

Allbirds began as a question in the mind of co-founder Tim Brown. After an eight-year professional soccer career, the native of New Zealand, a country where sheep outnumber people 6 to 1, began asking why wool, "such a remarkable, sustainable resource was virtually absent in footwear." Co-founder Joey Zwillinger, an engineer and renewables expert, partnered with Brown to perfect the fabric for their wool sneakers and the supply chain to bring an idea into fruition. Together, they created an original category of footwear inspired by natural materials (Figure 2-14.1).

Financial Beginnings

After retiring from soccer at age 31, Brown considered founding a sports-wear company. He grew up in New Zealand wearing homemade wool sweaters and socks—so he knew wool. By utilizing wool for a simple and sustainable sneaker, he could launch a marketable product.

The first financial backing for the project came from a group of New Zealand government agricultural scientists, along with a $200,000 development grant from a New Zealand wool industry research group. They gave Brown his start, and provided an early sense of credibility to future venture capital investors.

Once a sample shoe was made, Brown launched a Kickstarter campaign, hoping to raise $30,000. After four days and 1,064 pairs sold, the campaign closed with nearly $120,000 raised. Joey Zwillinger stepped in to bolster the financial operations and jumpstart the brand's sustainability programs.

"The World's Most Comfortable Shoe"

Another unorthodox step made by Brown and Zwillinger was to opt out of the shoe business's tendency toward a wholesale business model. Instead of creating a variety of products and selling them in bulk to distributors,

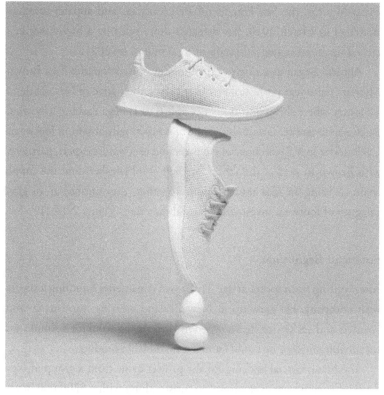

Figure 2-14.1 Allbirds' first shoe was the Wool Runner, made from New Zealand superfine Merino wool. The company is a certified B Corporation

Photo courtesy: Allbirds

they initially chose a direct-to-consumer model. When Allbirds launched, there was only one product available, the wool runner.

This revolutionarily simplistic tactic worked. The same day it became available, a profile in *Time* magazine anointed the sneaker "the world's most comfortable shoe." Later that day, the company received its first major fundraising round of $2.7 million.

A Silicon Valley Unicorn

In its first two years, the brand sold one million pairs of shoes. In the same year, the company's valuation reached a reported $1.4 billion—spurred by $50 million from investment firms that qualified them to be known as a "Silicon Valley unicorn" or privately held startups valued higher than $1 billion.

The company's collection offers both shoes and apparel for men and women in a variety of styles and materials. Products are available online, on the app, or in 33 brick-and-mortar locations in US, Asia, and Europe (Figure 2-14.2). Footwear styles are available in Allbirds Merino Wool, and in Allbirds Tree Material. Beyond shoes, Allbirds launched its first apparel collection in October 2020 with four styles and have since expanded the collection to include seven additional styles.

"Finding New Uses for Materials That Exist Right in Front of Us"

A single pair of running shoes is said to generate 30 pounds of carbon dioxide emissions, an unusually high amount considering the product does not use electricity. The source comes directly from the materials used.

In an industry that often favors cheaper, synthetic materials, Allbirds sticks to the natural material whenever possible. The three main ingredients used in their shoes are wool, tree fiber, and sugar. Allbirds' wool process uses 60 percent less energy than materials used in typical nylon. Another key material, TENCEL Lyocell, comes from ecologically friendly South African farms that minimize fertilizer use and rely on rainfall rather than irrigation. This tree fiber uses 95 percent less water than traditional materials like cotton and cuts the company's carbon footprint in half.

Allbirds uses southern Brazilian sugar cane to create their trademarked SweetFoam® material. Quick-growing and fully renewable resource, when manufactured into SweetFoam®, actually removes carbon from the atmosphere in its raw form. In the estimated $384 billion global footwear industry, a large majority of products contain a sole made of some form of EVA—rubbery foam made with petroleum. Allbirds' SweetFoam® uses an identical EVA polymer from the sugar plant instead of fossil fuel. Allbirds also incorporates recycled bottles in production of materials used for straps, interior materials, and anchors. Post-consumer recycled cardboard serves as an all-in-one shoebox and mailer.

The firm has launched its debut apparel collection with a line of T-shirts, sweaters, cardigans, and a puffer jacket for men and women. The T-shirt fabric is made from a fiber derived from crab shells.

Adidas and Allbirds Link Up

Globally, the footwear industry annually emits 700 million tons of carbon dioxide. Allbirds has joined forces with sportswear giant Adidas to not just lower emissions, but also work to eliminate them all together. In May 2021, the brands announced their first venture to create a high-performance sneaker with a carbon number of 2.94, which is lowest possible carbon number to date for either brand. Making a standard sneaker creates, on average, about 12.5 kg of carbon dioxide equivalent emissions, a common measurement for carbon footprint. Allbirds products average 7.6 kg of carbon dioxide equivalent emissions, according to the company's website.

"To envision a footprint that's even close to zero, we have to include technologies and solutions that don't exist yet. We readily admit that this is a marathon, not a sprint, and that there's much more work to be done," said Brown.

Figure 2-14.2 Exterior of Allbirds store, Philadelphia. Allbirds operates retail stores in United States cities plus Europe and the Far East

Photo courtesy: Chris Redmon

CHAPTER 2-15

Ministry of Supply

Hi-Tech Fabrics for Hi-Performance Apparel

Based out of Boston and born in the labs of MIT, Ministry of Supply fabrics are engineered for motion, comfort, and easy care. The product collection includes shirts, pants, outerwear, and other apparel items for men and women.

Its versatile Performance Professional dress shirt was introduced in 2014, with thermoset fibers that release wrinkles in the dryer, and subtle laser-cut underarm ventilation. Made with the same Phase Change Materials NASA invented to control astronauts' body temperature in space, Apollo's hyper-breathable knit regulates the user's core temperature in real time. Ministry of Supply implements 3D Print-Knitting, which reduces waste and helps to manage inventory. On-demand manufacturing was instituted in 2020.

Figure 2-15.1 Ministry of Supply retail store on Newbury Street, Boston

Figure 2-15.2 Aero Zero dress shirt

Figure 2-15.3 3D print dress

The firm's first carbon-neutral dress shirt is made of 100 percent recycled fabric milled under solar power. Through Aero Zero, the entire supply chain and operations became Climate Neutral Certified.

High Tech Masks

Ministry of Supply has experience in 3D printing performance clothing for a few years. Their seamless blazer 3D Print-Knit, for example, is constructed to enhance versatility and resilience. Through fabric prototyping, and rapid design testing, the company has become skilled in agile manufacturing. When the pandemic started, Ministry of Supply's knowledge of iterating new prototypes equipped them to collaborate with doctors, nurses, and engineers to develop an immediate solution. Partnering with high-tech Shima Seiki, a top manufacturer of computerized knitting machines, Ministry of Supply developed an open-source program to design and manufacture a new type of mask using 3D Print-Knit technology.

Ministry of Supply developed two models: 3D Print-Knit Mask and the Apollo Mask, lightweight and seamlessly knit. They are made of a viscose and PBT polyester blend, are machine washable, and the hygroscopic material pulls moisture to the core of the fiber, making it soft, breathable, and dry after even hours of wear. The Apollo Mask° uses NASA-developed Phase Change Materials and a pique-knit construction for advanced moisture management. By using non-woven material filters to make clothing, they can filter out particles when compressed. Gihan Amarasirwardena, Ministry of Supply co-founder explained that their non-woven fabric fuses together several layers of material, much like paper fuses together layers of cellulose fibers. While masks are designed by the Ministry of Supply team and partners, they are built by 3D printing machines. This means that the company can run multiple knitting machines to meet demand, without interfering with the design and production of their apparel and clothing. Test results by Nelson Labs showed that the masks provide higher than 95 percent Bacterial Filtration Efficiency.

Taylor Stitch

Producing Classics on Demand

This San Francisco-based brand that has its roots in men's shirting reduces its waste with a unique production and distribution model. The collection now extends to jackets and pants. Its Workshop model requires shoppers to order or reserve certain designs—insuring cost savings to the consumer as the product is manufactured for as many pieces as meets demand. According to co-founder Michael Maher, "Our hybrid selling model limits overproduction and guarantees early community buy-in, significantly reducing waste that would otherwise end in a landfill." More than 95 percent of the cotton used at Taylor Stitch is organic.

Classic Taylor Stitch staples are produced from environmentally friendly fabrics and constructed by responsible manufacturers (Figure 2-16.1). The designs in the collections are created to look and function as well in urban settings as in the great outdoors. Maher estimates that his firm's closely monitored production output has been responsible for saving nearly 57 million gallons of water, and averting hundreds of pounds of CO_2.

Wild Forever

"It's about protecting our places," says Maher. "No matter where you live, we only have one world to care for and we live in a global economy."

"We sponsor Wild Forever Days where we do things like blaze trails, clean up trash, help out on a farm and whatever else our community wants to learn about and participate in. It's about all of us coming together to protect our people and places through education and responsibility. We believe business is the best vehicle for change and we can have a lot of fun while doing it. No matter where you live, we only have one world to care for and we live in a global economy," Maher stresses.

Figure 2-16.1 Taylor Stitch Long Haul jacket in Cone Mills Reserve, and Chore Pants in British Khaki Boss Duck

Photo courtesy: Taylor Stitch

The brand's tough Boss Duck canvas mixes industrial hemp with polyester, organic cotton and a hint of stretch for fit. Industrial hemp can be grown without pesticides, requires one third the water of cotton, and yields more than double the fiber. "We're committed to using recycled and regenerative fibers wherever possible," Maher indicates. "This will help lower water usage, get rid of chemicals and pesticides which harm workers and leach into the rivers and help close the loop to create a cradle to cradle supply chain. It's going to take some time but we hope everyone joins us."

Best Buy

Committed to Community, People, and the Environment

Corporatewide Sustainable Practices and Employee Equality Programs Are Far-Reaching

At Best Buy, we aspire to drive forward the circular economy—a system in which nothing is wasted. We keep products in use for as long as possible, extract the maximum value from the products while in use, then recover and regenerate products and materials at the end of life.

Ongoing is our leadership role in addressing climate change, including reducing our carbon emissions by 55 percent. We continue to support teens from underserved communities through our 33 Teen Tech Centers.

—Corie Barry, Chief Executive Officer, Best Buy Co., Inc.

Figure 2-17.1 Best Buy Farmington, Utah

Photo courtesy: Best Buy

Sustainability has been a priority for Best Buy stores for more than a decade (Figure 2-17.1). Best Buy achievements make the annual lists of top-rated companies for its implementation of ethical business practices, sustainability programs, environmental impact, monitoring the sources of the products they sell, workplace diversity, ability to attract and retain talent, and responsibility to the community.

Its annual *Corporate Responsibility and Sustainability Report* supports the firm's progress for the expansive collection of their programs, and details the extent of their ongoing benefits.

Headquartered in Richfield, Minnesota, the company has operations in the United States, Canada, and Mexico. Founded in 1966, Best Buy now has more than 1,156 stores, employs approximately 125,000 people, and generated more than $47.3 billion in FY21. It has been the recipient of numerous awards for its corporatewide sustainable practices and employee equality applications.

- *Continuing programs:*
  - Prepare one million teens from underserved communities for tech-reliant jobs each year
  - Reduce carbon emissions by 60 percent and achieve carbon neutrality by 2050
  - Operate 16 Best Buy Teen Centers, with plans for 60
  - Achieved 50 percent carbon reduction over 2009 baseline
  - Collected 2 billion pounds of electronics and appliances for recycling since 2009, making Best Buy the largest collector of waste in the United States

Corporate Responsibility & Sustainability Governance

Best Buy advocates the circular economy: reduce, repair, reuse, and recycle. Products, the company believes, should be kept in use for as long as possible to extract maximum value, then recovered and regenerated.

Best Buy's corporate responsibility governance structure is comprised of the independent Nominating, Corporate Governance & Public Policy Committee of the Board of Directors that oversees Corporate Responsibility & Sustainability (CR&S). Some current programs include:

Damage Reduction: Specialized equipment to move TVs and appliances; training employees on correct product handling to avoid damage; placing additional safe-handling tips on all TVs 46in." and larger; providing a dedicated website for safe unboxing instructions.

Repair: To extend the life of their products, Best Buy can call on more than 20,000 Geek Squad Agents and repair partners, who can repair up to five million devices annually, keeping electronics in the "use" phase.

Trade-In Program: Best Buy recycles phones, laptops, tablets, and cameras so that customers can get value for products that are still in good working condition. Customers are able to upgrade sooner; products traded-in at a Best Buy and resold at a secondhand store allow purchase by users who might not be able to afford new products. Through its recycling program, Best Buy collects 409 pounds of electronics each minute its stores are open.

Sustainable Packaging: Modal cellphone case packages use bioplastics, a plant-based biodegradable material. Insignia packages use water-based coatings that are easily handled by a recycling facility.

Paper Procurement: 100 percent of paper is certified to an internationally recognized forestry standard; at least 30 percent recycled content for office paper.

Business Ethics Practices: All employees receive annual training based on realistic examples of ethical dilemmas that our employees have had or might encounter. Ethics training for new employees emphasizes the importance of acting with integrity in all decisions relating to the company. One-on-one meetings are held with each new officer to review key ethics and compliance policies. Annual roundtable training sessions on ethical leadership are held for all officers.

Community Outreach

Geek Squad Academy Camps. Best Buy partners with local nonprofits and other organizations to provide students ages 12 to 14 with two-day camps and one-day experiences to learn programming, complete challenges, and solve puzzles. Approximately 1,250 Best Buy employees engaged with GSA in the past year. Since its inception in 2007, GSA inspired more than 34,000 children from underserved communities to become engineers, entrepreneurs, teachers, and designers.

Best Buy Teen Tech Centers are free after-school programs that provide a creative learning environment where teens can build confidence, and gain employable skills through access to state-of-the-art technology, such as 3D printers, digital media, robotics, and coding. Best Buy plans to sponsors 60 Teen Tech Centers, including in communities hit hardest by natural disasters, including Puerto Rico and Houston.

Contributions: Since 1999, Best Buy and the Best Buy Foundation donated more than $366 million to services in communities in which they operate stores. Active programs include National Grants, Twin Cities Fund, and $125 million given to St. Jude Children's Research Hospital® since 2013. TagTeam Awards are monetary donations to nonprofit organizations where employees volunteer their time.

Supply Chain Sustainability Program

Best Buy's Chemicals Management Statement includes a Restricted Substance List for their branded products and for the use of chemicals in the manufacturing process. Best Buy launched a program with its nine TV suppliers requiring that each supplier indicates that all chemicals reported are within the limit of the restricted substances list. Plans are to expand this program to other product categories.

Managing Environmental Impacts

Reducing damage that occurs before it gets to our customers is the first step for us in this cycle. We have been working on initiatives to reduce damage for more than a decade, keeping products in the "use" phase longer.

—Corie Barry

Best Buy is the first US large-format retailer to earn ISO 14001-certified Environmental Management System (EMS) approval to assist in systematically managing progress toward achieving environmental goals and commitments. These include finding cost-effective solutions to save energy and directly reduce carbon emissions through operational improvements and sourcing renewable energy.

Energy-efficient operations. Technologies such as LED lighting and updated heating and cooling systems reduce carbon emissions in stores and distribution centers.

The new Geekmobile fleet and cars used by Best Buy InHome Advisors together comprise more than 1,500 Toyota Prius c hybrid model cars.

CHAPTER 2-18

Qwstion

A High-Performing Textile From Banana Fibers

Stylish Backpacks That Are Fully Sustainable

Qwstion started in 2008, when industrial designers Sebastian Kruit and Christian Kaegi joined forces with three colleagues to create an elegant, functional sports backpack. They founded their brand in Zurich, Switzerland.

"The vast majority of backpack materials are made from oil-based plastic fibers," says creative director Kaegi, "using environmentally harmful synthetics like nylon and polyester. We invested three years of research, testing, and development to create a truly sustainable material. The idea for us was to make a product that comes from plants that can eventually go back to plants and nature."

Producing Bananatex Yarn

Figure 2-18.1 Abacá fibers are air dried for two days before being bundled and taken to the warehouse for processing

The founders created Bananatex® (Figure 2-18.1), the first technical textile made purely from the fibers of Abacá banana plants, cultivated in the Philippine highlands. They are grown in organic mixed forestry cultures in the Catanduanes areas, in former jungles eroded by soil damage due to monocultural palm plantations that are now bringing economic prosperity to the region.

About 400 micro-farms are cultivating the banana fiber and transporting it to the warehouse for processing. Grown with a natural ecosystem of sustainable mixed agriculture and forestry, Abacá is sturdy and self-sufficient, requiring no pesticides or extra water. Abacá produces fibers that are long, strong, and lightweight. Abacá banana plants can be harvested up to three times a year, taking one year to regenerate naturally.

After cutting the stalk with a bamboo sickle, outer layers are separated from the inner ones, in order to prepare for fiber extraction. The inner stripped fibers extracted from the stalks are air dried and bundled before being transported and into the warehouse, where they are sorted by color grades. Separated fibers are boiled and pressed into sheets resembling cardboard. These sheets become yarn by Qwstion's production partner where it is woven into an extra high-density fabric. A natural beeswax coating makes it water-resistant.

Qwstion's Bananatex® Roll Pack and the Hip Pouch patterns were designed to maximize sustainability and recyclability, leaving zero waste after cutting the individual parts. The finished products are simply constructed, practical, and versatile. At the end of their life cycles, they leave no trace: their fabric is 100 percent biodegradable, and their component parts are recyclable.

Tencel threads are used for sewing. Bananatex bag owners, when they wish to purchase a new model, can remove the YKK-Zipper and metal hooks, which can both be recycled, and place the used bag in their compost. "We've tested it ourselves, and after about six months it's gone," reports Kaegi.

Qwstion Retail Stores

Qwstion's retail stores in Zurich, Basel, Lausanne, and Vienna (Figure 2-18.2) are elegant contemporary spaces that showcase their bag

Figure 2-18.2 Wall-hung display in Qwstion store in Vienna

Photos courtesy: Lauschsicht; Nico Schaerer; Qwstion

collections. Made from a fabric derived from banana plants, Bananatex, bags are individually hung from the walls with custom-made hooks.

The stores' boutique-like image is created by presenting the work of new local designers who relate to the company's own modernist design principles, including apparel, furniture and home accessories, footwear, jewelry, audio systems, sunglasses, and books. Qwstion products are sold in 45 countries.

CHAPTER 2-19

Picture Organic Clothing

A Pioneer in Sustainable Outerwear

Picture Organic Clothing, based in Annecy le vieux, France, creates bomber ski jackets, snow pants, wetsuits, swimwear, and other products (Figures 2-19.1–2-19.2) made 100 percent from recycled poly and plant-based materials that match the performance of traditionally made of less sustainable products. For the past 10 years, the fabric used for the firm's products contains polyester derived from recycling plastic bottles.

Technical outerwear is a whole different story.

Figure 2-19.1 Chase backpack

Figure 2-19.2 TANYA jacket

Photo courtesy: Picture Organic Clothing

Ski jackets typically require using fabric containing crude oil by products. Conventional technical polyester fabric (PET) consists of mono-ethylene-glycol (30 percent) and terephthalic acid (70 percent), both petrochemical compounds. Picture Organic Clothing has been using polyester derived from recycling plastic bottles since its founding in 2008.

Applying MEG Technology

"We are always looking for new solutions to directly or indirectly wipe out our dependence on fossil fuels," says co-founder Julien Durant. "Bio-sourcing represents one of these solutions. In the case of a snow jacket, it means creating a fabric partially made with plant material such as sugar cane or castor beans, to replace conventional petroleum-based mono ethylene glycol (MEG)," he says. He sees a future by incorporating plant-based bio-polyester.

In the sugar cane process, the sugar extract is refined by melting, bleaching, and crystallization to produce a colorless molasses mixture. Picture's technology introduces a specific bacteria that transforms the raw material to create through a chemical reaction to bio-ethanol. This can be converted into bio-mono ethylene glycol that through another process provides a non-petroleum-based MEG. MEG is an essential component used as raw material in diverse industrial processes such as the manufacture of resins, polyester, fibers, and various types of films. Next steps incorporate it into yarn to replace traditional polyester used in fabrics for Picture's apparel and accessories collections.

Recycling Used Clothes

Picture is embarking on a test program to recycle used clothes. A major challenge is that most products are made with several types of material; for most brands, this means a polyurethane membrane with a polyester face fabric. The company's goal is to create a polyester thread derived from recycled clothing that will then be used to make their products.

Ten recycling bins are in place in partnering Picture stores throughout France. Washed clothing and apparel from any brand is accepted. With the support of Techtera, Picture team sorts the piles of clothing to separate all technical apparel such as ski or hard-shell jackets, and sends it on to a recycling center to be treated to be turned into a reusable product.

Co-founder Julien Durant states that for his company, "Community service and social programs are just as important as the work we do for the environment. There are real human beings behind every Picture product. Picture is a member of the Fair Wear Foundation to improve working conditions for the people who make their products. Everything we do has an impact on the environment. What we have been trying to do since 2008 is to commit to a sustainable approach for every aspect of the brand."

Picture Organic Clothing is a certified B Corp. The brand is carried by 700 retailers in 30 countries.

CHAPTER 2-20

Tentree

An International Outreach to Offset Climate Change

Figure 2-20.1 The Tentree Juniper hoodie, which carries the firm's signature juniper tree logo, is breathable with insulating features

Tentree brand clothing is made from ethically sourced and sustainable materials including cork, coconut, and recycled polyester, and is produced in ethical factories. For each item purchased, Tentree lives up to its name and plants 10 trees in 42 countries around the world and provides customers a code so they can track the growth of their trees. The collection includes apparel and accessory products for men, women, and children, with styles for activewear, outerwear, backpacks, hats and caps, blankets and throws, and decorative pillow covers (Figure 2-20.1).

Vancouver, Canada-based Tentree by mid-2022 announced that it had been responsible for the planting of a total of 77 million trees worldwide, including Canada, Nepal, Senegal, Mexico, Indonesia, Haiti, Brazil, Peru, and Madagascar. "Tentree's goal is to become the most environmentally progressive brand on the plant," said co-founder and CEO Derrick Emsley. "Around the world, we work with 'agroforestry' farmers to plant fruit tress like pineapples and mangoes to help feed their communities," he adds.

"Our commitment to sustainability extends beyond planting trees. It is woven into everything we do … to identify priorities for actions and opportunities for improving environmental impacts, worker basic needs, and the well-being of communities," says Emsley.

The firm's 18-point Supplier Code of Conduct applies to the entire supply chain. One of the firm's goals for Tentree International Inc. is to become the most environmentally progressive brand on the planet. "Our commitment goes beyond planting trees," he says. He quotes the fact that the average fully gown tree produces the oxygen needed for two people to breath all year. It responds to this human well-being by absorbing as much as 48 pounds of carbon pollution annually.

1 Billion Trees by 2030

Tentree is a Certified B. Corporation. To achieve their certification, Tentree commissioned a life cycle analysis to measure and understand the key environmental impacts for its products, including fabric, garment, packaging, transport, warehousing, customer usage, and end of life.

The firm's long-range vision—to contribute to drastically reducing climate change—is to plant one billion trees by 2030.

"As environmentalists, our mission is to guide consumers and empower them to do their best when it comes to the environment," said Emsley. "It's the little things, like people riding their bike to work, bringing their own grocery bag, and buying an item that plants ten trees—they all add up. Especially when millions of other people start doing them too," he emphasized.

Tentree products are sold in stores operated by Urban Outfitters, Anthropology, and Nordstorm along with specialty outdoor outfitters.

CHAPTER 2-21

Li & Fung

The Supply Chain of the Future

Developing a 3D Design Library

The world's oldest and largest supply chain organization, Li & Fung Ltd, manages the Sustainable Sourcing division of its company by following several dozen precise directives, applicable to products ranging from furniture to hangtags on apparel. Founded in 1906 as a trader in Chinese handcrafts to the West, the Hong Kong-based company has expanded to 230 offices in 40 different markets, with a staff of 17,000.

In addition to its supply chain operations, Li & Fung extends its sustainability programs to engage their people and communities, and managing their footprint. Their three-pronged approach, involves managing risk and improving performance in the supply chain, adopting standards and best practices, and providing sustainable design, manufacturing, product and packaging options.

Programs instituted in 2019 that are directed by the firm's office in Norderstedt, Germany, included:

- P with Stop! Micro Waste, supplier of the Guppyfriend® washbag, which traps microplastics from entering the ecosystem during the washing process
- Received certification to the Responsible Wool Standard which combines aspects of animal welfare and traceability in the supply chain
- Supported customers who have committed to the Detox campaign to successfully phase out hazardous chemical groups from the production of materials
- Certification to the Global Recycling Standard of the use of polyester made of 100 percent recycled input for outerwear and swimwear brands

For one of its customers, Li & Fung sourced more than eight and one-half million units of denim made from recycled materials comprising the transformation of an estimated 25 million waster plastic bottles. For an outwear manufacturer, they sourced fabric that was the result of the treatment of three million, two-liter plastic bottles. For an order placed by a denim apparel maker, 1.5 million meters of recycled polyester was sourced.

Working with 75 wet-process production facilities in six different countries, the Norderstdet office specialists succeeded in eliminating the use of chemicals from the 11 groups banned according to the Detox Commitment.

Li & Fung provides content information to manufacturers of household items made from such wide-ranging materials as wood and paper to banana bark and water hyacinth.

Slashing Lead Time

Li & Fung sponsored research and development to reduce manufacturer's overall lead time and get the product right closer to the time of sale. They looked at the tools to digitize product development and design and developed a system that shortened it from months down to days, sometimes less. Their solution was 3D design. Photorealistic 3D digital samples can be used for wholesale catalogs, store merchandising, or the e-commerce site, eliminating the need for photo shoots and models.

To provide an industry resource, Li & Fung's Digital Product Development team is developing a materials library to serve high-quality 3D design. It will provide a database of super-high-quality scans of all kinds of physical fabric. Another module automatically calculates the cost and the impact of design changes during the development process.

The company plans to add capacity modules that help with finding available factories, fabric, and sourcing suppliers, potentially cutting a massive amount of time and decision making out of the process.

SECTION 3

Social and Cultural Programs

Introduction

Retail industry analysts agree that brands and retailers must respond to the values of new consumers, including being environmentally responsible, produced under humane conditions, paying fair wages, and being inclusive and equitable in hiring and compensation practices. Social justice has become table stakes.

Social justice and equity issues broke through to the boardroom. Social equity and justice lie at the core of action on sustainability and a just transition.

Getting the guardrails right for nature-based solutions is key to ensure sustainability and deliver real climate and other critical ecological benefits. Financial innovation can't run ahead of safeguards and governance. Nature-based solutions have important considerations beyond climate, including biodiversity, water, and the livelihoods of people who live near or work in forests and agriculture.

Many corporate entities are committing to be nature-positive. Natural solutions for sustainability are taking off. Investment and innovation are accelerating. Defined in broad terms, nature now offers some of the most exciting areas for sustainable investing. Regenerative solutions promise to heal and rebuild our ecological and social landscapes, going far beyond minimizing damage.

Reaching Out to the Community

Kroger Balances Food Donation Program with Increased Cash

Kroger adjusted a reduction in surplus food due to COVID-19 by increasing its charitable cash donations toward hunger relief organizations to $213 million.

The combination of rescued food—about 90 million pounds—and cash increased its total donations to an equivalent of 640 million meals in fiscal 2020, or a 29 percent increase from the 493 million meals it donated in fiscal 2019. Since kicking off Zero Hunger | Zero Waste in 2017, Kroger has donated the equivalent of 1 billion meals.

Zero Hunger | Zero Waste is a social impact plan built around addressing hunger by donating 3 billion meals in the communities in which it does business by 2025 and by achieving "zero waste"— diverting 90 percent of waste from landfills at all its owned facilities, by the same date.

Kroger is leveraging relationships with entities like the World Wildlife Fund to link disparities in global food production, access and waste to conservation challenges facing the planet's land, oceans, and wildlife; ReFED, the national nonprofit dedicated to addressing food loss and waste by advancing data-driven solutions; and Feeding America, the national network of food banks with which Kroger has been associated since it origins.

Publix Gives Back

More than 6,000 associates volunteered during a recent Publix Serves Week. Special attention to environmental sustainability. Associates helped keep our states beautiful by planting trees, cleaning beaches and parks, and much more. By the week's end, they'd spent over 22,000 hours helping our local communities.

When Publix Serves started, it was a day set aside to help those around us. Then we extended it a whole week. Now Publix Serves Week occurs twice a year—once in the spring and again in the fall. Environmental projects were emphasized in April, while the fall Publix Serves Week puts the spotlight on alleviating hunger. In April, 2022, Publix, which operates more than 1,200 stores, announced that the company has donated more than 50 million pounds of produce as part of its initiative to support farmers and food banks in the Southeast. Launched in response to farmers being forced to discard produce they could no longer sell due to the COVID-19 pandemic, Publix began purchasing produce directly from impacted farmers and donating it to food banks throughout the company's operating area.

As food insecurity continued to affect communities, Publix combined this initiative with a point-of-sale campaign to create Feeding More Together, which provides both produce and nonperishable food items to food banks. Through this campaign, Publix matches customer donations at the register, which provide nonperishable food items, with an equivalent value of fresh produce. "Providing nourishment to people facing food insecurity is fundamental to our mission of being responsible citizens in our communities," said Publix CEO Todd Jones. "In America, 1 in 8 people currently face hunger. With the help of Publix's customers and associates, we can do good together while supplying the foods individuals and families need to thrive." In a 12-year period, Publix's campaigns in support of hunger alleviation have resulted in more than $135 million in food donations.

CHAPTER 3-1

Galeries Lafayette

Reinventing Retail Standards With "Go For Good"

A Firmwide Label to Make a Social Contribution

Galeries Lafayette is no stranger to public recognition. Founded in 1894, its art glass-dome ceiling in its landmark 755,000-sq-ft Paris store is rated as the second most tourist destination after the Eiffel Tower. The Galeries Lafayette Haussmann, accounted for an estimated $1.42 billion in 2021.

Not satisfied to recline on its laurels, Galeries Lafayette in 2018 initiated the Go For Good movement. It is a collective, creative initiative aimed at offering the store's customers products that have style as well as sustainable consumption qualifications. Nearly 600 brands have already joined the movement to abide by these guidelines.

Environmental, social, and local-made production were the three key themes with which brands could participate. In order to maintain an ethical responsible standard, selected labels follow at least one of three criterions.

- Environmental criteria focused on the material used, the production processes, usage, and end-of-life benefit to the environment.
- The social element features brands that highlighted production and/or sale of goods that contribute to fighting poverty and exclusion while fostering social development.
- Local criteria focused on products manufactured in France, protecting jobs.

"It's not enough for our company to simply play an economic role anymore," said chief executive officer Nicolas Houzé, in a statement outlining the effort: "It's also our duty to make a social contribution. The store's investment is already understood and supported by consumers." He cites a report by consumer goods company, Unilever, that a third of consumers globally now choose to buy from brands that consider their social and environmental impact.

Promoting "Go For Good"

"Go For Good" is based on a strict set of specifications detailing precise criteria to build a range of more than 12,000 product references that feature one or more significant advantages over conventional equivalents to benefit the environment, social development, or support French manufacturing.

Kicking off with a series of responsible fashion-focused events, outposts across France hosted talks and in-store pop-ups, alongside products from accessory and homeware brands which are sustainably recognized. A dedicated corner is permanently settled on the second floor of the main building (cupola) and offers a Go For Good label, from ready-to-wear, to lingerie to accessories and shoes, to the gourmet food hall (Figures 3-1.1–3-1.3). By providing clear, transparent information about the benefits of each product, Galeries Lafayette shows that alternatives do exist in the fashion industry. Go For Good labels provide the consumer with information as to why these products were included.

By offering consumers the ability to experience a varied and extensive selection of ethical brands, Galeries Lafayette's initiative aims to start a revolution in sustainable commerce. "We are building the retail and fashion industry of the future, with a strong focus on experience and meaning," believes Houzé.

Figure 3-1.1 Information sign to the left of entry to Go For Good collection of men's apparel and accessories: "Galeries Lafayette is committed to more responsible fashion"

Figure 3-1.2 Girls apparel and accessory section. "The Good Spot for More Responsible Fashion"

Figure 3-1.3 Galeries Lafayette Haussmann, ReStore department, Paris

Photos courtesy: ©Thibaut Voisin, Galeries Lafayette

CHAPTER 3-2

ISAIC

Training for the Industry

Industrial Sewing and Innovation Center's (ISAIC) mission is to create a sustainable community-empowered ecosystem for apparel manufacturing with an innovative approach to facility design, application of technology, and advanced career path development. Chair and CEO Jennifer Guarino teamed up with change makers in the Detroit area to create the ISAIC.

"Ethical fashion is on its way to becoming a customer expectation," said Guarino. The fashion industry as a whole is beginning to understand what that means for production.

"We believe that sustainability must start with people. If your employees aren't making livable wages, that isn't sustainable. Development of an equitable workforce is at the center of ethical manufacturing."

Sources: Adapted from *isaic.org, michiganradio.org, crainsdetroit.com,* and *modelmedia.com*

ISAIC: Combining Technology and Skilled Labor

Creating a Career Path and Quality Work Environments

Interview by Ken Nisch with Jen Guarino, CEO and chair of ISAIC, Industrial Sewing and Innovation Center, Detroit.

KN: How is ISAIC developing an opportunity to teach and enhance skills to establish an ecosystem that is a new approach to manufacturing?

JG: Essentially, ISAIC is a Detroit-based academy and factory in one, defying the typical model that manufacturing has used to make products and treat the people who make them.

Our timing is good, reflecting the attention now being paid to sustainability issues. The apparel industry is being pressured to cut waste and produce output closer to its markets. It's a national problem. The industry has been shrinking for the last 30 years, after factories started closing and those that were left didn't have the resources to invest in training. We have to make up for a generation of not training people in the industry.

Two things are needed to make it competitive and make the cost of ownership reasonable—first, technology, and second, skilled labor. Traditionally in the apparel industry, people are taught how to sew and it is expected that they will do it forever. ISAIC is teaching the traditional required skills, but is also creating career paths toward higher-paying jobs by teaching workers how to use the available technologies, so they aren't left behind when new technologies emerge (Figures 3-2.1 and 3-2.2).

KN: How will this program be applied?

Figure 3-2.1 Here, workers are trained to cut and sew, and operate emerging technology such as robotics to create products, all while taking on contract work

Photo courtesy: John F. Martin Photography; ISAIC

Figure 3-2.2 Applying new technology skills at ISAIC

Photo courtesy: John F. Martin Photography; ISAIC

JG: Under development is a curriculum in partnership with academic institutions and industries to create flexible programs for the workers. For example, single moms can get paid during an apprenticeship while attending related classes that apply to a degree or other credentials.

A nonprofit learning center will be rolled into a facility co-owned by the workers. When it becomes self-sustaining, ISAIC will become co-owners, and be there to support them. Planned is an industrywide information program that can list career opportunities to develop talent pipelines.

KN: Are you setting an example for other industries to say, "There's a new way to do this?"

JG: The industry must begin to look at where they ask people to work. Think about it as a national institution for the trades, based in Detroit, supported throughout our country.

Envision this happening in a place where you would want to work: skylights, plants, music to replace the image of a sweatshop. The workers who make the product should have a wonderful place to work.

KN: Where have you found additional support?

JG: Social impact investors are looking at investing in a for-profit, worker-owned factory when it rolls out and promises to be self-sustaining. Social capital investors invest in for-profit companies all the time. We appeal to both the philanthropic and social impact investment communities. Philanthropic organizations are mostly interested in outcomes, that is, what will this do for people in a community?

KN: Has the ISAIC model been tried anywhere else?

JG: Our concept is different from incubators or maker-spaces. We are taking the responsibility and committing to people's development, rather than filling seats.

KN: Where did the ISAIC concept come from?

JG: It started when an industry contact called and told me about the many opportunities to grow a business in Detroit. Our response was to get a stakeholders group together. We met for three hours every other Monday night for six months. Together, we identified what was needed, and how to make it happen.

In 2009, I came to Detroit and opened a leather products factory for Shinola. With management's approval, we introduced a totally different energy environment in the worker's areas. There was music playing, window seats, natural light. It was a convergence of these different experiences that led to an improved production output.

It's our belief that we can help other industries look at our model as an example—jewelry, furnishings, home décor, technology, and so on, and show that it can be successful. If billions of pre-consumer garments go into landfills yearly, one reason is because cheap labor is being exploited. Stop overproducing, and turn those dollars into livable wages.

Consumers are beginning to understand that if they pay a little more, they can have information about the product: who made it, and whether it meets sustainable standards and won't contribute to landfills and exploited labor.

KN: You also want to take out carbon impact of transportation.

JG: If possible, lighthouse manufacturing, that is, source as far as your brightest light can shine. This means shorter lead time, fewer carbon emissions—not shipping all over the world and back—and use local materials. This sustainable model is at the very core, the DNA of change.

KN: What are the challenges in getting to a scale?

JG: There will be unknowns, and there are going to be things that worked better than we thought! Our job is to create the case that's believable enough that someone will want to invest in anything to start in a new way. In the tech industry, people do that every day for things that may or may not ever materialize. We have to convince people to do the same for manufacturing.

KN: Is it difficult to convince people to rally around your concept?

JG: We recently attended a conference called So-Cap and got a great reception. Many people are hoping that this model works. They are aware of many strategies that aren't working, and they see us as completely disrupting and successful.

KN: Is your model applicable to adapting products already made?

JG: Yes, it could, but we don't want to be in that business at the outset. But once someone else figures it out, we're all for it.

KN: Is Shinola a case study of what you are trying to achieve?

JG: Not quite. Shinola is a part of an ecosystem, with their factory located in the same building occupied by a college with dorms. We helped them to develop a curriculum, so that showed us what we can do. The ecosystem and the environment were the learning phases that we are now putting into practice.

CHAPTER 3-3

Kingsmen

A Focus on Sustainable Working Environments and Society

Implementing Corporate and Community Strategies

Established in 1976, Kingsmen Creatives Ltd. has grown from a local supplier of display fixtures to a global group with offices in 21 major cities across Asia Pacific, Middle East, and the United States, serving international brands in Research & Design, Exhibitions & Events, Thematic & Museums, Retail & Corporate Interiors, and Alternative Marketing.

As the retail landscape continuously reshapes, the Retail & Corporate Interiors division pursues opportunities in new emerging segments such as co-working spaces and online brands establishing an offline presence. The Group's current portfolio includes established markets of retail, corporate interiors, and other applications (Figures 3-3.1 and 3-3.2).

Figure 3-3.1 Kingsmen fixtures for Missoni, Milan, Italy

Photo courtesy: Kingsmen Creatives Ltd.

Figure 3-3.2 Kingsmen fixtures at Primark, Chicago

Photo courtesy: Primark website

Sustainable Working Environment

Kingsmen is an active practitioner in the global effort to sustain and better manage resources. Some conservation initiatives include adopting environmentally friendly practices into their processes; and as part of their standard operating procedures, reducing energy as well as water consumption.

Employees are actively involved in fulfilling the company's Green philosophy by engaging in green practices within their day-to-day operations. They also reduce their overall carbon footprint by promoting remote meetings and collaboration technologies, and limiting business travel. "Kingsmen's designers and project personnel advocate green design during the planning process, and develop methods to make projects more eco-friendly by the use of innovative products and materials," says Andrew Cheng, Group CEO of Kingsmen Creatives.

Sustainability Guidelines

1. Incorporating the method of 5 Rs (Reuse, Reduce, Recycle, Repair, and Rethink) to reduce any pollution impacts.

2. Consistently enhancing the performance monitoring processes and improving the type of data that is collected.

3. Emphasizing Kingsmen as a green organization by encouraging employees to reduce the usage of toxic products such as foam and plastic.

4. Incorporating waste management measures in daily work.

5. Committing to the sustainable development goals throughout all procedures, from production to waste management.

Contributing to the Next Generation

Kingsmen believes they have a responsibility to improve the lives of those in the communities in which they operate. The focus is on initiatives that will contribute where it matters—and have a positive impact. Beyond corporate work, their community strategy involves areas of education, design, and youth.

The focus on supporting youth empowerment is an extension of the motto of continuous learning which has been actively supported by Kingsmen. This program connects employees with marginalized youth through support for the beneficiaries' community engagement work. Apart from partnership with SHINE Children and Youth Services in Singapore, Kingsmen's Vietnam office initiated a campaign to benefit disadvantaged youth in selected social centers and orphanages in Ho Chi Minh City and nearby areas. The objective was to increase creative self-exploration by providing a creative platform for the disadvantaged youth and concurrently raise public awareness about the support that society can lend to these young people.

Through a series of public activities, including a design contest, a charity walk, pop-up store road show, and a charity auction, Kingsmen proactively promotes public interest to raise funds and engage youth through school-based program activities.

Care the Bear

Kingsmen's Thai office, Kingsmen C.M.T.I. Plc., joined 22 other organizations in "Care the Bear: Change the Climate Change by Eco Event" organized by the Stock Exchange of Thailand in 2018. Its purpose was to campaign with partners to prevent global warming by reducing the carbon footprint from event organizations.

Green Industry

Kingsmen C.M.T.I., Plc., has been honored with the "Green Industry" certification from Thailand's Ministry of Industry. The recognition acknowledged the company's efforts to comply with the policies on sustainability, resource control, climate change mitigation, and pollution prevention with the common aim of contributing to the environment and society both within and beyond the enterprise.

CHAPTER 3-4

Shinola

Made in a New Detroit

An Unconventional Manufacturing Company Is a Major Factor in the City's Successful Repurposing

In 2013, the city of Detroit filed the largest public-sector bankruptcy in the U.S. history. Its debt totaled $20 billion, stemming largely from its drastic population decline. From its 1.8 million residents in 1950, the current population is reported as 662,000.

But today, its has a new nickname: "Comeback City."

An iconic driving force in the city's change of fortunes is the Shinola multibrand collection of products and services. Founded by Tom Kartsotis, who in the early 1980s initiated Fossil watches and, with its retailing offshoot, drove its volume in 10 years to $3.2 billion, adding clothing and accessories to the mix. In 2003, he founded a private equity and brand management firm, Bedrock Manufacturing Co., assembling a diversified portfolio of U.S.-made brands.

Eight years later, he launched Shinola, Bedrock's vehicle for doing something completely new. Shinola's corporate identity derives from the specialty shoeshine products manufacturer, Seattle-based Shinola, which operated from 1907 to the 1970s. Shinola's objective is to turn traditional American manufacturing with skills to the production of goods for a contemporary lifestyle range, including luxury handmade bicycles, time-pieces, stationery, and leather goods. Kartsotis is credited with fashioning a brand that feels authentic despite being a largely promotional assemble.

Today's Shinola employs over 500 people, with an average of 100 in manufacturing at any given time depending on the production needs. They follow a practice of globally sourcing the best possible components for all of their products, and work with a community of independent manufacturers across the country and around the world who share Shinola's commitment to using materials of an enduring nature.

A Dedicated Workforce

Shinola management is reminded by founder Kartsotis that with a healthy degree of humor and tenacity, the firm can get a lot of great things done when they work together. Through skilled training, Shinola creates opportunities for team members, and supports the local workforce to manufacture products such as world-class timepieces. They receive substantial support from the Detroit business community and from the public sector, contributing to Shinola's growth.

Shinola's initial expansion push was to open a 30,000 sq.-ft. watch factory in Detroit's historic Argonaut building, built by General Motors and now the A. Alfred Taubman Center for Design Education (Figure 3-4.1). Set up in collaboration with Swiss watch movement maker Ronda, the factory trains locals, many ex-auto workers, through Shinola-sponsored

Figure 3-4.1 Shinola watch production facility, Detroit

Photo courtesy: Shinola

classes. Shinola has located its corporate headquarters on the fifth floor in the same building.

Founder Kartsotis brings in outside partners to train his U.S. workers in complex manufacturing skills that were long ago offshored. He says the more the company grows, the more new job posts he'll have to fill, the more skills training he'll provide, and the more supply chains he can help restore.

Shinola Boutiques

Customers at the Detroit flagship store could enjoy artisanal entertainment, watching dial makers through plated glass (Figure 3-4.2).

Its Manhattan retail store, designed with the Rockwell Group, in the heart of Tribeca, New York (Figure 3-4.3). Architect David Rockwell Group helped to implement a sophisticated amalgam of old and new accents, dividing the 1,400-sq.-ft. space into multiple sections to capture the Shinola ethos. Features include a custom-made steel spiral staircase, which leads up to a mezzanine catwalk, while another wall features a row of stadium-style bleacher seating, on which products are displayed.

Figure 3-4.2 Shinola retail store, Detroit

Photo courtesy: Shinola

Figure 3-4.3 Shinola retail store, New York City

Photo courtesy: Shinola

Kartsotis has looked beyond Detroit, visiting other cities across the country that Shinola might colonize next. "Through skilled training, we create opportunities for our team members and support local workforces by partnering with US companies to manufacture specialty items," Kartsotis emphasizes. "We show our respect of thoughtful design and the beauty of industry through every product we make," Kartsotis affirms.

CHAPTER 3-5

Bottletop

Fashion Collections from Bottletops and Ring Pulls

A Foundation to Support Youth Training Programs

BOTTLETOP is a London-based sustainable fashion brand. Beginning in 2012, its line of handbags covered with upcycled bottletops was made in Kenya and lined with leather offcuts. The co-founders, Cameron Saul and Oliver Wayman, then discovered the versatility of upcycled aluminum ring pulls, held together by crotchet, which developed into their signature chain mail fabric collections.

Figure 3-5.1 The Bottletop Maxi bag

Photo courtesy: Bottletop

Through a collaboration with the established producer and retailer Mulberry, the designs became international bestsellers, generating local employment and raising vital funds for grassroots education projects in Africa. The product line has been extended to include a selection of bags, accessories, and jewelry (Figure 3-5.1).

The firm's management established the Bottletop Foundation launched in 2002 by co-founder Cameron Saul and his father Roger (founder of the Mulberry chain) to provide funds to disadvantaged young people for health education and vocational training projects (Figure 3-5.2), which in turn support their wider communities. An atelier and training programs were established in Brazil and Nepal. The Bottletop Foundation also supports programs for young people in Malawi, Mozambique, Rwanda, and the United Kingdom. Bottletop programs also promote sustainable design and creative culture, using film, youth newspapers, drama, music, and peer education to engage young people.

Figure 3-5.2 Creating Bottletop products by workers trained as part of the company's community employment programs

Photo courtesy: Bottletop

Benefitting Youth and Communities

Running costs of the Foundation are covered by Bottletop, enabling 100 percent of additional funds raised to be spent on empowering young people and their communities. Funding for each partner projects is for a minimum of three years, and to offer supplementary support and guidance to our partner organizations where possible. Projects based upon their demonstrated potential to equip young people with the skills and attitudes to be agents of change in their own lives and their wider communities. Support is lent to the creation of fair wage employment and for organizations that work to meet the UN Sustainable Development Goals.

To raise money for the United Nations' COVID-19 Solidarity Fund for WHO and Médecins sans Frontières, Bottletop launched the #TOGETHER FUND as well as existing beneficiaries who need support to deliver the Global Goals. All of the #TOGETHERBANDs are handmade in the Nepalese atelier by a collective of women who have been rescued from human trafficking. They are made from Humanium Metal and 100 percent Parley Ocean Plastic®.

Figure 3-5.3 Product displays at the Bottletop London store at 84 Regent Street

Photo courtesy: Bottletop

Bottletop retail stores are located in London at 84 Regent Street in Northpark Center, (Figure 3-5.3) and Dallas. The interior of the London Bottletop store has a 3D printed interior made from 60,000 upscaled plastic bottles. It is said to be the world's first zero-waste retail location, created using 3D printers and recycled plastic waste.

CHAPTER 3-6

Fabindia's Corporate Social Responsibility (CSR) Policy

The CSR Philosophy

Comments Supplied by Prableen Sabhaney

Fabindia Overseas Private Limited (referred to here as "Fabindia" or "the Company") was formed by John Latane Bissell with a mission to provide a platform to artisans who are based in rural parts of India, to produce and market the traditional handicraft products (Figures 3-6.1 and 3-6.2) made with age-old techniques. This mission created a base for providing skilled, sustainable employment to rural artisans, weavers, and local communities, and in turn preserving India's traditional handicrafts in the process.

Distinctive Fabindia Apparel

Figure 3-6.1 Fabindia's dress collection features styles created by classic techniques in bold hues. Cotton printed short and long length kaftans shown in hand-blocked prints have flared sleeves and round necks

Figure 3-6.2 Fabindia's men's patterned shirts feature roll-up sleeves and Chinese collar; (left) cotton kalamkari printed cotton cambric kurta shirt with blue background pattern. (right) geometric pattern cotton printed kurta shirt

Photo courtesy: Fabindia

Fabindia has been operating as an ethical and trustworthy brand, promoting a stakeholder-based community model of inclusive capitalism and fostering founder John Latane Bissell's vision—"In addition to making profits, our aims are constant development of new products, a fair, equitable and helpful relationship with our producers, and the maintenance of quality on which our reputation rests."

"We believe that corporate social responsibility (CSR) is the responsibility to conduct business in a socially responsible, ethical and environment friendly manner and in turn contribute to the economic and social growth of the nation."

CSR mission: We have identified the following focus areas as our CSR mission:

1. Promotion of Education and Vocational Skills: To promote education, employment-enhancing vocational skills among children, especially girls in rural areas and children with disabilities, children of families who have financial constraints by providing access to high-quality education, scholarships, other incentives such as supply of books, stipends, awards, and so on, without any discrimination on the basis of caste, creed, religion, or sex.

2. Social Welfare: To help and assist the needy, poor, aged, homeless, destitute, orphans, and widows in case of any emergency by providing financial assistance or aid including medical aid and provide other welfare facilities to reduce the inequalities faced by the socially and economically backward groups.

3. Empowerment of Women: To participate in programs or projects that promote gender equality, support creation of opportunities, and facilitate employment for women and provide financial support with a view to make them more educated and thus socially and economically empowered.

4. Sanitation and Health care: To support campaigns and awareness programs initiated by the governments, local bodies, nongovernment organizations, trusts, societies, or companies to educate people in rural areas on the importance of maintaining hygiene which in turn will prevent occurrence of various diseases.

5. Conservation of Environment: To ensure environmental sustainability, ecological balance, protection of flora and fauna, conservation of natural resources, animal welfare, and maintaining quality of soil, air, and water; help in providing safe drinking water and to support clean air and sustainable mobility initiatives or programs.

6. Rural Development Projects: To promote rural development projects that help in skill development, community development, generation of employment opportunities, and eradication of poverty in rural areas.

7. Disaster Relief: To provide financial assistance and other humanitarian and medical aid to help rehabilitate persons hit by floods, earthquakes, or any other natural disaster or calamity, and to undertake any other general public utility service.

8. Conservation of National Heritage, Art, Culture, and Other Related Activities: To support and participate in projects, campaigns, and programs that help in protection and conservation of national heritage, art, and culture including maintenance and restoration of buildings and sites of historical importance and works of art, setting up of public libraries, promotion and development of traditional arts and handicrafts, and so on.

CSR activities and implementation: The CSR activities to be undertaken by the Company shall be in line with our CSR Mission stated in this CSR Policy and shall include activities prescribed under schedule VII of Companies Act, 2013.

Our identified CSR implementing partners will be Bhadrajun Artisans Trust and Centre for Science and Environment, both of which are registered societies. We may further identify and collaborate with other organizations, registered trusts, registered societies, or companies incorporated under Section 25 of Companies Act 1956 or Section 8 of Companies Act 2013 to implement our CSR Mission.

We shall either directly or through BAT implement the mission of providing disaster relief to victims of natural calamities or force majeure events like floods, cyclones, earthquakes, and so on, by way of contribution to the Prime Minister's National Relief Fund or any other fund set up by the Central Government for socioeconomic development.

The Company also helps in rehabilitation of persons affected by natural calamities in any other approved form.

CHAPTER 3-7

El Palacio de Hierro

The Department Store as a Community Asset

The Veracruz Store Is Customer-Centric

In Mexico, El Palacio de Hierro can trace its origin back to 1850 as the Las Fabricas de Francia in Mexico City. It now numbers over two dozen free-standing stores around the country (Figure 3-7.1).

Figure 3-7.1 With its striking blue exterior, El Palacio de Hierro Veracruz integrates with its coastal environment

Photo courtesy: Jaime Navarro; El Palacio de Hierro

Figure 3-7.2 The central circular atrium opens to the store's two selling levels

Photo courtesy: Jaime Navarro; El Palacio de Hierro

The store's name was first attributed when the five-story flagship was under construction in Mexico City in the mid-1890s and the structural iron and steel frameworks were exposed. Passersby were reported to comment, "What iron palace are they building?" The owners took marketing advantage of the interest generated by the identification given to their project and named their store, El Palacio de Hierro.

Juan Carlos Escribano, CEO of El Palacio de Hierro, believes in the continuity of the department store concept as interpreted by his organization. "Mexicans still take pride in their department stores. Visiting them becomes a family outing," Excribano pointed out in a recent interview. "Latin families like to go out a lot. They embrace the place where they can meet friends and family and walk around. They do not like to stay by themselves. We love to socialize. We are very family-oriented. We hang out with our families every weekend. At El Palacio, we fulfill that family experience," he indicated.

"Each Palacio store is built differently to accommodate the community, and tells its own story. It gives shoppers, regardless of social or financial status, a sense of belonging. The first thing they think is, 'This is my store,'" said Escribano.

Veracruz, Mexico's largest port city, borders the Gulf of Mexico. El Palacio de Hierro is situated in the Andamar lifestyle center in the upscale Boca del Rio community (Figure 3-7.2). "Veracruz is a wealthy place. Twenty percent of the population is A-plus," said Escribano. Veracruz Palacio and the other Palacio department stores offer a true full-line assortment of hard and soft goods and services, from fashion, jewelry, and food to technology, toys, and tequila, along with beauty, appliances, and services such as getting prescriptions, barber shops, gourmet food halls, and even separate ice cream stands to encourage lingering after the main course.

"You can buy a sandwich that's not very expensive and sit on the terrace by the water, or you can buy a pair of designer shoes. Customers can 'mix and match' styles at all price points," Escribano said. "We have full travel services and a service called Palacio Solutions. If you have a problem with your watch, your phone or computer or you want a solution for your house or your car, you come to us for Solutions," he added.

"But because of our luxury brands, there has to be a luxury environment—the whole store. Construction cost for Veracruz was $40 million for a population of about 500,000. It is a complete department store," said Escribano. "We have all the categories," Escribano affirmed.

El Palacio de Hierro in Veracruz: Inspired by the Sea

El Palacio's 170,000-sq.-ft., two-level department store by the sea serves a population of 500,000. Veracruz is Mexico's major port. The country's 430-mile-long shoreline along the Gulf of Mexico has several other import/export centers where Mexican goods and produce are shipped worldwide.

Working with a team of merchants, visual experts, TPG Architects, and historians, JGA as the interior store planning consultant identified two inspirations that were deeply rooted in the Veracruz community. The first was the sea: water, the semi-tropical landscape, and sea life. The second was their influence on the region's architecture and design. Each of these attributes influenced the selection of materials, lighting, art, and particularly, shopping experiences in the Veracruz store. It is filled with aquatic-inspired decorative and architectural elements and artwork (Figure 3-7.3).

Figure 3-7.3 Andalus, the store's informal dining facility, welcomes groups of all sizes

Photo courtesy: Jaime Navarro; El Palacio de Hierro

Palacio Veracruz's overall environment was influenced by its seaside location. With its striking blue exterior, El Palacio de Hierro Veracruz is integrated into its surroundings. Dramatic facades are a Palacio signature. "When we talk about luxury, we talk about quality. So quality is food. Quality is experiences. Fashion is central—it's 40 percent of our business. But our concept of luxury is bigger than fashion. We run this luxury concept through all the categories and lifestyle divisions," said Escribano.

El Palacio de Hierro, with an annual sales volume in the range of $1.6 billion, is one of the holdings of the Grupo BAL conglomerate, which has interests in mining, financial, insurance, agribusiness, health, music sectors, as well as retail. El Palacio de Hierro's growth is outlined in its ambitious five-year plan.

For Escribano, the department store has to be more like entertainment, and a place where you really like to go because there is always something happening. "Young people especially want everything immediately. They will be our engine. We have to adapt to that," said Escribano.

CHAPTER 3-8

The "Mahindra Challenge"

Making a Case for Global Sustainability

I visit countries around the world to discuss why it makes sense to be sustainable, to take on projects that are great for the environment and also great for business.
—Anirban Ghosh, Chief Sustainability Officer, Mahindra Group

Editor's Note: Started in 1945 as a steel trading company, the Mahindra Group presently operates 11 business sectors and 20 key industries, that is, it's a $19 billion global federation of companies. The Group has a leadership position in utility vehicles, information technology, financial services, and vacation ownership. Mahindra Retail Private Limited operates as a retail store, offering toys and game, maternity wear, mother and baby wellness products, and kids' apparel and accessories, serving customers throughout India. It has a strong presence in agribusiness, components, commercial vehicles, consulting services, energy, industrial equipment, logistics, real estate, steel aerospace, defense, and two-wheelers. Headquartered in Mumbai, India, Mahindra employs over 200,000 people across 100 countries.

Mahindra Lifespace Developers Ltd. (MLDL) (Figure 3-8.1) focuses on inclusiveness, the art of living, and responsible citizenship. The MLDL is a pioneer of sustainable urbanization, to not only create value for all its stakeholders but also to influence the larger ecosystem. The company is proactively contributing to the cause of sustainable urbanization by demonstrating at their sites how systematic sustainability is not only good

Figure 3-8.1 Evolve, a building from Mahindra World City, Jaipur, is in a multi-product Special Economic Zone (SEZ) based on the concept of an "Integrated Business City."

environmentally and social but also economically, and by advocacy and leadership where they further sustainability within the industry. Their residential portfolio has a total green footprint of 8 million sq. ft., of ongoing projects, and 7 million sq. ft., in the completed stage.

Mahindra is a founding member of the Sustainable Housing Leadership Consortium (SHLC), a voluntary, private sector-led consortium, formed to ensure that at least 20 percent of India's new housing developments are green by 2022 (Figure 3-8.2).

Interview by Ken Nisch with Anirhan Ghosh, Chief Sustainability Officer, Mahindra Group.

KN: What is Mahindra's goal to accelerate the construction of green buildings in India?

AG: Mahindra has been building only green buildings for 25 years. Ratings of buildings have gone from silver to gold to platinum. It is not possible to build platinum-grade buildings without incremental cost, so we

Figure 3-8.2 Rendering of Mahindra Happinest Palghar, planned to meet the need for low-cost, high-quality homes. The design applies innovative technologies and contemporary construction methods to maximize utility per square foot

enhance the adoption of green buildings. It is estimated that 70 percent of the buildings required by India in 2050 have not been built yet.

The International Finance Corporation formed the SHLC using the World Bank's "Eco-cities" program to bring like-minded developers together to set a goal to build only green buildings. Technologies brought into the mainstream and added to India's building codes for any builder to implement green technologies for construction. *That's the dream we are trying to pursue.*

Numerous technologies have been identified which can be applied today. The Cement Sustainability Initiative in India has made access to much greener cement than was previously possible. Mahindra has built a couple of small cities and industrial clusters—near larger urban areas—adopting all of the principles of green construction.

KN: Have these directives come from engineers and architects to give builders a similar program to follow?

AG: Everything that the coalition has done is vetted by designers, architects, and members of the coalition. Representatives examine projects from all practical points of view to determine what is or isn't feasible, or commercially acceptable. These sustainability practices make complete business sense.

KN: Have these plans and designs been applied to habitable structures in India? Are they more far-reaching?

AG: An India-wide footprint would be the largest in the world. However, because it is done under the umbrella of the World Bank, there are enough opportunities to go outside the country, wherever there are relevant technologies that can be verified by the Consortium.

KN: Where is environmental sustainability placed within Mahindra's long-term management structure?

AG: We have two major construction businesses: Mahindra Life Spaces and Mahindra Holiday Resorts; the latter builds resorts around India. All are certified green resorts, designed for double energy efficiency using 100 percent renewable energy.

We are committed to be carbon neutral by 2040 for every Mahindra Group company. The coalition is working closely within the relevant government ministries and agencies to bring these commitments to companies outside the group and to pass the necessary legislation. Building codes are evolving. Over the last 2–3 years, there have been a numerous enhancements to these codes, citing greener elements of construction as a regular element of buildings being constructed in India.

KN: How can Mahindra influence other corporations to take this sustainable approach?

AG: A number of organizations have already adopted sustainability, but there are millions more companies of all sizes which need to come on board. It isn't easy to get people to start looking at sustainability in a holistic way.

I spend a great deal of time talking to peers and other organizations about why it makes sense to follow green principles in doing business. I visit countries like Peru to discuss why it makes sense to be sustainable, to take on projects that are great for the environment and also great for business. As soon as an organization understands that, we get them started to move forward. *There are questions about overhead costs, they have no time to implement, and so on. While the solutions are often industry- and business-specific, it is very rare to not find solutions with overlap benefits to the planet and profit for any business today.*

KN: What arguments do you cite when you address these groups? How do you answer the tough questions?

AG: The Confederation of Indian Industries and Federation of Indian Chambers of Commerce and Industry are two places where we speak to many other Indian corporations and share with them how following sustainability principles are useful for business. At large international conferences, we speak to CEO groups about leveraging sustainability principles and doing business better.

We are members of the World Business Council of Sustainable Development, where 15–20 percent has committed to becoming carbon-neutral, along with the World Economic Forum CEO Alliance. By sharing stories with other companies, we show that doing what is sustainable makes business sense, and conversely, that not doing this is an opportunity lost.

I've found that speaking to the board or senior management has significant impact; usually because someone believes that the company can do better. They bring in an expert to share their experience in a way that does not make the board feel threatened. Instead of telling them what they are doing wrong, we show them how spending a little bit more money will bring in returns of approximately 24 percent, which Mahindra has implemented in India, citing preventing water pollution and promoting health, and volunteer to show them how to do it.

Depending on their response, we present project details. We invite people to our factories, where they can speak to people to get a firsthand sense of how things really work. We have a certified carbon-neutral factory and a certified real waste to landfill program at 12 sites within the group that serve as good examples of what is possible.

For a conference in San Francisco, our chairman issued in January 2018 what has come to be known as the "Mahindra Challenge." There are now more than 650 companies who have signed onto what we identify as SignSpace targets. Mahindra representatives spoke at 12 different locations during that conference. SignSpace targets went from committing to 2-degree centigrade targets to 1.5-degree centigrade targets. If it gets stricter, we will be the first ones to join. Pursuing this work quickly, we stress, gives fantastic returns to business, so it doesn't make sense not to do it.

KN: How are tenants evaluating buildings based on Mahindra's programs?

AG: Very positive! We are asked, "How will green buildings save energy and water, and how do we know if this is actually happening?" We commissioned a study called the "Living Building Study," a survey of residents living in our green buildings. The results clearly show that from their past experiences living in other buildings, they now confirm the anticipated energy and water savings.

We are happy to share our results. Go to "Sustainable Housing Leadership Coalition" on the Mahindra website, send us a request, and we will get you what you need.

KN: Is there international interest in the benefits of Mahindra's programs to help find solutions to the climate change crisis?

AG: I certainly believe so. This book will contain other examples of organizations which have done great work. We hope your book will help with spreading the message. Ultimately, it's up to individual companies like Mahindra to affect meaningful change!

Photos courtesy: Mahindra Group

CHAPTER 3-9

Kering Group

A Far-Reaching Biodiversity Strategy

Luxury and sustainability are one and the same.
—Francois-Henri Pinault, CEO, Kering Group

Kering Group's sustainable initiatives date back to 1996, when the firm established its first Code of Ethics. "Far more than an ethical necessity, it is a driver of innovation and value creation for the Group, its houses, and its stakeholders," said Francois-Henri Pinault, CEO of Paris-based Kering Group designated as 13 Houses. They include Gucci, Saint Laurent, Bottega Veneta, Balenciaga, Alexander McQueen, Brioni, and Boucheron.

Kering's (Figure 3-9.1) inclusive biodiversity strategy identifies a wide-ranging series of targets to achieve a "net positive" impact on biodiversity by 2025. It has initiated with Conservation International, the Kering Regenerative for Nature Fund with the long-range objective of supporting the fashion industry's transition to regenerative agriculture. By 2025, the aim is to have a significant net positive impact on biodiversity by driving a shift toward farming practices that operate in harmony with natural ecosystems.

Figure 3-9.1 Logo, Kering Group

Kering's $6.1 million grant is directed to restore and regenerate 840,000 hectares, which will ultimately be transformed into regenerative agricultural spaces and a million hectares for its supply chain and protect an additional one million hectares of critical, irreplaceable habitat. The in-depth program encourages the prevention of biodiversity degradation, the promotion of sustainable and regenerative farming practices favoring soil health, and the protection of global ecosystems and forests that are vital for carbon sequestration. It is estimated that the project will engage up to 60,000 people around the globe.

The final seven recipients of the funds are located in South America, Central Asia, India, Europe, and Africa. They represent small- and large-scale farming operations to turn land into a regenerative supply source, including:

- The Good Growth Company—partnerships with cashmere goat herders in Mongolia
- Organic Cotton Accelerator—transitioning conventional cotton farmers to regenerative ones and organic production processes in India
- Solidaridad—works with indigenous smallholder cattle producers in Argentina and restoring native forests and vegetation
- Fundacion Global Nature—restoring traditional grazing systems alongside goat shepherds in Spain
- Wildlife Conservation Society and the Wildlife-Friendly Enterprise Network—focusing on co-existence with wildlife and sheep wool production in Patagonia
- Epiterre—the increase in plant diversity for positive ecological outcomes
- Conservation South Africa—implementation of regenerative agricultural practices in South African biodiversity

"Global change always begins at the local level, which is why we support grassroots conservation efforts on four continents with Kering under the Regenerative for Nature Fund," explained Dr. M. Sanjayan, CEO of Conservation International. "We know that the path to a sustainable, nature-positive future must include indigenous peoples and local communities. Progress will be continually monitored together with Kering to ensure that initiatives are delivering measurable outcomes for the environment, and just as critically, for local livelihoods."

CHAPTER 3-10

Kohl's

$750 Million for Community Support

Implementing Operational Sustainability

Figure 3-10.1 Kohl's pop-up in New York City

Kohl's, which operates 1,165 stores in the U.S., has given more than $750 million throughout its history to support communities nationwide (Figure 3-10.1). In 2020, it donated $1 million to Milwaukee nonprofits serving Black and Hispanic residents.

Kohl's has been named one of the World's Most Ethical Companies by the Ethisphere Institute. It rated high on five key categories including its ethics and compliance program, culture of ethics, corporate citizenship and responsibility, governance, and leadership and reputation.

Since 2001, Kohl's has offered customers four seasonal collections featuring Kohl's Cares merchandise that supports their communities. One hundred percent of the net profit generated from Kohl's Cares merchandise is donated to charitable organizations, including children's hospitals across the country, in each state where the company does business. The merchandise is available year round, in all stores and online at Kohls.com/Cares. To date, Kohl's has raised nearly $340 million through this program.

Community Spring Volunteer Initiative

More than 100,000 hours of associates' personal time has been contributed to more than 3,000 active and wellness organizations to inspire communities to be active and stay well. Kohl's continued its support of Boys & Girls Clubs of America during the back-to-school season to benefit children across the country.

Kohl's has donated $1 for each pair of jeans sold in store and online, up to $1 million. Kohl's received the Boys & Girls Clubs of America 2017 Cause Marketing Award for these efforts.

Hometown Partnerships

Based in Milwaukee, Wisconsin, Kohl's maintains strong partnerships with nonprofit organizations, including more than 20 hometown and affiliate partners.

Kohl's and Kohl's Cares have given more than $100 million to nonprofits in the Milwaukee metro area. The support initiative expands afterschool and summer programs at learning centers, adds programming to include school off-days and introduces vital science, technology, engineering and math curriculum through the Kohl's Explore Your Future program. More than 4,500 youth are engaged in Kohl's supported programs at COA.

Sustainability Initiatives

Kohl's acknowledges that climate change can alter the way they currently do business, from energy expenses to sourcing, even to shifting seasonal weather conditions that impact their customers' shopping habits. Kohl's is a founding circle member of the Sustainable Apparel Coalition, a group of apparel manufacturers, retailers, brands, and nongovernmental organizations working together to standardize sustainability measurements in the apparel and footwear supply chain.

It utilizes the Higg Index, an indicator-based tool for apparel that enables companies to evaluate material types, products, facilities, and processes based on a range of environmental and product design choices. Kohl's benchmarks itself against peers and engages suppliers to improve their textile supply chain and factory performance.

Lighting and HVAC

Eighty-eight percent of Kohl's stores are Energy Star (Figure 3-10.2), which Kohl's promotes to associates and customers through overhead announcements, customer receipts, banner ads on envelopes, screensavers, websites, and internal reports.

Figure 3-10.2 The Women's Activewear department, Kohl's, Brookfield, Wisconsin

Replacing lights with LEDs has allowed Kohl's to reduce its emissions and save on both electricity and maintenance costs. Sales floor lighting upgrade program in 2017 was based on the retrofitting of fluorescent fixtures in 130 stores with LED lighting, reducing total consumption by more than 38 million kilowatt-hours. Newer, more efficient HVAC models were installed in stores across the country. Kohl's plans to continue to maximize efficiency by continually upgrading their facilities to LED lights and newer HVAC systems.

As a retailer, Kohl's sees first-hand how climate change affects their business. Frequent or unusually heavy snow, ice or rain storms; natural disasters such as earthquakes, tornadoes, floods, fires, and hurricanes; or extended periods of unseasonable temperatures shift consumer shopping patterns. It can also cause physical damage to their properties as well as customers and associates. Kohl's is a signatory to the American Business Act Pledge on Climate Change in 2015.

Kroger's Zero Hunger | Zero Waste

A Social Impact Plan That's Good for Business and Society

Our Purpose and Promise guide everything we do, how we live that Purpose every day.
—Rodney McMullen, Chairman and Chief Executive Officer,
The Kroger Co.

The Kroger Co., the largest supermarket chain in the United States, has since 2006 tracked its objective to becoming more sustainable. The *2020 Kroger Environmental, Social and Governance Report* highlights the year's advances in nearly two dozen various categories and the development of new performance targets for 2025, 2030, and beyond.

Based in Cincinnati, Kroger's family of companies comprises 3,242 Kroger owned retail locations, occupies 179 million square feet of space, employs 453,000 people, and is serviced by 34 manufacturing plants and 44 distribution centers. Total sales in 2021 was $137.9 billion.

Kroger's Social Impact Plan includes Zero Hunger | Zero Waste; along with Zero Heroes Among Us; Climate Impact; Food Waste; Zero Waste; Packaging; Water; Product Sustainability; Food Safety; Associate Health & Safety; Community Engagement; and Supply Chain.

Established in late 2018, The Kroger Co. Zero Hunger | Zero Waste Foundation is a nonprofit public charity that aims to fill the gap in philanthropic funding needed to support entrepreneurs and creative thinkers with solutions to improve food security and end food waste.

In 2019, the Foundation directed $10 million in 349 grants to advance their mission to create communities free of hunger and waste.

The following are responses adapted from: "Q&A With Rodney McMullen, Kroger's Chairman and Chief Executive Officer," published in the *2020 Kroger Environmental, Social and Governance Report*

"**Kroger is America's favorite grocer.** We are committed to delivering fresh food at a fair price, simplifying the customer experience, and meaningfully giving back to the communities in which we operate. We Live Our Purpose—to Feed the Human Spirit™—in big and small ways through Kroger's Zero Hunger | Zero Waste plan, our commitment to help create communities free of hunger and waste. I'm proud of our Associates—together we achieved our three-year goal to direct 1 billion meals in food and funds to our communities by 2020. These include commitments to reduce greenhouse gases (GHGs) by 30 percent and transition to 100 percent recyclable, compostable, or reusable Our Brands packaging by 2030. Together, we can achieve a meaningful change that transforms our communities."

"**Kroger has a rich history** of investing in communities and being there for our customers. Strategic investments in our Restock Kroger plan, including alternative shopping modalities, proved critical as customers turned to lower-contact shopping during the pandemic. Similarly, our Zero Hunger | Zero Waste Food Rescue and Dairy Rescue programs, as well as our charitable giving, were amplified by our community support at a time when many people were struggling."

"**We invested more than $830 million** to reward our Associates and safeguard our teams, customers, and communities during the first four months of the COVID-19 pandemic. We also created 'Sharing What We've Learned: A Blueprint for Businesses,' which captured our best practices in retail operations, sourcing, supply chain and more, to help others."

"***We seek and embrace difference*** in the backgrounds, cultures, and ethnicities of all associates, customers, and vendors. We encourage and expect collaboration, teamwork, and the active involvement of all associates. We are also taking deliberate action to be a catalyst for change in our communities, in part through a $5 million fund in The Kroger Co. Foundation to advance diversity, equity, and inclusion."

"We are driving the integration of key ESG topics into our business plans and decisions over time. Our Zero Hunger | Zero Waste plan, for example, reflects the concept of shared value in action—working collectively toward a common goal that is good for both business and society. I'm incredibly thankful for our Associates' continued dedication and service."

"We are deeply committed to our brand ethos—Fresh for Everyone™— and to advancing diversity, equity, and inclusion in our company and communities. We believe no matter who or where you are, you deserve affordable, easy-to-enjoy, fresh food. That represents our egalitarian brand and underscores our commitments to our customers. We encourage and expect collaboration, teamwork, and the active involvement of all associates. We seek and embrace difference in the backgrounds, cultures, and ethnicities of all associates, customers, and vendors."

"We plan to accelerate our digital and ecommerce efforts, applying customer data and personalization to more aspects of the business, and building the success of Our Brands Partner for customer, using more capital to fund technology and infrastructure upgrades and create alternative revenue streams that will redefine the Grocery Customer Experience."

Zero Waste Recipe Series

Households waste more than $1,300 in unused food each year. But consumers don't have to throw food (and money) away any longer. Kroger's Zero Waste recipe series, published electronically every month, provides ways to transform produce that's "on the edge" (and other food items might normally be thrown out) into delicious dishes. Recipes are accompanied with photos of serving the finished dishes.

CHAPTER 3-12

Stella McCartney

The Power to Affect Change

Stella McCartney Ltd (Figure 3-12.1), founded in 2001, is a luxury multi-label apparel, accessory, and related products organization with eight stores worldwide, whose collections are sold in 77 nations through 863 specialty shops and department stores, and shipped to 100 countries via online.

    (*Note: The following comments were adapted from the 39-page, Stella McCartney: ECO IMPACT REPORT 2020.*)

A Message from Stella

In releasing this report, we believe information is power and necessary to guide action. We face some hard truths: 75 percent of terrestrial land has been altered by human activities, wildlife populations have declined by 60 percent, and we have, until 2030, to cut our global emissions in half and combat dangerous climate change.

    At Stella McCartney, change has always been about being more conscious, in tune with Mother Earth and her creatures—and using the fashion industry as a powerful platform to make that message desirable. We believe we all have the power to affect change. Our planet is at a turning point, and we are committed to making every action count. In publishing this report, we hope to inspire others to consider their natural capital and

Figure 3-12.1 Stella McCartney logo

Photo courtesy: The Stella McCartney logo by iconspng.com

account for the value of the "hidden" services that nature provides us all. Not only is climate change a growing threat to species and ecosystems, but also to people and communities worldwide, especially those that depend most directly on Mother Earth and the services she provides. **Coming together has never been more necessary than it is in this moment. We believe we are responsible for the resources we use and the impact we have on people, animals, and the planet.**

We are constantly exploring innovative ways to become more sustainable, from designing to product manufacturing to our retail practices. We have never used any leather, fur, skins, or feathers for both ethical and environmental reasons. Business models under development will transform how clothes are produced, sold, shared, repaired, and reused; promoting long-lasting products with extended use to reduce environmental impacts.

The Value of People

Each person is vital to the creation of our products and we have a responsibility to ensure every worker is respected, valued, and heard. We are committed to empowering women and supporting workers' rights to create the world we want to see. We aim to have a positive impact for everyone that we depend on and for those who depend on us in return. We want to live in a world free of discrimination, poverty, and exploitation, where everyone has a voice that can be heard.

The fashion industry and Stella McCartney rely on people—those who make our clothes, the farmers who grow the crops for our materials, our employees, and our customers. Everybody in our supply chain should be treated fairly, and with respect and dignity.

Each person should be recognized and valued equally. We aim to build modern and resilient supply chains that provide desirable jobs, foster people's skills, strengthen workers' voice, and advocate for vulnerable groups. We endeavor to collaborate with suppliers, NGOs, and other local stakeholders in a way that brings value to the workers that sustain our supply chain. This year, working in partnership is more important than ever; we are looking at how we can use partnership to accelerate activities and progress.

Feedback into our program will ensure that we and the suppliers are always keeping channels open and are able to listen to and learn from workers. The women in our supply chain work hard and build their lives around making beautiful products. We aim to support these women to feel empowered to give feedback, to raise concerns or grievances, and speak out when things are not as they should be, fundamental principles of the United Nations Guiding Principles for Business and Human Rights. We are committed to ensuring that all workers and communities in our supply chain have the opportunity to be heard and listened to.

Setting Standards

We are entering into the most consequential decade for humanity. The choices that we collectively make between 2020 and 2030 will determine what the future of life on our planet looks like. As a business, we think this means a move from managing and reducing impacts to conserving and restoring nature and its services and doing what we can to transform the industry, creating the systemic change that is needed.

Policies and guidelines have been supplied to our suppliers outlining requirements and expectations relating to social sustainability. These include the Code of Conduct; Responsible Sourcing Guide, Modern Slavery Policy, and Subcontracting Policy. We partner with suppliers in key sourcing countries such as Italy, Hungary, Portugal, China, and India.

We are stubborn optimists who celebrate life. Nothing is ever achieved by starting with an attitude of defeatism; optimism is the starting point of success.

CHAPTER 3-13

Sponsored Education

Several major retailing organizations offer financial support for educational programs to prepare employees for careers of their choice.

Amazon: Full College Tuition for Frontline Employees

Amazon's more than 750,000 operations employees in the United States are eligible for fully funded college tuition, including cost of classes, books, and fees.

Figure 3-13.1 An Amazon employee in a break room, working on an assignment as part of the company's Upskilling 2025 program

Photo courtesy: Amazon media library

Since the launch of Upskilling 2025 in 2019, more than 70,000 employees have participated in one of Amazon's upskilling programs including Amazon Technical Academy, a program that helps Amazon employees from all backgrounds become software engineers in nine months (Figure 3-13.1).

Amazon is expanding the education and skills training benefits it offers to its U.S. employees with a total investment of $1.2 billion by 2025. Through its Career Choice program, the company funds full college tuition, as well as high school diplomas, GEDs, and English as a Second Language (ESL) proficiency certifications for its frontline employees—including those who have been at the company at least three months. Amazon's three new education programs provide employees with the opportunity to learn skills within data center maintenance and technology, IT, and user experience and research design.

Amazon is now the largest job creator in the United States. "We launched Career Choice in 2011 to help remove barriers to continuing education—time and money—and we are expanding it further to pay full tuition and add several new fields of study," said Dave Clark, CEO of Worldwide Consumer at Amazon.

Starting in January 2022, Amazon frontline employees have access to more education benefits through Career Choice.

New Skills Training Programs

In addition to the expanded Career Choice benefits, Amazon initiated three programs—tuition-free for participants—to provide more career-advancement opportunities:

- **AWS Grow Our Own Talent**: On-the-job training and job placement opportunities to Amazon employees and entry-level candidates with nontraditional backgrounds
- **Surge2IT**: Designed to help entry-level IT employees across Amazon's operations network pursue careers in higher-paying technical roles through self-paced learning resources
- **The User Experience Design and Research Apprenticeship Program**: Combines instructor-led training and real-world

experience in a one-year program offering employees the
opportunity to learn and develop skills in research and design
on Amazon teams

Source: Amazon website, September 9, 2021

Gap, Inc.: P.A.C.E. Education Program

Gap has reported that more than 800,000 women and girls completed
its Personal Advancement and Career Enhancement (P.A.C.E.) education
program to-date; it aims to reach one million individuals by 2022. The
company set new goals for 2025 that include improving gender parity at
the supervisor level at its strategic factories, and gaining more participants
in its Empower@Work program.

Walmart: Live Better U

Walmart, through its Live Better U education program, will pay for full
college tuition and book costs at 10 designated schools for its U.S. workers, the latest effort by the largest private employer in the country to
sweeten its benefits as it seeks to attract and retain talent in a tight job
market. Participants must remain part-time or full-time employees at
Walmart to be eligible. An estimated 28,000 workers participate in the
program, which Walmart began in 2018. Walmart employs approximately 1.5 million workers.

Walmart is offering more degree and certificate options in areas like
business administration, supply chain, and cybersecurity.

Employees of Walmart have incentive to participate in the program.
Those who have participated in the program are twice as likely to get
promoted and are retained at a significantly higher rate than other workers.
The move comes as retailers around the country face challenges hiring
employees to staff stores and warehouses.

Target: Debt-Free Education Assistance

Target Corporation will offer its more than 340,000 U.S.-based part-
time and full-time frontline team members a comprehensive debt-free
education assistance program. This education assistance program is part

of Target Forward, Target's sustainability strategy that includes goals to create an equitable and inclusive workforce.

Beginning Fall 2021, all part-time and full-time team members working in Target stores, distribution centers, and headquarters locations in the United States are eligible for debt-free assistance for select undergraduate degrees, certificates, certifications, free textbooks, and more with no out-of-pocket costs on their first day of work at Target. Target will invest $200 million over the next four years in the program.

"A significant number of our hourly team members build their careers at Target, and we know many would like to pursue additional education opportunities. We don't want the cost to be a barrier for anyone, and that's where Target can step in to make education accessible for everyone," said Melissa Kremer, chief human resources officer, Target. A Target objective is to eliminate student debt and promote equitable access to education for its team as part of Target Forward sustainability strategy.

Team members have options for assistance through a program with education and upskilling platform Guild Education. Target supports team members taking courses for high school completion, college prep, English language learning and select certificates, certifications, boot camps, and associate and undergraduate degrees. More than 40 schools, colleges, and universities, choosing from an industry-leading 250 business-aligned programs from Business Management and Operations to IT, Computer Science, Design, and more. Team members who opt into this program will not have any out-of-pocket costs and will have flexibility to find opportunities that fit with their interests, schedules, and career goals. Academic institutions include the University of Arizona, Oregon State University, University of Denver and Cornell along with Historically Black Colleges and Universities (HBCUs), Morehouse College, Paul Quinn College, and more.

For team members pursuing educational opportunities outside of the select business-aligned programs within the Guild network of schools, including master's degrees, Target will provide direct payments to their academic institution of up to $5,250 for non-master's degrees and up to $10,000 for master's degrees each year.

Minneapolis-based Target Corporation operates 1,931 stores and Target.com. Since 1946, Target has given 5 percent of its profit to communities.

Starbucks: College Achievement Plan

After five years, more than 3,000 Starbucks employees have earned bachelor's degrees through its College Achievement Plan. It covers all education costs remaining after traditional financial aid for Arizona State University's online programs. Currently, 13,000 Starbucks employees are enrolled in ASU online classes, with two-thirds of the stores having at least one participant. Starbucks has set a goal of 25,000 graduates by 2025.

To show gratitude to veteran partners for their service, they can extend an additional Starbucks College Achievement Plan benefit to a qualifying family member of their choice. The participating family member will receive all of the same benefits as partners in the program, with access to over 100 different degree programs. Tuition coverage does not include other educational expenses, such as textbooks and laptops. Financial aid may help cover these costs.

Every benefits-eligible U.S. partner working part- or full-time receives 100 percent tuition coverage for a first-time bachelor's degree through Arizona State University's online program. Over 100 diverse undergraduate degree programs are available.

Taco Bell: "Start With Us, Stay With Us"

In partnership with Guild Education, a specialist in organizing employer education benefits, Taco Bell offers personalized college advisors and pays up to $5,250 per year upfront toward the education costs at a network of universities, including online partners such as Bellevue University, Brandman University, University of Denver, University of Florida, and Wilmington University. An initial pilot in 2017 saw a 34 percent increase in retention for employees enrolled in the program. In 2018, Taco Bell extended the benefit to all 210,000 corporate and franchise employees in its 7,000 U.S. restaurants.

Macy's: Corporate Partnerships

Macy's Corporate Partnerships and The New School's Parsons School of Design launched a new custom executive education program for Macy's Merchandising colleagues within the curriculum of the Macy's Fashion Academy. Part of The New School's Corporate Partnerships Initiative, and led by Parsons' faculty, the multifaceted program is designed for a changing retail landscape to offer innovative, discipline-based curricula to provide Macy's merchants and designers with new skills, knowledge, and methodologies.

Through a series of master classes, lectures, and workshops, the partnership offers Macy's merchants exposure to today's most pressing business issues. Parsons scholars and practitioners identify emerging challenges and opportunities in retail to help shape best practices and stimulate new ways of thinking in the workplace. Using an interdisciplinary approach, Macy's merchants engage with the School's world-class design expertise.

In addition to skills-based learning, the curriculum offers Macy's colleagues a fresh way of looking at the inner workings of the fashion industry from a global perspective. Macy's fashion designers and merchants participate in immersive master classes to inspire new work processes and methodologies.

Terra Carta Design Lab

Designer Sir Jony Ive is partnering with Prince Charles to open a design lab through London's Royal College of Art. Called the Terra Carta Design Lab, its goal is to work with students to "create designs that can make a big impact for the world's transition to a sustainable future," according to the announcement.

It provides an environmental innovation framework to be backed by $10 billion in planned investments raised from the private sector including sources such as Amazon.

American Eagle

American Eagle Outfitters, Inc., established the AEO REAL Change Scholarship for Social Justice, a $5 million commitment created to advance educational opportunities for full and part-time AEO, Inc., associates, for actively driving anti-racism, equality, and social justice initiatives.

Scholarships are open to all full-time and part-time associates based on academic performance, financial need, and a demonstrated commitment to advancing social justice issues that will create lasting and positive change. The AEO REAL Change Scholarship began to accept applications in spring 2021. In its first year, the program selected 15 recipients, each eligible for up to $40,000 during their pursuit of a post-secondary education. Recipients are assigned an AEO, Inc., mentor to serve as a resource. AEO, Inc., offers tuition reimbursement to qualifying associates to further promote and build upon education and recruiting opportunities at the company.

"The REAL Change Scholarship for Social Justice demonstrates AEO's commitment to help end racism, discrimination and inequality while providing educational support for the next generation of leaders," said Jay Schottenstein, Executive Chairman of the Board and Chief Executive Officer, AEO, Inc. "Together we are making real—and lasting—change to build an even stronger, more diverse workplace that provides opportunities for our associates to continue to develop and grow within our AEO family."

In 2020, AEO, Inc., made a $500,000 pledge to the NAACP Legal Defense and Education Fund to support their education equity work and scholarships for exceptional African-American students. The company matched up to $100,000 in donations made by AEO associates to organizations fighting against racism and for social justice. A program was initiated with the National Retail Federation to provide retail career education for students attending HBCUs. It supports work with The Pittsburgh Promise, It Gets Better Project, and Big Brothers Big Sisters Workplace Mentoring, among others.

The Mahindra Group

The Mahindra Group is a diversified retail, manufacturing, construction, and consulting organization based in Mumbai, India.

Mahindra Leadership University. Home to 10 academies including Healthcare, Life Sciences, Sales and Marketing, Service Excellence,

Manufacturing, and Quality Control, among others, to develop leaders to build future leaders.

The Future Leadership Program (FLP) is an 18-month program in leadership development and talent management, conducted in collaboration with the Institute of Management Development, Switzerland, and Yale School of Management. Participants are recruited from different businesses and positions across the group.

Nanhi Kali was established in 1996 by the K. C. Mahindra Education Trust. It provides academic, material, and social support to underprivileged girl children across India.

Naandi Foundation was founded in 1998 as a Public Charitable Trust with the aim to eliminate poverty. It provides educational support to elementary school children and skilling programs for unemployed youth.

Door Step School was established in 1988. It provides education and literary services to socially and economically disadvantaged children in urban slum communities of Mumbai and Pune.

Women Leaders Program (WLP) bridges the gender gap in the workforce and builds mid-level women leadership pipeline. It is focused on advancement of women in the workforce, encouraging women employees in the middle management cadre. The professional development journey spans 18 months, specially designed to help participants develop competencies needed to advance into future leadership positions.

Mahindra Pride Schools train and place socially and economically disadvantaged youth on a yearly basis from a total of nine campuses that graduate approximately 6000 students annually. Mahindra Pride School is an initiative by K. C. Mahindra Education Trust that provides Livelihood Training to the less-privileged youth.

Mahindra Institute of Quality (MIQ), based in Nasik, India, was created to offer Quality Management competencies across the Group in areas like TQM and Manufacturing Excellence programs like Lean Manufacturing and Supply Chain improvements.

Mahindra Universe Program, an annual on-campus event, gathers 35–40 top global managers of Mahindra and their spouses at the Harvard Business School. Aimed at fostering a whole-brained approach, this program aims to broaden managerial views while engaging with noted faculty.

Chipotle: Will Send Employees to College

Chipotle Mexican Grill is expanding its Chipotle Cultivate Education benefits program, which the retailer says has provided employees with over $20 million in tuition assistance in the past two years. The company now pays 100 percent of tuition costs upfront for 75 different types of business and technology degrees through a partnership education benefits company named Guild Education.

After 120 days of employment, employees are eligible to pursue degrees from nonprofit, accredited universities, including The University of Arizona, Bellevue University, Brandman University, Southern New Hampshire University, and Wilmington University.

Qualifying employees can also take advantage of a full suite of benefits including access to health care; fitness discounts; and free ESL and GED classes for employees and family members.

Chipotle had over 2,836 corporate restaurants as of June 25, 2021, in the United States, Canada, the United Kingdom, France, and Germany.

IFM-Kering Launches Certificate In Fashion Sustainability

Global luxury group Kering and the Institute Français de la Mode, Paris, have established the IFM-Kering Sustainability Chair. It is the basis for research and teaching center for the fashion industry. The program incorporates all aspects of sustainability, from traceability to eco-friendly new business models. Upon completion of the course, students will earn a Certificate in Fashion Sustainability.

Supported by Kering's experts, the Certificate's curriculum has been designed to provide Masters Students with the knowledge and skill across the main areas integral to advancing sustainability and corporate social responsibility. It will focus on scientific research on a wide range of topics. Aspects of creative ecology will be studied to identify ways in which creative teams can develop new and attractive sustainable offerings. "The IFM-Kering Sustainability Chair means students can develop a 360° understanding of the challenges of sustainability, so that they can participate as future professionals in the industry's transformation," said Xavier Romatet, Dean of Institute Français de la Mode.

SECTION 4

The Retail Environment

Introduction

The Future Lies In Sustainability

Interview by Petr Simek, Managing Director of Wellen, Operators of Huckberry Sustainable apparels and other brands, and Ken Nisch.

PS: How can designers champion sustainability and supply chain transparency?

KN: An open mind and open eye out for new companies or resources, and their influence to promote and nurture suppliers who support this effort, is one way. Organizationally, it means using a more universal language. In the environmental aspect, we need to find a set of shared goals and measurement. On the cultural side, and the diversity, equity and inclusion (DEI) sides, professional organizations have an opportunity to champion this.

PS: Customers themselves are changing the new retail paradigm. As part of the Covid-19 pandemic, consumers confirmed the use of omnichannel as a diversification of sales channels. Retail is not a battle between the online and offline world. Omnichannel is the necessity of every brand or retailer to survive. Sustainability in this direction is next in line.

Brands that incorporate sustainability efforts into their operations and customer experiences are poised to reap the benefits. Consumers are increasingly educated and as their expectations for brands to champion sustainability increase, retail designers should create value by responding to their demands.

Sustainability is a trend which has endured long enough to now be considered an eventuality rather than a possibility for retail.

PS: Industry experts predict sustainability will be a major driving force behind the retail experience by 2030. What should designers consider to prepare?

KN: 2030 is too late. Designers should think about the broader aspect of sustainability that speaks to DEI now. While environmental sustainability is a longer process and bigger investment, consumers are demanding a much faster response around human and action (*i.e.* the DEI aspect) not just the environmental aspect. Consumers are somewhat skeptical if you set the timeline out too much. In the near-term, people expect real-time change, not 10 years from now. They are passionate about the human impact. Change has to happen now.

PS: The Covid-19 pandemic affected perceptions of sustainability and the circular fashion economy and will affect shopping after Covid-19. From products and services, to the environment and communication inside stores, sustainability will becomes a standard prerequisite, not only a marketing tool. How should designers incorporate sustainability efforts into the in-store experience?

KN: Focus on more of the human aspect. They should think about building environments that can change and evolve without being disposable. Think about not just the lifecycle of brand obsolescence, but also about physical obsolescence. Can we build something that serves longer, considering choice of fixtures, systems, and materials? We have to think more generationally, especially of the big box retailers, that represents the longer cycle investment-oriented companies.

CHAPTER 4-1

Simons

A Corporate Embrace of Sustainability

From Buildings to Bees

Doing the right thing and being proud of what we are doing is the force that drives us.

—Peter Simons, Chief Merchant, La Maison Simons

La Maison Simons is a Canadian institution. Founded in 1840 by Scottish immigrant John Simons, the current president, Peter Simons, is the fifth generation of the family to lead the company, now a chain of 16 department stores across Canada. Privately held, current sales are estimated at $456 million.

Its extensive, stylishly edited assortments of apparel, accessories, and home products are sourced internationally, with a specific emphasis on Canadian talent and technology. Each store's design is different, with furnishings and artwork reflecting the local culture and environment.

Simons' concern with improving the environment involves subscribing to reducing energy use in its stores and sourcing from companies with strict sustainable operational guidelines. Simons supports far-ranging movements to counter effects on humans and nonhumans alike, brought on by global warming and other harmful environmental circumstances.

Figure 4-1.1 *Alvéole rooftop beehive*

Photo courtesy: Stéphane Groleau; La Maison Simons

- In 2018, Simons created an apparel collection featuring bee-related designs from which funds from sales were directed to the installation of urban beehives on the roofs of Simons stores to help prevent the worldwide decline of the bee population (Figure 4-1.1). Operated by the Canadian company Alvéole, honey gathered from the hives is sold in Simons stores. "It's our way of protecting the species in our ecosystems and improving our actions in response to the different problems that are arising," said Peter Simons.
- The Simons team that merchandises the contemporary Twik collection adopted a beluga whale from the St. Lawrence River and an orca from the Pacific Ocean. Their goal is to support different research programs to protect these animals in their natural habitat. A recent report carried news of the beluga whale with a newborn calf (Figure 4-1.2).

Figure 4-1.2 Twik display with "From Sea to Sea" with whale illustration signage

Photo courtesy: Stéphane Groleau; La Maison Simons

- In association with Stockholm-based Swedish Stockings, Simons installed collection receptacles in most Simons stores to receive donations of used hosiery of any brand, color, and composition. Swedish Stockings states that typical nylon yarn is produced from an environmentally harmful petroleum derivative process that leads to carbon emissions and wears poorly. From donated products, the company has innovated a system for a high-quality yarn, using environmentally friendly dyes, water treatments, and solar power.

Simons Galeries de la Capitale Is the First
Net-Zero Energy Store in Canada

Figure 4-1.3 Exterior of Simons' net zero energy Galeries de La Capitale store, Quebec

Photo courtesy: Stéphane Groleau; La Maison Simons

Simons opened in 2018 its 80,000-sq.-ft. store in Québec which is the county's first retail-use building with proven net-zero energy consumption, producing as much energy as it uses (Figure 4-1.3). Project management and exterior architecture was by Québec-based architecture and design firm Lemay Michaud. Implanted into an existing c. 1981 building, it used the envelope as backdrop and the design was molded onto to it. The brick was preserved with the integration of a weaving of colorful steel elements. The superimposition of the elements brings depth and relief, and generates interesting moving shadows on the facade.

The interior, designed by Toronto-based Designstead, is situated on one floor and divided into two sections, with women's fashion on one side, and men's fashion and Simons Maison on the other. Between these two spaces is the shoe section.

Combined technologies reduce the store's energy consumption and greenhouse gas emissions. In the mall's parking lot, 27 geothermal wells were dug generating the equivalent of 80,000 kWh of energy. A heat pump extracts warmth from the ground and transfers it in store for heating, or removes heat from the store and sends it back into the ground to keep the interior air-conditioned. The energy-recovering heating, ventilation, and air-conditioning system combined with the LED lighting control program allows a 60 percent reduction in energy consumption compared to the previous location.

The parking lot contains 133 spaces equipped with awnings on which are 1,020 double-sided solar panels to capture direct as well as reflected light. By combining this with the 2,308 double-sided solar panels on the store's roof, the solar electricity system generates enough k/h/y to power 50 houses.

The project reflects Simons' values, working to present its green philosophy, both in the physical environment and in its operational choices. The store stands out in two ways: by its consumption reduction and by its energy production, relating to the environmental values of the project.

"Building a net-zero energy store is the culmination of a six-year voyage of learning, understanding and discussing what our company's roles and responsibilities are regarding environmental impact," says Peter Simons. "It takes extremely committed partners to achieve a goal like this. Oxford Properties stepped up, allowing us to make significant structural changes like drilling geothermal boreholes outside the shopping center," he adds.

Do Canadians believe that companies have a responsibility toward the communities in which they do business? Do Canadians make a conscious effort to shop at retailers that are making an effort? I hope so.
—Peter Simons

CHAPTER 4-2

Closed Loop Partners

Building a Circular Economy

Closed Loop Partners is a New York City-based hybrid investment firm comprised of venture capital, growth equity, private equity, project finance, and an innovation center focused on building the circular economy, a new economic model for a more profitable and sustainable future. Their extensive network connects entrepreneurs, industry experts, global consumer goods companies, retailers, financial institutions, and municipalities, building an ecosystem that accelerates circularity across entire value chains. Investors include the world's largest retailers, consumer goods companies, family offices, and financial institutions.

The firm works to align capitalism with positive social and environmental impact, investing in solutions that reduce waste and greenhouse gas emissions via materials innovation, advanced recycling technologies, supply chain optimization, and diversion of materials from landfills. Across the firm's verticals, their investments and initiatives span multiple sectors, including plastics and packaging, food and agriculture, fashion, and technology to meet a surging demand for more eco-friendly products and services.

Closed Loop Partners, founded in 2014, has a successful investment track record. It has provided equity and debt financing to help develop numerous circular design innovations, as well as bolster recovery infrastructure to capture materials after use. The firm's unique fund structure allows it to finance and invest in companies at any part of their growth journey, starting as early as seed venture capital, to private equity, buyouts, and project finance. By accelerating the growth of early-stage companies, through to established companies, the firm's funds build upon one another, bridging gaps and fostering synergies to scale the circular economy.

The Center for the Circular Economy

The firm's Center for the Circular Economy is at the fore of research, analysis, and precompetitive collaborations toward building a more circular economy. Consortia managed by the Center, including the NextGen Consortium and the Consortium to Reinvent the Retail Bag, convenes leading brands and industries to solve seemingly intractable material challenges, harnessing design, innovation, and powerful partnerships to reimagine products and packaging for sustainable impact at scale. For example, the NextGen Consortium is a partnership of food-service industry leaders to identify innovations and investment opportunities for single-use food packaging waste globally, launched in partnership with Starbucks and McDonald's.

The Consortium to Reinvent the Retail Bag is a multi-year collaboration across retail sectors that aim to identify, test, and implement viable design solutions and models that more sustainably serve the purpose of the current retail bag. CVS Health, Target, and Walmart are Founding Partners of the Consortium to Reinvent the Retail Bag.

Closed Loop Partners takes a holistic, end-to-end approach to innovating, testing, and scaling the circular solutions of the future. Their expertise spans the full lifecycle of a product, connecting upstream innovation to downstream recovery infrastructure and end markets. Working across brands, countries, sectors, and industries, they create the systems change necessary for the advancement of the circular economy. Closed Loop Partners has made investments across the globe, with portfolio companies in four continents, five countries, and 24 U.S. states.

As a result of the investments, the firm has kept 1.3 million tons of material in circulation and out of landfills, avoided three million tons of greenhouse gas emissions, and catalyzed $270 million of co-investment in support of circular supply chains.

CHAPTER 4-3

Fashion for Good

To Bring Together the Entire Fashion Ecosystem

Figure 4-3.1 Fashion for Good, based in Amsterdam, promotes the messages that how good fashion is socially, economically, and environmentally beneficial

Figure 4-3.2 Exterior of the building in Amsterdam housing Fashion for Good with the banner, How Can We Make Fashion a Force for Good?

Launched in March 2017 with founding partner Laudes Foundation and an open invitation to the entire apparel industry to join, Fashion for Good (Figure 4-3.1), based on Amsterdam, aims for brands, producers, retailers, suppliers, nonprofit organizations, innovators, and funders to work together in their shared ambition to make the fashion industry a force for good (Figure 4-3.2).

"What the industry lacks are the resources, tools and incentives to put it into practice," says Katrin Ley, Managing Director for Fashion for Good. "Our mission at Fashion for Good is to bring together the entire fashion ecosystem through our Innovation Platform as a pathway for change."

By providing the inspiration and information needed to make it possible, they champion the system where companies and the planet can flourish together. They see their role as reimagining the way fashion is designed, made, worn, and reused. Their activities include exhibits, events, and information.

The "Good" in Fashion for Good™

Fashion for Good cites industry statistics indicating that on average of 60 percent more clothing is purchased today than 15 years ago—but is kept only half as long. Nearly 60 percent of all clothing produced is estimated as being burned or in landfills within one year of being made. Fashion for Good proposes an approach that is restorative and regenerative by design in five important "Goods": Good Materials—safe, healthy, and designed for reuse and recycling; Good Economy—growing, circular, shared, and benefiting everyone; Good Water—available to all; Good Lives—living and working conditions that are just, safe, and dignified.

> *The Five Goods represent an aspirational framework we can all use to work toward a world in which we do not simply take, make, waste, but rather take, make, renew, restore.*
>
> —William McDonough, Co-founder Fashion
> for Good Innovation Platform

The Fashion for Good hub in Amsterdam houses the Fashion for Good Museum and the Resource Library (Figure 4-3.3). Exhibits are staged and educational sessions for professionals and the public are conducted. A co-working space is utilized by the Circular Apparel Community. Fashion for Good's programs are supported by founding partner Laudes Foundation (formerly C&A Foundation), co-founder

Figure 4-3.3 Display at the "A Cut Above" exhibit, Fashion for Good headquarters, Amsterdam, July 2020–January 2021

Photo courtesy: Presstigieux

William McDonough, and corporate partners Adidas, C&A, Chanel, Bestseller, Galeries Lafayette, Group Kering, Otto Group, PVH Corp., Stella McCartney, Target, and Zalando, and affiliate partners Arvind, Norrøna, vivobarefoot, and Welspun. Visitors are shown how to reimagine the way our clothes are designed, made, and worn.

"A Cut Above," July 2020 to January 2021

Due to restrictions around the COVID-19 pandemic, the launch of "A CUT ABOVE" was presented as an online event that featured the owners of the curated brands, whose products would be available in the Netherlands for the first time in the Fashion for Good-Good Shop. Using a PechaKucha-style visual presentation, the brands introduced themselves, speaking on how they are taking fashion to the next level—from sourcing, using sustainable materials and zero-waste patterns, to assembly—with 3D weaving techniques; through to use. They created infinite styles through modular garments, or designing virtual fashion that exists in digital space.

The Fashion for Good Experience runs guided digital tours, giving access to their museum for visitors from around the world to discover the stories behind their clothes and to explain how they can make more sustainable choices. Fashion for Good hosts explain the fashion industry and the innovations that are making fashion better. Gwen Boon, general manager, for the museum, explains: "Guided tours of the museum are always incredibly popular. We've developed interactive tours with a quiz and personalized one-on-one guidance." Schools, associations, groups, and individuals can book a tour at fashionforgood.com/tours.

The Cradle to Cradle (C2C) Certified™ How-To Guide

The Cradle to Cradle C2C Certified How-To Guide demonstrates how good fashion is socially, economically, and environmentally beneficial. Fashion for Good created a practical and in-depth *How-To Guide* to help apparel manufacturers and brands begin their process toward only good fashion. The *How-To Guide* was developed in collaboration with McDonough

Innovation MBDC and two Indian apparel manufacturers, Pratibha Syntex and Cotton Blossom.

The *How-To Guide* outlines the principles and criteria of the C2C Certified Products Program to inspire apparel manufacturers, brands, and retailers:

- Sharing our experience and learnings from the C2C Certified pilot project
- Showcasing best practices from real apparel manufacturers in short videos and in a more in-depth downloadable handbook
- Demonstrating what pursuing C2C Certified means for a business
- Providing a self-check tool that gives a first indication of an apparel manufacturer's potential level of achievement in C2C Certified

Fashion for Good Fund

Fashion for Good sponsors the Good Fashion Fund, directed by investment specialist Bob Assenberg. "The Good Fashion Fund is the first investment fund focused on driving the implementation of innovative solutions in the fashion industry," explains Assenberg. "While sustainable solutions do exist today, there's a lack of capital available to scale these technologies within the supply chain," says Assenberg.

Fashion for Good has expanded the program to South Asia, offering the Accelerator Program that gives promising start-up innovators the expertise and access to funding needed to grow. The Scaling Program supports innovations that have passed the proof-of-concept phase, initiating pilot projects with partner organizations and guided by a Fashion for Good team that offers support and access to expertise, customers, and capital.

"The Good Fashion Fund connects the most promising technologies to the industry, to collaboratively tackle its challenges. We invest in the adoption of high impact and disruptive innovations to finance a shift to more sustainable production methods," Assenberg reports, "creating an opportunity for a regenerative closed loop system that eliminates waste."

Fashion for Good Reports

Representative subjects:

Tracing Sustainable Viscose: Industry-Wide Implementation

The Rise of Reusable Packaging: Understanding the Impact & Mapping a Path to Scale

Financing the Transformation in the Fashion Industry

Tracing Organic Cotton from Farm to Consumer

The Future of Circular Fashion

CHAPTER 4-4

Whole Foods Market

A Holistic Approach to Sustainability

Supporting Energy Conservation, Green Building, Job Training, and Community Food Programs

Interview by Ken Nisch with Christine Sturch, Whole Foods Market, Midwest Store Development, Design, and Décor Coordinator

Figure 4-4.1 Whole Foods, Addison, Texas

Photo courtesy: Whole Foods Media Library

KN: Describe Whole Foods Market's sustainability programs you have been involved in.

CS: Our core values have always been based on a holistic approach, on a health and well-being way of doing business, not just about the food or the design of stores. It is part of the concept of caring for our communities and the environment.

We've pushed the bar not only in retail design, but in food standards as well.

KN: What are your policies about construction and the environment of the stores?

CS: From the actual lease signing, we commission ground and environmental studies. Over the years, we've cleaned up existing real-estate to improve the environment around it. For example, at the Kingsbury store in Chicago, located off the Chicago River, we cleaned up the site, built parkland, walkways, sustainable green walls, roads, water diversion, and used pavers instead of concrete.

We make sure our landlords and developers are on board to protect the environment, through to the building products used, including energy-conserving materials.

KN: Quality of materials is one reason Whole Foods stores do not need remodeling as often as other retail food stores. That's another element of sustainability.

Your repurpose and recycle systems are signature elements of Whole Foods' sustainable programs (Figure 4-4.1).

CS: Yes. We'll pay slightly more for a tile with 75 percent recycled content, or support upcycled materials on their second life. It applies from decorative elements to equipment.

It's beneficial from an ROI standpoint, and for environmental reasons. We have two recent stores in the Midwest region alone where all of the refrigerator cases inside were refurbished, repainted, and reused.

KN: Whole Foods customers socialize, hold meetings in the stores, and of course, grocery shop. Your environments work really hard, to fully optimize their use throughout the community.

Figure 4-4.2 Whole Foods coordinates product displays and identifying graphics by adjusting the light level during store hours

Photo courtesy: Whole Foods Media Library

CS: Retail space is very valuable. We weigh how much space to assign to a product versus the user experience which adds to our bottom line over the long run.

Today, a Whole Foods store means far more to our customers. It's not just women shopping anymore. Demographics show that many more men are involved in the family grocery shopping. Our reach has spread to meet changing shopping trends.

Skylights help to provide illumination in the morning. LEDs that are dimmed in the morning area are programmed to keep the store bright the rest of the day (Figure 4-4.2). In the evening, the light level is electronically adjusted creating the relevant ambience for visitors who come in for dining as well as shopping.

KN: How does Whole Foods become catalytic to affect positive community change?

CS: Whole Foods has three foundations.

- The Whole Planet Foundation is a private, nonprofit organization established by Whole Foods Market and dedicated to poverty alleviation. Whole Foods aims to empower the world's poorest people with microcredit in places where we source products.

- The Whole Kids Foundation supports schools and inspires families to improve children's nutrition and wellness.
- The Whole Cities Foundation works to improve individual and community health through collaborative partnerships, education, and broader access to nutritious food.

At a school in Englewood, we partnered with classrooms and kitchens outside of the store to provide needed education and training. Foods that the kids had never seen before were brought in. We handed out colored pencils so they could draw them, and then we all talked about them.

Our Local Producer Loan Program offers low-interest loans to local producers to help grow their business. Through the program, we have provided over 350 low-interest loans, representing more than $25 million in capital, to independent local farmers and food artisans. We will also provide equipment and resources to kick-start their company, everything from a UPC sticker to additional production space, to signs that identify a local producers or product.

We want our Team Members to learn about retail as a whole: about food production, about leadership, and about conscious living. Some Team Members that have been with the company 20, 30 years, have moved up in their responsibilities. I started out bagging groceries 23 years ago.

We've achieved economies of scale, but have kept our uniqueness. There are 11 regions, all with store development teams. In the Midwest, we went from 22 to 62 stores in four years. Creating connections in the individual communities has been a factor in achieving this expansion.

KN: Some retailers use sustainability as a promotional tool, whereas Whole Foods Market has a history of taking a long-term operational investment view.

CS: In California, 45 Whole Foods Market stores were honored with Global Stewardship Certification for sustainability practices. California is an industry leader for sustainability.

Figure 4-4.3 A Whole Foods in-store coffee and tea dispensary

Photo courtesy: Whole Foods Media Library

Our founder, John Mackey, made advancing environmental stewardship a core value for the company. It comes from his conscious leadership and holistic mindset. The underlying effect is an overall harmonious, holistic environment for food (Figure 4-4.3). It's a circular argument.

We rely on our vendor partners. Whether it's our architects, MEP, lighting vendors, or consultants, we ask a lot of questions of their expertise, and put that knowledge to use. We are always willing to try something new.

CHAPTER 4-5

EHI

Sustainability in Shopfitting

An Emphasis on Flexibility and Transparency

Comments by Claudia Horbert, Director, Research Store Planning + Design, EHI Retail Institute, Cologne, Germany, adapted from Euro-Shop 2020 panel discussion, Dusseldorf, led by Ken Nisch.

EHI interviewed the heads of store planning departments in 50 leading retailing companies in Germany, Austria, and Switzerland to obtain insight into trends and developments in their businesses. One of the topics was sustainability in store planning and shop construction: What could these retailers do to consider sustainability when planning to build and furbish a store?

Sustainability has a high priority by the retailers we spoke to, who first have to overcome the first steps concerning shop construction and furnishing, they pointed out that they face very high competition and cost pressures in retail businesses in these German-speaking countries. Shopfitting, they affirmed, is becoming a growing consideration in evaluating strategies to grow store traffic.

Shopfitting Options

The four key trends in shopfitting we examined were: flexible spaces, omnichannel retail, showrooms, and personalization. Physical retail spaces are tending to become more fluid in their structure. Exhibitions, cafés, social, and educational spaces are intertwined with more traditional retail setups. Omnichannel retail is impacting shopfitting because retailers are connecting the online and offline experience in new ways, installing in-store devices for online searches and augmented reality mirrors.

Nearly half of the retail companies surveyed reported that they are reducing the number of products when using furnishing elements, particularly relevant to visual merchandising, where theme and concept have a short lifetime. The length of time during which store furnishings and materials can be utilized is a consideration in the planning stage. Especially for retailers in the fashion and other lifestyle areas, it is an important aspect of sustainability. According to the retailers interviewed, the systems should be modular and flexible so that they can be upgraded when improvements are introduced. Examples are slot systems in rear walls for installation of different surfaces, and compatibility with fittings of a range of manufacturers.

Refurbishing and reusing existing shopfittings have long been a common money-saving technique employed by food stores, drug stores, and other specialty retailers. Now fashion retailers with shorter-term tenancy agreements are extending the life of their store furnishings, enabling them to extract additional life from their amortized assets. However, if when the need to relocate, and problems with damages occur, during disassembly, transport, and reassembly, retailers reported that the purchasing of new display and storage pieces would be preferable and less costly in the long run.

Supplier Relationships

Sustainability is becoming increasingly transparent in shopfitting. It has become common to ask suppliers where a product is manufactured and under what conditions. They ask about the energy used for production and transport, particularly for international retail companies. If they purchase all or part of their shopfittings from other countries, they can insist on transparency relating to production conditions that ensure compliance with the country's environmental and social laws.

Purchasing of shopfittings by retailers operating in Europe from European sales subsidiaries or from domestic-based suppliers typically provides a warranty of compliance with applicable environmental and social standards. Efforts are underway to develop supplier evaluation systems for multi-country adaptation.

For retailers who have such strategies in place, particularly in the food business, they mount programs to inform customers of their sustainable practices, utilizing POS as the communication medium. To the retailers' benefit, they boost their public image by explaining their commitment to the environment and climate protection. Aspects relating to sustainability and the environment are also important in obtaining building certification for facilities selling food products.

In the nonfood sector, sporting goods retailers who promote their commitments to sustainability count on it to achieve a competitive edge in the marketplace. For retailers who are tenants in a shopping center, compliance with the center's policies for sustainability and tight controls on energy use contributes to the center's closely monitored operating efficiencies.

CHAPTER 4-6

James Avery Artisan Jewelry

90 Stores Across the South

James Avery was a self-taught jeweler who built a Southern retail empire, selling his creations starting with his first store in Dallas in 1973. The company now employs more than 3,500 people in 90 stores in five states across the South. Their extensive collection is sold on the company's website and in 229 Dillard's stores in 29 states. Total estimated annual revenue is $156 million.

Figure 4-6.1 James Avery headquarters, Kerrville, Texas

Photo courtesy: James Avery Artisan Jewelry

Figure 4-6.2 A James Avery retail store, displaying the company's
extensive jewelry collection

Photo courtesy: James Avery Artisan Jewelry

James Avery is a vertically integrated, family-owned company based
in Kerrville, Texas (Figure 4-6.1). Their collection offers finely crafted
jewelry designs for men and women in sterling silver, 14K and 18K gold,
gemstones, and leather wallets—designed by the firm's own skilled artists
and assembled in Kerrville and four other studios in Texas.

JGA, Inc., assisted the firm in the development of a new store concept that could be applied to the next generation of James Avery stores
as future expansion of the chain was implemented (Figure 4-6.2). James
Avery's granddaughter, Lindsey Avery Tognietti, manager of strategic initiatives, became part of the management team. "There has always been an
enormous amount of pride from family members about the business," she
said. John McCullough is the firm's CEO.

Upgrading of the Store Design

Lindsey has been a leading member of the team guiding the installation
of three key stores as incubators for new digital integrations and new lines
of merchandise. Each has added an experiential area where customers can
personalize the product. "The James Avery theme is 'celebrating life'. The

brand strongly believes in building relationships and creating experiences with our customers. Our store's design reflect and influence our shared values with the customer, and our brand of connecting people through the products we offer," said Tognietti.

Forging Hope

The James Avery charitable giving program, Forging Hope, serves local communities. "Our goal is to support our associates and customers," Tognietti indicated. "Since 2003, the firm has given $18.5 million through our charitable giving program that provides direct support to the arts, craftsmanship, military personnel, first responders, people with special needs, and the environment," she pointed out.

To commemorate its 65th anniversary, the firm sponsored the donation of a total of $165,000 to be distributed to charitable causes. Customers were encouraged to vote for their favorite of three eligible organizations. Funds were divided according to the number of votes they received.

A Team of Passionate and Dedicated Employees

Ken Nisch Interview with John McCullough, CEO

KN: James Avery is both a company and culture. Where does James Avery fit into today's social, environmental, cultural, and sustainability approaches?

JM: When James Avery was still involved with the company, as recently as a few years ago, he never imagined this would be what it has become, 90 stores around the South. His own value system was based on an appreciation for nature.

That influences everything we do. The environment for our main campus in Kerrville, Texas, is spread over 40 acres. As the company grew, we added more buildings that took into account very beautiful oak trees that were native to the property. He wanted to make sure the placement of any development respected their protection.

James Avery had a deep appreciation for beauty around it and he didn't want to do anything to compromise or diminish future generations' ability to enjoy it. He was focused on doing things the right way. It's how we treat people, and also drives how we approach sustainability. We want to do no harm, be sensitive to those working at James Avery, leave the world the same, if not better, than how we found it.

KN: How did you repurpose the building on the campus?

JM: The design studio is an old farmhouse that we acquired from the farm adjacent to the original land. It was converted into a beautiful work space for the designers. Locally sourced materials like limestone, and barn and timber woods were used.

KN: Describe the workforce at James Avery.

JM: We have four manufacturing facilities—one at our headquarters in Kerrville and three others within an hour's drive. We are often asked: "How do you find all these people to make jewelry?" The reality is, we don't technically need people who have experience producing jewelry. We've been able to bring people on who have basic skill sets. They go through a training period where we teach them the skills they need in order to actually make the jewelry.

This has proven to achieve a high success rate among our production staff. Over time, we further invest in them and provide them with opportunities to enhance the complexity of their skill set. They become involved in working on new projects such as hand-hammered pieces or gemstone setting. Financially, we are able increase their earnings.

We have numerous multigenerational families, people who have worked here for decades. Their brothers and sisters work here, their spouses work here, we have grandfathers and grandsons working next to one another. To me, it's amazing. I don't know how often this happens, but we are fortunate to have such passionate and dedicated employees.

James Avery's product selection is directed to the customer who looks for a design that embodies and encapsulates their memories, milestones, and feelings … not disposable qualities. Rather, it's about longevity and long-term value (Figure 4-6.3).

We feel honored to be part of people's lives. Mr. Avery wanted to make beautiful things that people could share with each other that reflect them and their lives. His jewelry was simply a medium.

Figure 4-6.3 A James Avery charm bracelet and necklace design

Photo courtesy: James Avery Artisan Jewelry

It is important to us to take care of the environment that we are in. We try to capture every piece of metal and recapture and repurpose it to make jewelry. None of it is lost. When an item has run its course and is no longer keep-it-in-the-line, it sells down in anywhere from six to 12 months. Then, rather than discounting it, we bring it back to one of our plants. They are melted down and repurposed into a new design.

KN: The company has a Christian, faith-based background. How does it influence your products?

JM: Part of Mr. Avery's influence in his career was his Christian faith. Approximately 15 percent of our sales come from items that are Judeo-Christian based themes. Our mission statement to celebrate life through the beauty of design, allowing us to personally determine if there is a faith-based element to it or not. We want everyone to celebrate what's important to them in their lives. For many people, that can be their own faith. Mainly, we focus on these values of how we treat other people from employees, to customers, to the beauty of the environment around us.

There's a whole library of our designs that have their origin from the beauty of nature around us. The Texas Hill Country is an area where people flock to during the spring when the wildflowers are in bloom. That has influenced a portion of work. We have other nature-based designs as well.

From around the 1980s, the World Wildlife Federation sells our products and all proceeds go to their funds. When Hurricane Harvey hit the Gulf Coast in 2017, many of our associates and customers were devastated. We donated 100 percent of the sales from the proceeds of a James Avery design called "Deep in the Heart of Texas" for five weeks after the storm. A total of $1.8 million was raised for the assistance fund by this effort.

KN: Do you look into the methodology of the firms/companies you source raw materials from?

JM: We have strict standards of conduct that apply to our dealings with our vendors. They are expected to meet them in terms of working conditions and more. Our ongoing relationships are evaluated by us, making sure that it is very clear to them about their understanding of our expectations.

Levi's® and David Jones Open Sustainability Shop in Shop

Collections with Material and Technology Innovations

Levi's® in partnership with David Jones Australia have launched the Sustainability Shop in Shop to present sustainable fashion collections and offer consumers a conscious and sustainable way to shop (Figures 4-7.1 and 4-7.2). The dual sponsorship brings together two long-established retail icons. Levi Strauss & Co. was founded 1873. Its jeanswear and accessories collections are available in more than 110 countries, around the world. David Jones first opened its doors in 1838 and currently operates 47 department stores through Australasia, the oldest continuously operating department store in the world still trading under its original name.

Figure 4-7.1 Mutually sponsored by Levi's and David Jones, the Sustainability Shop in Shop offers customers a variety of styles made from sustainable sources

Photo courtesy: Levi Strauss & Co.

Figure 4-7.2 Men's and women's collections by Levi's displayed at Sustainability Shop in Shop at select David Jones stores

Photo courtesy: Levi Strauss & Co.

Sustainable Shop in Shops are located in David Jones stores at the Bourke Street Mall, Melbourne, and six other locations.

"We are partnering with Levi's on this sustainability initiative," says Bridget Veals, General Manager of Womenswear, Footwear and Accessories for David Jones. "We are committed to considering new ways of doing business to support a transition to the low-carbon and circular economy of the future. Working with our brands and investing in programs and activities that optimize our use of energy, increase diversion of waste from landfill, and reduce natural resource consumption are parts of this commitment and our broader Good Business Journey."

The unique space within David Jones will house Levi's Made & Crafted, Wellthread™, and a number of other collections with material and technology innovations such as Cottonised Hemp, Tencel™ x Refibra™, Water>Less™ and F.L.X. They represent the company's commitment to sustainable cotton production processes with the Better Cotton Initiative, and building a sustainable supply chain with the Worker Wellbeing program. The Levi's garments are displayed on 100 percent recyclable Arch & Hook BLUE® hangers—the world's first hanger made of Marine Plastics®, collected from the world's five most polluted rivers.

The Sustainability Shop in Shop was designed using premier Tasmanian wood supplied by Hydrowood. It was sustainably sourced and crafted by Australian industrial designer, Jaron Dickson, into custom structures, furniture, shelving, and signage for the new shop. To minimize the environmental impact of the building process, the structures used water-based products for gluing and finishing.

"The new retail concept is a physical representation of our ongoing commitment to craftsmanship, innovation and sustainability," says Paul Sweet, Managing Director ANZ for Levi Strauss & Co. "We're placing environmental considerations front and center of the shopping experience and inviting consumers to shop more consciously," Sweet affirmed.

CHAPTER 4-8

David Jones

Mindfully Made a One-Stop Shop for Sustainable Goods

Sustainable Products and Information

Australian department store chain David Jones has launched Mindfully Made, a merchandise hub where consumers can shop for sustainable fashion, beauty, and selected food products, all in one place in selected stores. The goal for the shopping experience is for David Jones customers to be able to identify the techniques that brands are adopting to be more responsible, whether socially or environmentally, and support the firm's far-reaching program to help protect the environment.

David Jones and Levi's also co-sponsor Sustainability Shop-in-Shop (see Chapter 4-7).

In order to be part of the carefully curated Mindfully Made hub, the brand must meet a minimum of one sustainability attribute of the following five benefits representing sourcing and production. Many meet more than one.

- *Australian Made* is a label assigned to a brand that manufactures its goods at home and supports the local industry and community.
- *Sourced with Care* brands focus on using responsibly sourced materials like regenerated nylon or vegan leather, and production processes to minimize environmental impact.
- *Reduce and Recycle* are brands with innovative and conscious ways to upcycle, recycle, and reduce waste, such as packaging made out of recycled materials.

- *Community Minded* is for ethical brands that actively support their communities and the welfare of workers, uphold fair working conditions, and offer supply chain transparency.
- *Kind to Animals* is earned when a brand uses cruelty-free production methods and ingredients that do not harm animals.

Sources featured in the shop are such Australian and overseas brands as Veja, Weleda, Bec + Bridge, Waverly Mills, Grown Alchemist, Outland Denim, KitX, Bianca Spender, Country Road, R.M. Williams, Cue, and KeepCup.

"It's not just about offering customers the ability to shop by their values, we see it as a place for consumers to learn important information about shopping sustainably," says Eloise Bishop, the head of sustainability for David Jones. "For example, the hub includes information about caring for and prolonging the life of their purchases as well as decoding terminology around fabric, sustainability, and ethics, including terms such as circularity, cellulose, vegan leather, and more," Bishop says. The hub is on the David Jones website as well as in seven stores across Australia.

CHAPTER 4-9

Starbucks

Investing in Communities

Starbucks $100 million fund is aimed at investing in community development projects and small businesses in areas populated by Black, Indigenous, and people of color. The company's Community Resilience Fund is part of a broader plan to step up its commitment to racial and social equity, particularly in the communities where it operates cafes. The Starbucks Foundation has pledged $1 million in neighborhood grants, joining numerous companies that would give money to fight against racism.

Figure 4-9.1 A Starbucks farmer support center, San José, Costa Rica

Starbucks plans to use the new fund to invest $100 million over the next four years in 12 U.S. cities with populations that are Black, Indigenous, or people of color. The cities are Atlanta, Detroit, Houston, Los Angeles, Miami, Minneapolis, New Orleans, New York, Philadelphia, San Francisco Bay Area, Seattle, and Washington, DC. The money will go to impact-focused financial institutions, such as community development financial institutions, which provide financial services to low-income people. Small businesses and neighborhood development projects are beneficiaries of the program.

Starbucks is collaborating with the Smithsonian's National Museum of African American History and Culture to share the museum's educational resources and digital volunteer opportunities, and invite partners and customers to participate in the Freedmen's Bureau Transcription Project. Volunteers helped digitally transcribe handwritten records containing information about Black Americans newly emancipated during the Reconstruction era. A museum exhibition is planned.

Starbucks joins other major retail companies and financial firms that have pledged funds to groups focused on social and racial justice including: Walmart/Walmart Foundation; Nike; MasterCard; Citigroup Inc.; and Coca-Cola.

Starbucks invests in financial institutions, such as CDFIs (Community Development Financial Institutions). Community lenders focus on providing access to capital and promoting economic development. In addition to offering loans, CDFIs provide services to support individuals and community-based organizations through mentorship and technical assistance.

Starbucks opened its first farmer support center San José, Costa Rica (Figure 4-9.1), in 2004 just as it was launching its groundbreaking CAFE (Coffee and Farmer Equity) Practices verification program. Working one-on-one with farmers in the field, supporting coops, and suppliers, Starbucks agronomists build upon traditional growing methods to help farmers improve both the quality and profitability of their crops.

Today's farmers are facing constant challenges to their long-term future. Starbucks currently operates eight farmer support centers and one satellite agronomy office in coffee-producing countries around the world, providing farmers with free access to the latest findings of Starbucks agronomists, including new varietals of disease-resistant trees and advanced soil management techniques. Its original Costa Rica agronomy office has relocated from an office building in downtown San José to the Hacienda Alsacia farm on the slopes of the Poas Volcano, the company's global agronomy research and development center (Figure 4-9.2).

(*Sources*: CNN, January 12, 2021, Amelia Lucas; Starbucks website)

Figure 4-9.2 Starbucks is participating in the development of disease-resistant coffee trees

Photo courtesy: Starbucks

CHAPTER 4-10

Harrods

Fashion Re-Told Pop-Up Brings Luxury Resale to the Upmarket

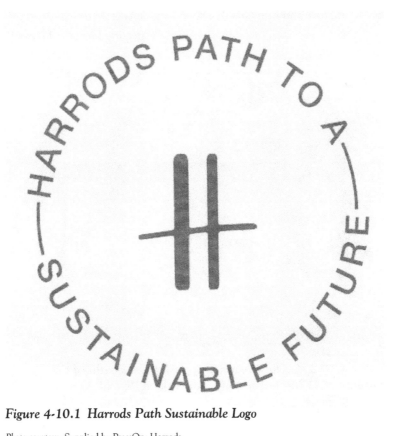

Figure 4-10.1 Harrods Path Sustainable Logo

Photo courtesy: Supplied by PressOn; Harrods

Harrods Path to a Sustainable Future

"Our sustainability logo represents the journey we're on to drive positive change—protecting our planet, communities and people. Whenever you see it across our platforms and in our stores, you'll know that you're looking at one of our sustainability initiatives.

Our strategy–Harrods Path to a Sustainable Future–is built on four pillars, each working towards a clear sustainability goal aligned to Harrods' people, products, partnerships and operations. Initiatives under each pillar are closely aligned with our broader strategy and values, ensuring that a commitment to becoming sustainable and responsible is part of our tapestry.

We have made huge progress but will continue to push ourselves every day to improve and think big in our sustainability journey."

Michael Ward, Managing Director, Harrods"

Figure 4-10.2 A colorful garland of fresh flowers outlined the entrance at 51 Marleybone Street to Fashion Re-told

Photo courtesy: Supplied by PressOn; Harrods

Retail icon Harrods (Figure 4-10.1) sustainability program extended to joining the reuse and resale market in its own singular world-class style by hosting Fashion Re-told in London in both 2018 and 2019. In this widely supported month-long event that featured Harrods artfully designed luxury charity pop-up store, Fashion Re-told, the benefactor of funds collected from the sales of donated luxury apparel and accessories was the National Society for the Prevention of Cruelty to Children (NSPCC). For the two years in operation, 2018 and 2019, Fashion Re-told collectively raised the equivalent of $385,000 at current exchange rates for the NSPCC. COVID-19 forced cancellation of the 2020 event.

Surrounding the arched entry to the store was a thick luxurious border of live blooms, designed by the noted floral purveyor, Flowerbx (Figure 4-10.2). Harrods visual merchandising team developed the store's design concepts. On display were high-end fashion items donated by luxury brands, as well as donations from the public, celebrities, and Harrods employees. Open seven days a week during its run, it was staffed by NSPCC members and Harrods employees who donated a total of 1,400 hours. PressOn was responsible for the distinctive image and sales-stimulating environment.

Figure 4-10.3 Flowers on walls and floors, designer apparel, and accessories

Photo courtesy: Supplied by PressOn; Harrods

In an atmosphere of flowing oversize flowers on walls and floors, designer apparel and accessories were offered on the shop's street-level (Figure 4-10.3). Decorative and functional items for the home were displayed on the lower level. All proceeds from Fashion Re-told went to the NSPCC.

The designer selection represented styles by such labels as Stella McCartney, Chloé, Missoni, Calvin Klein, and Balmain, among others. The store hosted an expanded selection of items across womenswear, menswear, childrenswear, accessories, and home. In the lower level were displays of decorative and functional items for the home. An area in the pop-up was set aside for Harrods- and NSPCC-staged events to generate traffic for the store. Presentations were given by *British Vogue* staffers, Harrods fashion editorial director Stacy Duguid, and the manager of Flowerbx.

Michael Ward, Harrods managing director, stated in an announcement of the opening of Fashion Re-told, that Harrods, by offering a Harrods-level of service, product range, and distinctive shopping environment, would serve to change the public's perception of charitable shopping. "We want customers to leave knowing that not only have they raised money for a highly important cause, but that have purchased a luxury item as part of a truly unique shopping experience," Ward said.

"The success of Fashion Re-told demonstrated that luxury consumers have become increasingly aware of the negative impact of fast fashion and its unfortunately fast disposal, and as a result are looking to invest in long-lasting quality pieces," said a Harrods merchandising executive. "We are seeing a broad acceptance of shopping vintage, sustainable pieces, as well as the support of evolving social enterprise brands."

The Corporate Social Responsibility (CSR) Manager for Harrods is Ankita Patel, who joined Harrods in 2018. Her management role involves leading the CSR and Sustainability strategy for Harrods.

CHAPTER 4-11

Grupo Advance

Contributing to a Cyclical Economy and Social Well-Being

Figure 4-11.1 *Grupo Advance in San Martin, Argentina, urges the establishment of point-of-purchase industry standards*

Photo courtesy: Grupo Advance

Figure 4-11.2 *Product display for KitKat*

Photo courtesy: Grupo Advance

Figure 4-11.3 Product display for Patagonia

Photo courtesy: Grupo Advance

Questions posed by Ken Nisch; responses from Jimena Seoane, Sustainability Manager for Grupo Advance, with CEO Gustavo de Freitas

KN: Please describe some of your company's activities as related to sourcing, validation of sustainable products, and practices in your own communities around recycling and upcycling, including skilled training to improve the communities in which your businesses are based and/or sourced from.

GA: Grupo Advance is a design, development, and manufacturing company of permanent P.O.P. elements, located in San Martin, Argentina, near Buenos Aires (Figure 4-11.1). Our customers include AB InBev, Unlever, Nestlē, Cervecería y Maltería Quilmes, and Mondelez, among others (Figures 4-11.2 and 4-11.3). We earned several certifications that endorse our operating on a responsible and caring path with our planet, both from the environmental, social, and economic perspectives.

Our business model not only aims at social impact to reverse the local conjuncture of violence, lack of opportunities, and inequality, but also to transmit the responsibility for the environment that we have individually and as a community. We work with productive processes with sustainable durable materials and promoting the recycling of waste treatment that contributes employment and new life cycles of materials. It is believed that these activities contribute to social well-being and a cyclical economy, where the environment is a goal to preserve and care for everyone.

Long-term functionality will contribute to taking care of the planet and our life on it. We are a certified Company B, and by ECOVADIS, one of the most important certifiers worldwide, and also part of the UN Global Compact.

We implement our objectives through such programs as hiring and training. These include people with high job barriers; former prisoners; low-resource residents; disabled people; members of the LGBT community; and those with limited education. Other programs involve mentoring, and workshops on gender equality and on financial education.

KN: Are your company's sustainability efforts a major business advantage? How do you respond to unique RFP requests, as part of its mission and values?

GA: We work with and encourage the use of durable and resistant materials, whose durability properties have resistance to the different agents that cause deterioration.

- **Waste Reduction**: We design by determining how different materials will be implemented, according to the characteristics in which the raw material is available, to optimize the productive use of the material, and make maximum of its use. Recycling allows the generation of new raw materials, or their reuse, in the manufacture of new products.

- **Recycling Network:** Funds resulting from the recycling of materials from the production processes and packaging are directed to the public hospitals of San Martin. Wood is donated to local prisons, where the learning of craft jobs is promoted, transforming it into toys distributed to kindergartens and other end uses.

So far, our long-term emphasis on sustainability hasn't yet constituted a business advantage. One of our major customers, AB InBev, has placed a certified B company Corp seal on the products we make for them.

We are beginning to see some changes in the market but they are still small and recent. Despite all our years of promoting sustainability—teaching, explaining, and boosting among our clients, the old concept of business still prevails in the market. Sustainability is unfortunately not part of many companies' agenda. In certain sectors, empathy is generated, but it only goes so far; it does not go through formal processes of action.

When sustainability is talked about in the P.O.P. world, there is still no knowledge in large companies about this, considered only words. The appreciation of the actions and processes carried out by our company is undervalued.

KN: Would a system similar to which SHOP! is looking to develop be helpful in having a common and shared retail focused approach to sustainability, in arriving at more predictability and consistency for suppliers and purchasers?

GA: The support of a certification is very important, but even more so that this certification not only audits administrative or agency processes, but actually where those materials are produced. When P.O.P. material is fully considered, the impact is real and integral.

Certification is useful and provides clear parameters, but we believe in the need for it to thoroughly audit every aspect to ensure that the impact is real and is not the part of a discourse. It is key that the certification audits the production process in each company, and consider not only about the environment but also about the social aspects. The sustainable agenda is organized through Sustainable Development Goals (SDGs), which involve environmental as well as the social economic aspects, including strategic alliances between the public and private sectors to carry out a real and integral impact.

At the UN Global Compact Leaders Summit 2020, these topics were discussed. We observed that companies only focus on a few SDGs. There is need for action by each company to implement a greater number of SDGs as the way to achieve the agreed-upon goals for 2030.

KN: What are some examples in the supply chain where the producer such as your firm, who live in the "last mile" of the supply chain, that is, translating raw materials into finished product, can innovate to enhance sustainable practices, across environmental, social, and cultural activities?

GA: At Grupo Advance, we work with each P.O.P. element, from durability to functional and communicational needs, to fulfill its objective of standing out in the market, and its function and useful life over many years. Reduction and reuse are necessary, at the same time to reverse logistics dealing with excess waste, and emissions impacting global warming.

Currently, the P.O.P. market is a prisoner of long-established programmed obsolescence. Adoption of the SHOP! Program will help to reverse these practices, supported by investment, research, and application.

CHAPTER 4-12

H&A

Innovations for Sustainable Display Fixtures

Driving Change, Generating New Ideas

Chris Hewitt founded Hewitt & Associates (H&A), based in Durban, South Africa, to not only design and build traffic-generating product displays, but to build them by sustainable practices in a sustainable working environment. With a staff of 250 operating in a 71,000-sq.-ft. facility, H&A's design team serves regional and international clients.

"It's our goal to do business the way we live, by using no more than we need, respect those around us, and tread lightly with a small footprint," says Hewitt. "We believe that design, creativity, and innovation can drive change, generate new ideas, and leave things in a better state than the way we found them."

The H&A site has 15 percent of its footprint allocated to trees and garden. Cognitive lighting—that combines intelligence, sensors, and energy-efficient sources—reduces the energy spent on lighting. The factory makes use of natural lighting and automated ventilation on the ridgeline for climate control. A solar installation was completed at the close of 2020. In addition to Energy, H&A monitors four other sustainable categories: Health, Resources, Environment, and Respect. For the latter, Hewitt points out that the firm partakes in socially responsible investments, and works with four other green businesses.

To innovate, stay competitive, improve speed to market and conserve resources, H&A employs 3D printing, virtual modeling, and value engineering on every project undertaken.

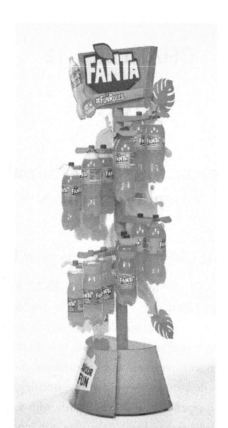

Figure 4-12.1 Freestanding display fixture by H&A for Fanta, Coke, South Africa

Photo courtesy: H&A

The 360-degree display unit by H&A emphasizes new twist packaging and the launch of new flavors. Designed with a steel core and other sustainable fittings, the fixture occupies minimal space for the amount of product shown (Figure 4-12.1). Life expectancy is five years.

CHAPTER 4-13

Bish Creative Display

An International Approach to POS

Questions Posed By Ken Nisch; Responses from Jerry Fox, CEO, Bish Creative Display, Inc.

KN: **Please describe some of your company's activities and relating to sourcing, validation of sustainable products, and practices around recycling and upcycling, including skilled training to improve the communities in which your businesses are based and/ or sourced from.**

JF: Bish Creative, founded 60 years ago and based in Lake Zurich, Illinois, outside of Chicago, has six offices, four in the United States and one each in Paris and China. Our customers for our POS (point-of-sale) displays include Bacardi, Jack Daniels, Beeluxe, Absolut, Mattell, ABINBEV, Pepsico, Kellogg's, Coty, Milwaukee Tool, and Goose Island (Figures 4-13.1 and 4-13.2).

We are committed to higher standards in the selection of the manufacturing materials we source. Each project is unique which allows us the opportunity to collaborate with our customers to provide designs with sustainable options. Working cohesively with our customers, we actively strive to reduce our carbon footprint.

Figure 4-13.1 Sustainable in-store displays from Bish Creative Display; for holiday tree for Jack Daniels

Photo courtesy: Bish Creative Display, Inc.

Within our offices and warehouses, we have instituted layout and design upgrades, monitoring our recycling, waste ratio, water usage, and transitioned every light to LED. This has resulting in savings of 39,702 kWh per year, or 28.1 tons of CO_2 annually, equivalent to:

- Greenhouse gas emissions from 6 cars / year
- CO_2 emissions from 3,159 gallons of gasoline consumed
- CO_2 emissions from 4.9 homes' electricity use per year
- Greenhouse gas emissions avoided by 9.8 tons of recycled waste instead of landfilled
- 464 tree seedlings grown for 10 years

(Source: U. S. Environmental Protection Agency)

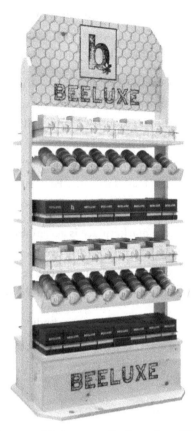

Figure 4-13.2 Sustainable in-store displays from Bish Creative Display; here is a Beeluxe candle rack

Photo courtesy: Bish Creative Display, Inc.

Our goal is to reach our target audience with designs that are unbiased and will promote fairness. We support education internally and in the industry by participating in educational sponsorships. Additionally, we offer internships and shadow days to students in the community.

We belong to SEDEX, one of the world's leading ethical trade service providers, working to improve working conditions in global supply chains. To offer employees a beneficial work-life balance, we allow work from home (WFH days) and staggered schedules.

Whenever possible, we select environmentally friendly products and also freecycle to keep waste out of landfills. Personally, I try to lead by example through volunteering and community outreach.

KN: Are your company's sustainability efforts a major business advantage? How do you respond to unique RFP requests? Is your organization's commitment to sustainability part of its mission and values?

JF: I have a strong personal commitment to sustainability which is reflected in Bish Creative's corporate commitment to the adoption of sustainability practices within our industry. Many of the displays we produce are recyclable. The key to building and maintaining a significant environmental program is to educate raw material suppliers to use more sustainable materials in their core manufacturing. For example, 3D resin could be improved to utilize more plant-based materials vs. chemical.

KN: Do you find that the marketplace is acceptably developed, when it comes to the ecosystem of your locating products and suppliers that meet or exceed your company's commitment to sustainability? Are there categories where the market is being underserved?

JF: We haven't experienced any shortages in finding products. However, the technology is not yet advanced to make biodegradable materials at a comparable cost to raw materials.

CHAPTER 4-14

Shanghai Zhitao Cultural Innovation Co., Ltd.

Creating Sustainable POS for the Upscale Market

Shanghai Zhitao Cultural Innovation Co., Ltd., based in Shanghai, has built a worldwide client base of high-end shopping malls, showrooms, branded product in-store designs, and outdoor promotions. It is a major supplier of point-of-sale (POS) product display and retail marketing materials for leading brands. Clients include L'Oreal, LVMH Group, Estèe Lauder Group, LG group, Shiseido Group, Amore Pacific Group, Swatch Group, P&G, Clarins, KOSE, Elizabeth Arden, and Pernod Ricard China (Figures 4-14.1 and 4-14.2).

Figure 4-14.1 Merchandise display projects produced by Shanghai Zhitao Cultural Innovation include a free-standing jewelry counter

Figure 4-14.2 Merchandise display projects produced by Shanghai Zhitao Cultural Innovation include Givenchy fragrances display unit

The firm has offices in Shenzhen, Shanghai, Chengdu, and Beijing in China and in South Korea. In the future, CEO Yuan Dong indicates that the firm's business network is planned to expand to Singapore and Malaysia.

Guidelines that focus on environmental protection have been established for production facilities it operates. These include:

- Use of recycled acrylic, wood, FSC paper, metal, photopolymer, visual for display, and packing materials made from repurposed PET, and from easily degradable materials.
- Eco-friendly processing during production, such as water-based paint, vacuum electroplating, 3D print
- Efficiently operating waste treatment equipment for water, gas, and solid waste
- Verification by inspection organizations: ISO14001, ISO9000, SA8000, and ECOVADIS
- LED illumination for permanent POS installations

The firm has instituted guidelines dealing with the weight of materials used, by reducing the thickness of the materials without compromising their technical performance. For products constructed of multiple materials, specifications are followed so that the materials are separable for recycling.

Social Responsibility

CEO Dong affirms that the company will continue to undertake social responsibility as an important sustainable development task. Representative programs include nursing homes and homes for the elderly; donations to special needs staff, and underprivileged residents; assistance to the Disabled Persons Federation; cooperation with local colleges, including East China University of Science and Technology, Seoul National University; and Shanghai Art & Design Academy to cultivate talents; cultural communications with overseas markets. Cross-industry traditional handcraft design is encouraged for adaption into creating the POS design concepts.

"As a co-organizer of SHOP!, our company has been cited for its original designs for retail environments. It will be our policy going forward to contribute to society as much as we can, supporting environmental protection and social responsibility," stated CEO Dong.

CHAPTER 4-15

Will Sustainability Become a Law?

The Proposed "New York Fashion Act"

In January, 2022, the Fashion Sustainability and Social Accountability Act (or Fashion Act) was unveiled to the state's legislature in Albany. If passed, it would make New York the first state in the country to pass a legislation that would effectively hold the biggest brands in fashion to account for their role in climate change.

Sponsored by State Senator Alessandra Biaggi and Assemblywoman Anna R. Kelles, and backed by a powerful coalition of nonprofits focused on fashion and sustainability, including the New Standard Institute, the Natural Resources Defense Council, and the New York City Environmental Justice Alliance, as well as designer Stella McCartney, the law will apply to global apparel and footwear companies, with more than $100 million in revenues, doing business in New York. That extends to large multinational fashion names—LVMH, Prada, and Armani—to such fast-fashion giants as Shein and Boohoo.

Specifically, it would require such companies to identify a minimum of 50 percent of their supply chain, starting with the farms where the raw materials originate through factories and shipping. They would then disclose where in that chain they have the greatest social and environmental impact when it comes to fair wages, energy, greenhouse gas emissions, water, and chemical management, and make concrete plans to reduce carbon emission numbers in accordance with the targets set by the Paris Climate Accords.

Companies would disclose their material production volumes to reveal, for example, how much cotton or leather or polyester they sell. All information would be made available online.

The bill is expected to make its way through Senate and Assembly committees, with the sponsors aiming to bring it to a vote in late spring after state budget negotiations are complete. "Before officially introducing the bill, we built a broad coalition of support that includes leaders in the fashion industry, manufacturers, labor rights activists and environmental activists who are passionate about seeing the bill become law," Ms. Biaggi has emphasized.

"A Groundbreaking Piece of Legislation"

Though she said she expected "that some companies impacted by this legislation won't initially support these new standards," she added: "This diverse and active coalition makes me confident we can pass this legislation in both chambers later this legislative session."

"As a global fashion and business capital of the world, New York State has a moral responsibility to serve as a leader in mitigating the environmental and social impact of the fashion industry." Ms. Biaggi called the law "a groundbreaking piece of legislation that will make New York the global leader" in holding the fashion industry "accountable," ensuring that "labor, human rights, and environmental protections are prioritized."

Companies would be given 12 months to comply with the mapping directive (18 months for their impact disclosures), and if they are found to be in violation of the law, they would be fined up to 2 percent of their annual revenues. Those fines would go to a new Community Fund administered by the Department of Environmental Conservation and used for environmental justice projects. The New York attorney general would also publish an annual list of companies found to be noncompliant.

"Fashion is one of the least regulated industries," said Maxine Bédat, the founder of the New Standard Institute. "Its sprawling supply chain can include multiple countries and continents, so efforts at sustainability vary widely. Imposing government regulation would regularize the reporting and make sure there isn't a competitive disadvantage to doing the right thing," Ms. Bédat said. "Often, there is a reaction by businesses against the idea of regulation," Ms. Bédat said, noting that numerous stakeholders were consulted while drafting the Fashion Act. "Even the auto industry, which initially rebelled against fuel efficiency standards, has now embraced them."

The Fashion Act, Ms. Bédat said, "is an effort to recognize the good faith efforts they are already making and come up with a common standard, but do so with some teeth."

Efforts to rectify the situation so far have been left up to the companies and an assortment of nongovernmental watchdog consortiums such as the Fair Labor Association, which addresses wage issues, and Higg, which addresses supply chain reporting. Ralph Lauren, Kering, LVMH, and Capri Holdings, for example, are among the companies that have already committed to using the Science-Based Targets Initiative, a tool for reducing carbon emissions created by the CDP , the United Nations Global Compact, World Resources Institute, and the World Wide Fund for Nature.

Elsewhere, Carbon Labels, and Other Requirements

A similar legislation is being debated in the European Union, and while Germany, France, Britain, and Australia have laws requiring due diligence relating to human rights and slavery, there is no general legislation in any country governing the greater social and environmental actions of the fashion industry and mandating change.

The French Parliament approved in July 2021 an expansive climate bill to introduce mandatory "carbon labels" for goods and services, including clothing and textiles, to inform consumers about the environmental impact of their purchasing decisions. A decade-old Extended Producer Responsibility Law requires businesses to provide or manage the recycling of their clothing, textiles, and footwear products at the end of their lives. France bans brands from destroying leftover stock under an "anti-waste" law. In 2018, the French Agency for Environment and Energy Management (ADEME) instituted a labeling system that grades garments from A to E, with A being the most sustainable and E the least.

The 2021 Climate Law sets requirements for environmental and social labeling for certain goods and services sold on the French market. Such a labeling will be implemented in a pilot phase for a period of up to five years and then will become mandatory. The environmental impact taken into account labeling that includes greenhouse gas emissions and impact on biodiversity and/or water over the entire lifecycle of the product or service. The list of goods and services subject to environmental labeling will be detailed in an upcoming implementation decree for clothing items, food products, furniture, hotel services, and electronic products.

Enforcing Ecocide

The French Lower House of Parliament approved in April 2021 the creation of an "ecocide" offence as part of a battery of measures aimed at protecting the environment and tackling climate change. It will, once it becomes law, apply to "the most serious cases of environmental damage at national level," said Environment Minister Barbara Pompili. Transgressors will be liable to up to 10 years in prison and a fine of 4.5 million euros ($5.4 million).

Pompili stressed that the draft bill is aimed at national events, such as the pollution of a French river. "When we think of the attacks on the Amazon rainforest, that is not something we can tackle within our own laws," she said. "The aim is to strengthen the sanctions available to deal with 'serious and durable' cases of intentional pollution of water, air, or soil," she indicated.

France banned plastic packaging for nearly all fruit and vegetables starting in 2022 in a bid to reduce plastic waste.

CHAPTER 4-16

Aquafil

Repurposing Used Nylon With Econyl®

In 2011, Aquafil developed a regeneration system to produce nylon from waste instead of oil, creating fabrics for products ranging from distinctive back packs and totes to designer runway garments. Research and innovation led Aquafil to launch the ECONYL® Regeneration System project, a proprietary industrial system that turns disused nylon into a secondary raw material which is processed into yarn for consumer and industrial use.

Reprocessed ECONYL has been adapted by Gucci for its designer apparel and accessory collections. Gucci Off The Grid selections are created from recycled, organic, bio-based, and sustainably sourced materials, including ECONYL, to assortments for footwear, luggage, accessories, and ready-to-wear. Product packaging to the consumer includes a card with information about the products and the story behind the Gucci Off The Grid sustainability project.

Stella McCartney, a long-time proponent of sustainability for her firm's products, is moving away from using virgin nylon, switching all of her current nylon to ECONYL regenerated nylon. The firm's Falabella GO bags that are made with ECONYL yarn have linings of a silky-like version of the yarn. ECONYL is also used outerwear designs.

Renewing Old Nylon Carpeting

Each year in the United States, four billion pounds of carpet are discarded in landfills or are incinerated. Aquafil USA Inc. recognized the

Figure 4-16.1 Aquafil Building in Phoenix

Photo courtesy: Aquafil USA Inc.

opportunity to give these fibers new life, and currently operates carpet recycling plants that disassembles used carpets to recycle carpet waste for reuse.

Aquafil started by using preconsumer waste and then added postconsumer waste as well as spent carpets and used fishing nets. In the beginning, Aquafil was sheering old carpets to recover only a small fraction of useable material. It then changed to shredding them, via a process that involves water and friction, to prepare the components for reuse. Through their technology, the waste is split into their three main components: polypropylene, calcium carbonate, and nylon 6. Each component enters a different stream: polypropylene goes into the injection molding industry; calcium carbonate is directed to road construction or concrete stream; and nylon 6 feeds the ECONYL regeneration process.

The first U.S. carpet recycling facility in Phoenix, Arizona (Figure 4-16.1), went into operation in 2018, and the second in Woodland,

California, in 2019. Each facility will annually recover 36 million pounds of old carpets to retrieve their three main components. The California Carpet Stewardship Program develops uses for used carpet, backed by incentives based on the amounts of material the suppliers put into the recovery system.

SECTION 5

Resources & Services

Introduction

Retailers Face More Investor Scrutiny

Investors may push major retailers for more details on their long-term climate goals. Pressure is likely to be in the form of increased shareholder resolutions, as federal agencies place a renewed emphasis on environmental matters.

Even at companies that have already made significant environmental commitments, observers believe that investors will want near-term evidence of process in areas such as decarbonizing supply chains and transitioning away from natural gas and other fossil fuels.

"Sustainable Fashion." What Does It Actually Mean?

Econyl®, in its Newsletter of July 6, 2021, observed that "sustainable" has recently become something of a buzzword in fashion. Together with words like "eco-friendly," "conscious," and "green," the language used to describe fashion's sustainability credentials often falls short of adequately explaining what it is about a certain brand or product that makes it a better choice. As a result, consumers face some confusion when evaluating data to make informed purchases.

For shoppers, this means learning exactly what to look for in the brands they buy from. Seeking out environmental, social, and cultural criteria can help to accurately assess impact of clothing, going beyond taking the word "sustainable" at the face value. New perspectives on sustainability in the fashion industry appear on services that can be accessed on Instagram:

- The OR Foundation (@theorispresent) consistently raises awareness about the damaging aftereffects of overproduction.
- Anna Sacks (@thetrashwalker) and Lizzie Carr (@lizziecarr) address the important issue of waste in the industry and beyond.
- Sites such as @thatcurlytop and @rosannafalconer provide inspiration for colorful, environmentally conscious outfits.

CHAPTER 5-1

Services

CLEANTECH'S 2020 50 To Watch

The 2020 50 to Watch is the second annual list of the top international early-stage private companies delivering innovative solutions to combat the climate crisis published by Cleantech Group. The entrepreneurs in the list are creating new technologies and business models that could solve the plastics crisis, regenerate soils, seed new forests, create climate-positive buildings, and end desertification.

Sustainable Apparel Coalition

The Sustainable Apparel Coalition (SAC) is an industrywide group of more than 250 leading apparel, footwear and textile brands, retailers, suppliers, service providers, trade associations, nonprofits, NGOs, and academic institutions. Its objective is to promote social justice throughout the global value chain and reduce the environmental impacts of products. Through multi-stakeholder engagement, the SAC seeks to lead the industry toward a shared vision of sustainability built upon a common approach for measuring and evaluating apparel, footwear, and textile sustainability performance that emphasizes priorities for action and opportunities for technological innovation. The Higg Index suite of tools that was developed in 2011 was spun off in May 2019 as a technology platform for the Higg Co.

Social & Labor Convergence Program

The Social & Labor Convergence Program (SLCP) is a multi-stakeholder initiative of over 200 signatories including leading brands, manufacturers, standard holders, and other concerned professionals. The SLCP signatories developed a Converged Assessment Framework (CAF) to eliminate duplicative and repetitive proprietary social and labor audits with a single verified assessment that can be used by all stakeholders.

The Good Trade

"35 Ethical & Sustainable Clothing Brands Betting Against Fast Fashion"

The company reports on companies that approach fashion in an ethical and transparent way that considers both people and the planet. It also publishes guides to responsibly made shoes and fair trade jewelry, apparel sources in the United Kingdom, and affordable places to shop secondhand clothing.

Glamour

"27 Sustainable Fashion Brands You Can Shop Confidently"

This publication believes the fashion industry's greenwashing problem is real—so, it recommends brands actually doing the work.

The Honest Consumer

A creative advocate for fair fashion, social impact, mental health awareness, and conscious living.

Elle

"55 Sustainable Clothing Brands That Are Anything But Boring"

Elle identifies green and sustainable clothing, shoe, and underwear brands. To put them up for resale, *Elle* provides a guide to resale sites.

Eluxe

The Best Sustainable Fashion Stores Online

Eluxe promotes sustainable fashion stores online to make more ethical purchases from anywhere.

Restitchstance

Where to Shop Eco & Ethical Fashion

Restitchstance is a sustainable and ethical lifestyle blog.

The Best Vegan Clothing Brands: 2021

There are 50 ethical and sustainable clothing brands.

Good On You

The 41 Most Ethical and Sustainable Clothing Brands from the United States and Canada

Also publishes guides to Europe, the United Kingdom, Germany, France, the Netherlands, Australia, and New Zealand.

Harper's Bazaar

Their Favorite Sustainable Brands

"Look good with a clear conscience."

Good Housekeeping Institute

"20 Best Sustainable Fashion Brands You Can Actually Trust"

The Good Housekeeping Institute's Lab Textile's top brands addresses environmental and social concerns.

U.S. Cotton Trust Protocol

The U.S. Cotton Trust Protocol is a new system for responsibly grown cotton that will provide annual data for six areas of sustainability in line with the UN Sustainability Goals. This year-over-year data, available for the first time, will allow brands and retailers to better measure progress toward meeting sustainability commitments.

TÜV SÜD

TÜV SÜD, the technical testing organization based in Munich, Germany, launched a vegan product certification program for the producers of apparel, footwear, and home textiles. It will certify brands and permit them to portray their animal welfare credentials.

The certification ensures that the final textile product does not contain animal-driven materials through a series of material composition tests. They also monitor the production process and conduct regular audit tests.

Sources: YarnsandFibers News Bureau 12–16 2020, used with permission; TÜV SÜD

Top 10 Sustainable Fashion Schools

High fashion and street brands a like value designers and market strategists with expertise in sustainability. These most often recognized 10 fashion schools offer degrees, certificates, or courses on sustainable fashion.

1. Parsons, The New School for Design, New York
Parsons course on Sustainable Systems is mandatory for all incoming freshmen.

Program: Option to specialize in sustainability is open to all majors.

Special projects: Partnership with Loomstate to create jeans close to zero waste.

2. Fashion Institute of Technology (FIT), New York
FIT was one of the nation's first higher education institutions to work with the government to reduce carbon emission.

Program: Minor in Ethics and Sustainability, an interdisciplinary study that equips students to apply sustainability in all areas: materials, economics, aesthetics, theories, and social responsibility. A noncredit certificate in Sustainable Design Entrepreneur, a series of four-week classes, equips participants to learn about and practice sustainable business ideas.

Special projects: Annual Sustainable Business and Design Conference; Sustainability Awareness Week with talks and exhibitions on sustainable fashion.

3. California College of the Arts, San Francisco

California College of the Arts has the longest-running sustainable fashion design program in the country. Sustainability is included in the curricula in all levels of degrees, from bachelor's to master's degrees.

Program: BA in Fashion Design and MBA in Design Strategy are about fashion and design in general, but sustainability is deeply embedded into the curricula. MBA in Design Strategy focuses on teaching students to create design strategies for "total value creation" or "something much more than mere profitability."

4. Pratt Institute, New York

Pratt Institute integrates sustainability across multiple studies. The Center for Sustainable Design Strategies serves as research and resource center for any faculty or students interested in sustainable design.

Program: Minor in Sustainability Studies, an interdisciplinary study that looks at sustainability with environmental, economic, and social lens; Certificate in Design Entrepreneurship.

Special project: The Pratt Design Incubator for Sustainable Innovation, founded in 2002, has four sectors: clean energy, fashion, design, and design consulting. The incubator hosts 12 businesses, and operates the Pratt Pop-up shop in Brooklyn, New York.

5. Otis College of Art and Design, Los Angeles

Otis offers students a wide network of industry leaders specializing in sustainable fashion and design, throughout different departments, from Fashion Design to Toy Design.

Program: BA in Fashion Design. A minor in sustainability is available for all majors.

Special project: The Fashion Design Department founded the Otis Sustainability Alliance, a group of creative leaders including fashion, design, art, and higher education.

6. Academy of Art University, San Francisco

San Francisco's Academy of Art University is the largest accredited private art and design school in the country. It has implemented environmental and sustainable design options into the curriculum in the past 25 years. It provides both in-class and online courses centered on sustainability.

7. Fashion Institute of Design & Merchandising, Los Angeles

As it is located in California, the U.S. denim capital, students majoring in the business of denim learn about sustainable methods for developing denim products. It includes developing and promoting more sustainable practices, from growing cotton to engineering yarn and fabrics.

Special project: Exhibitions featuring green textiles and raw materials; partnership with Guess to mentor students on sustainable design.

8. Central Saint Martins College of Art and Design, London

Central Saint Martins provides instruction in innovation in sustainable fashion, citing that it is not only ethical, it is the future of fashion.

Program: MA in Material Futures is a multidisciplinary study that focuses on developing smart, eco-friendly textile technologies to respond to emerging environmental awareness.

Special project: Textile Futures Research Community is a research group that studies ways to make textiles and materials more sustainable through technological and innovative means.

9. London College of Fashion, London

London College of Fashion offers its students in-depth knowledge and expertise in sustainability, across different departments.

Program: MA in Fashion Futures focuses on fashion practices and theories.

Special project: The Centre for Sustainable Fashion (CSF) established the United Kingdom's first sustainable fashion lab, launching Shared Talent India, which encourages designers to exchange expertise with other experts across the supply chain. They sponsor the annual Fashioning the Future Awards, for innovative sustainable designs from students and graduates worldwide.

10. AMD Academy Fashion & Design: Hamburg, Düsseldorf, Munich, Berlin, and Wiesbaden, Germany

Established in 1989, AMD Academy Fashion & Design offers a curriculum focused in sustainability.

Program: MA in Sustainability in Fashion and Creative Industries, an international program offered in English, covers such areas as sustainable design strategies, sustainable production, and sustainable business.

Source: The University Network

France and Europe Unveil Their Plan for Sustainable Fashion

The strategic committee of the Fashion and Luxury sector (CSF) has submitted to the French government a study on "Prospects for Relocation and Support for Sustainable Fashion."

Sustainable fashion, using less-polluting natural resources, serves to make French designers and manufacturers stand out. Several startups have positioned themselves in this niche but it remains up to the State to boost this dynamic. "The fashion sector has a strong environmental impact. Its model must evolve," notes the Minister of Ecological Transition, Barbara Pompili. "The Government is alongside the players to support them in this transformation: exemplary public order, support for investments, and implementation of environmental labeling."

While the French government evaluates proposals from the fashion and luxury sector, other European countries are moving ahead. Brussels is currently working on a roadmap to make the Belgian textile sector more sustainable. "This strategy will facilitate the European Union's transition to a circular, climate neutral economy, in which products are designed to be more sustainable, reusable, repairable and energy efficient," explains the Commission.

The European Green Deal is the action plan for the circular economy and the industrial sovereignty strategy. The textile industry, which employs 1.5 million people in Europe, is taking the collective path of sustainability toward recovery.

CHAPTER 5-2

Books and References

Books

Unraveled: The Life and Death of a Garment, By Maxine Bédat. Penguin Random House, 2021.

A chronicle by the founder of the New Standards Institute of the birth—and death—of a pair of jeans, which exposes the fractures in our global supply chains, and our relationships to each other, ourselves, and the planet.

Making Money Moral: How A New Wave of Visionaries Is Linking Purpose and Profit
Judith Rodin and Saadia Madsbjerg, Wharton School Press, 2021.
Rodin, a former president of the University of Pennsylvania, was president of The Rockefeller Foundation. Madsbjerg is a global leader in the field of sustainable and impact investing and is a former managing director of The Rockefeller Foundation.

The authors explore a rapidly growing movement of bold innovators unlocking private-sector investments to solve global problems, attempting to tackle environmental challenges, social issues, poverty, and inequality, among others, and reimagining capitalism in the process. They point out that making money moral happens when the world of financial markets meet the world of impact. Then capitalism benefits stakeholders in addition to shareholders, including consumers and employees, suppliers, and the environment.

Sustainable and impact investing has grown from a small niche market to one that now deals in the trillions. The challenge, say the authors, is also to ensure that it's growth with integrity, with robust tools and reliable data that drive confidence in the impact that's coming from these investments, not just in the financial returns.

MEND!: A Refashioning Manual and Manifesto,
Kate Sekules, Penguin, 2020.

Apparel is among the most polluting and exploitative of all industries. It creates 93.7 million pounds of waste each year. Visible mending (VM) is more than darning a hole. Changing the way we think about clothes is a revolutionary act. It's a protest movement and an art form and a fashion statement. Buying less and better, and vintage curation is within everyone's reach. Mending is the missing link, the key to it all, especially visible mending, because of its sheer usefulness, and high style quotient. This is a true style revolution.

A Practical Guide to Sustainable Fashion Basics Fashion Design, 2nd Edition,
Alison Gwilt, Bloomsbury Visual Arts, 2020.

With examples from designers such as Vivienne Westwood, Stella McCartney, Edun, and People Tree, *A Practical Guide to Sustainable Fashion* is an overview of current models of fashion design and production. Gwilt introduces the key issues associated with the production, use, and disposal of fashion clothing, and gives step-by-step guidance on how to identify and evaluate the potential impacts of a garment during the design process.

There is in-depth coverage of design thinking, materials manufacture, practical techniques for creating "faster" recyclable fashion, and new ways forward for fashion, such as including the circular economy and the UN's sustainable development goals.

Fibershed, Growing a Movement of Farmers, Fashion Activists, and Makers for a New Textile Economy
Rebecca Burgess and Courtney White, Chelsea Green Publishing, 2019.

Fibershed describes how natural plant dyes and fibers such as wool, cotton, hemp, and flax can be grown and processed as part of a scalable, restorative agricultural system. It shows how milling and other technical systems need to make regional textile production possible. *Fibershed* is a resource for fiber farmers, ranchers, contract grazers, weavers, knitters, slow-fashion entrepreneurs, soil activists, and conscious consumers who want to join or create their own fibershed.

Sustainable Business: A One Planet Approach,
Edited by Jean-Paul Jeanrenaud, Sally Jeanrenaud and Jonathan Gosling, Wiley, 2017.

A textbook for contemporary business, this book recognizes the realities of global sustainability challenges, covering the knowledge, frameworks, and techniques that will underpin emerging solutions to those challenges. It was published in association with WWF, The World Wide Fund for Nature. This book offers a wealth of insight and interpretation into new ways of doing business that have a positive impact on people, planet, and prosperity.

How to Avoid a Climate Disaster: The Solutions We Have and the Breakthroughs We Need,
Bill Gates, Alfred A. Knopf, 2021.

Microsoft co-founder turned philanthropist, Bill Gates spent a decade investigating the causes and effects of climate change. His book focuses on what must be done in order to stop what he believes is Planet Earth's slide to certain environmental disaster.

Drawing on his understanding of innovation and what it takes to get new ideas into the market, Gates's goal is to get from the 51 billion tons of greenhouse gasses added to the atmosphere annually down to zero. This includes transportation's "zero-carbon future," meaning using "electricity to run all the vehicles we can, and getting cheap alternative fuels for the rest." (Such alternatives include electrofuels, under development.)

He has invested in companies trying to slow down the rate of global warming, and launched Breakthrough Energy, an effort to commercialize clean energy and other climate-related technologies.

References

CFDA Sustainability Initiatives

The Council of Fashion Designers of America (CFDA) provides open access resources and information specific to fashion design business sustainable strategies. These resources are intended for everyone: for the CFDA members, educators, students, professionals, designers, and anyone interested in learning more about sustainability and sourcing relevant contacts. Through its Sustainability Initiative program, the CFDA offers references, relevant information and data, and case studies.

- **Sustainability A-Z Resource Directory**
- **CFDA Guide to Sustainable Strategies**
- **Sustainable Strategies Toolkit**
- **CFDA A-Z Materials Index**
- **KPI Design Kit: A Sustainable Strategies Playbook for Measurable Change**

Climate Justice Playbook for Business

B Lab launched a new *Climate Justice Playbook for Business* to provide companies with a resource to actively incorporate racial justice and equity considerations into climate projects and corporate priorities. Created by the Climate Collaborative, a global collaboration of private sector and climate leaders, the partnership included: B Lab, the COP26 Climate Champions Team, Provoc, and the Skoll Centre for Social Entrepreneurship at the University of Oxford.

The Playbook stresses that a fundamental mindset shift is essential. It emphasizes that the global business community must make a fundamental mindshift on climate action—from extractive and exploitative approaches that perpetuate a cycle of harm and injustice to equitable and regenerative ones. In its basic description, the message points out that Climate Justice recognizes that those who are least responsible for climate change are more likely to suffer its gravest consequences, a disproportionately negative impact on the historically marginalized and underserved, primarily people of color and low-income communities around the world.

The Sustainable Fashion Glossary

Condé Nast launched *The Sustainable Fashion Glossary*, a global digital resource on sustainable fashion and the fashion industry's role in the climate emergency. It is designed to strengthen and develop sustainability literacy by providing guidance on key sustainability terms and emerging topics.

Produced by the CSF at London College of Fashion, University of the Arts London (UAL), with input from *Vogue* editors, it was reviewed by a network of academics and sustainability researchers. The text is divided into four key themes: climate emergency; environmental impacts of fashion; social, cultural and economic impacts of fashion, and key elements of fashion and sustainability. New definitions reflect the evolving debates about climate emergency, fashion, and societal change.

CHAPTER 5-3

Reports

The Best Sustainable Fashion Brands

For consumers looking for something new, sustainable fashion brands that can reduce each individual's carbon footprint, while ensuring that the people making jeans, dresses, and bags are treated fairly, now have expanded choices.

One industry observer suggests to prioritize both environmental and social responsibility throughout the life span of a garment, from raw materials all the way to how long a piece of clothing will last in your closet. Another expert on sustainable fashion sourcing says some brands are going as far as disclosing the wage of the lowest paid worker in their supply chain.

For a sustainability-minded consumer, instead of trying to find the perfect company that's accounting for everything, it's easiest to think about what is most important—better labor practices, less waste, or renewable raw materials—and focus individual purchasing power on a brand with similar aims.

There are organizations that vet the so-called sustainable brands and online resources such as Good On You and The Fashion Transparency Index. Consumers can avoid greenwashing (brands marketing themselves as environmentally conscious without backing up their claims) by looking for third-party certifications such as bluesign, GOTS (Global Organic Textile Standard) certified organic, OEKO-TEX, fair trade, and B-Corp.

Here are some manufactures to consider, based on aspects of most concern.

Responsibly Sourced Raw Materials

Knickey. This NYC-based direct-to-consumer brand uses GOTS-certified organic cotton for both environmental and reproductive health reasons.

Christy Dawn. Best known for their flowery floral dresses that are hand-made from upcycled materials in Los Angeles

Babaà. Spanish brand Babaà sources the wool for its chunky sweaters from northern Spain. Its wool is spun and dyed by Spanish artisans, as is most of their cotton, which comes from organic farmers in Andalucia. The brand's yarns are never mixed with acrylics or any other synthetic fibers.

M.Patmos. Brooklyn designer M.Patmos uses organic materials and innovates with dead-stock fabric to eliminate waste.

Nicholas K. This brother-sister design duo uses undyed natural fibers and vegetable dyes from roots, leaves, bark, and berries.

Environmentally Responsible Production

Marimekko. All of the fabrics from this Finnish company with a 70-year history of colorful and bold patterns are screen printed by hand in Helsinki in a facility that operates on biogas and renewable electricity.

Mate the Label. In addition to using organic cotton, Mate the Label reduces its carbon footprint by keeping its supply chain local; everything is cut, sewn, and shipped from Los Angeles.

Reducing Waste

Another Tomorrow. Another Tomorrow has partnered with the company EVRYTHNG to assign a digital ID to every item of clothing in their collection so consumers can scan their garment's QR code and see its entire journey from raw materials to fabric mill to final quality control.

Mara Hoffman. The brand's website has detailed instructions for how to get the most out of their garment; they will take back a dress or bathing suit that is no longer wanted.

Fair Labor Practices

Brother Vellies. Based in NYC, Brother Vellies uses renewable and recycled materials to create some of the industries most coveted boots and shoes, emphasizing products from Black entrepreneurs.

Fashion & Interiors Brands Empowering Women Around the World. For any brand, being truly sustainable means thinking beyond the environmental impact of each item it creates. Rather, it's about actively seeking out problems to solve, and developing products that turn a business into a force for good in the world.

Alongside using low-impact materials and eco-friendly packaging, going one step further means prioritizing the people on the ground. Educating women and girls, for example, is one of the most important things that we can do to protect against the climate crisis. Mothers, daughters, sisters, and grandmothers form the backbone of whole families and communities. Investing in their empowerment sets in motion a circle of sustainable development that will last through generations.

From funding the projects of female entrepreneurs to educating about sexual health, or empowering artisans to earn financial independence, these are some of the brands put female empowerment firmly at the center of their business models.

Fashion as a Force for Good

Progetto Quid: Progetto Quid is the sister brand of Verona-based social enterprise Quid. Women from vulnerable backgrounds often find themselves out of work. Quid embraces the design, production, and distribution of fashion collections.

RubyMoon: The all-women team behind RubyMoon has two objectives: helping to clean up our oceans and raising the voices of female entrepreneurs around the world. The brand's Gym To Swim clothing is designed using ECONYL®, regenerated nylon made from plastic waste.

Sirohi: Sirohi's furniture is woven by women in India through the Skilled Samaritan Foundation. Since 2012, Sirohi has grown its workforce from one single weaver into a 200 artisans around northern India. It provides access to design support through technology and partnerships with international designers. Its women workers create traditional designs from recycled yarns made with textile and industrial waste from local factories.

Indego Africa: Each beautiful basket has been woven by women across Rwanda and Ghana, using local indigenous fibers such as sweetgrass, banana and palm leaves, and bolga straw. Indego has begun working with women refugees in the Mahama Refugee Camp in Rwanda.

Sarawagi Rugs: The Nepalese hand-knotted rug company teaches female survivors of violence and abuse the traditional art of weaving in the country's capital, Kathmandu. Women weavers have also created rugs made from ECONYL®.

Labels to Know When Buying Sustainable Fashion

Sustainability is Coming to the Fashion Industry, Bringing With It a Plethora of Labels

With so many labels and so many standards, it can be hard for consumers to know what to look for—and why. What do they say about a manufacturer on the earth and on their employees?

This list provided by Commonshare has 27 sustainability labels that consumers should look for when buying sustainable fashion.

1. **Better Cotton Initiative** A global not-for-profit organization and the largest cotton sustainability program in the world.
2. **BLUESIGN®** Represents the vision and mindset of responsible and sustainable manufacturing of textile consumer products.
3. **Content Claim Standard (CCS)** A chain of custody standard that provides companies with a tool to verify that one or more specific input materials are in a final product.

4. **Cotton Made in Africa** An initiative of the Aid by Trade Foundation that serves as a leading standard for sustainably produced cotton

5. **COTTON USA™** An association of family cotton growers who own their own land and want to protect their fields for future generations.

6. **Cradle to Cradle Products Innovation Institute** A global nonprofit dedicated to transforming the safety, health, and sustainability of products through the Cradle to Cradle Certified Product Standard.

7. **DETOX TO ZERO by OEKO-TEX®** A verification system for the textile and leather industry that aims to implement the criteria of the Greenpeace DETOX Campaign within production facilities.

8. **ECO PASSPORT by OEKO-TEX®** An independent certification system for chemicals, colorants, and auxiliaries used in the textile and leather industry.

9. **Fair Trade** The Fair Trade Certified™ seal represents thousands of Fair Trade Certified™ products, improving millions of lives, protecting land and waterways in more than 45 countries.

10. **Fair Wear Foundation** Based on the belief in a world where the garment industry supports workers in realizing their rights to safe, dignified, properly paid employment.

11. **Global Recycle Standard Originally** developed by Control Union Certifications in 2008, ownership was passed to the Textile Exchange on January 1, 2011.

12. **Global Organic Textile Standard (GOTS)** Developed by leading standard setters defines requirement, and ensures the organic status of textiles that would be recognized worldwide.

13. **LEATHER STANDARD by OEKO-TEX®** An internationally standardized testing and certification system for leather and leather goods at all production levels, including accessory materials.

14. **Leather Working Group (LWG)** An international, not-for-profit membership organization that is responsible for the world's largest leather sustainability program.

15. **LENZING™ ECOVERO™** Viscose fibers are derived from certified and controlled sources of sustainable wood and pulp.

16. **MADE IN GREEN by OEKO-TEX®** A traceable product label for all kinds of textiles, including garments and home textiles, and leather products, as well as nontextile and nonleather accessories.

17. **Naturtextil IVN certified BEST** Defines the highest level of textile sustainability by applying the maximum currently achievable parameters to production and product.

18. **Organic Content Standard (OCS)** An international, voluntary standard that sets requirements for the third-party certification of certified organic input and chain of custody.

19. **Organic Content Standard Blended Applies** to any nonfood product containing 5 to 10 percent organic material.

20. **PETA-Approved Vegan** Over 10,000 companies are using the PETA-Approved Vegan logo to highlight clothing, accessories, furniture, and home décor items made of vegan alternatives to animal-derived materials such as leather, fur, silk, feathers, or bone.

21. **RCS (Recycled Claim Standard)** A chain of custody standard to track recycled raw materials through the supply chain.

22. **Responsible Down Standard** Ensures that down and feathers come from animals that have not been subjected to any unnecessary harm.

23. **Responsible Mohair Standard (RMS)** A voluntary standard that addresses the welfare of goats and the land they graze on.

24. **Responsible Wool Standard (RWS)** For farmers to demonstrate their best practices to the public, and a means for brands and consumers to have the certainty that the wool products they buy and sell are in line with their values.

25. **STANDARD 100 by OEKO-TEX®** Every component of the article, every thread, button, and other accessory have been tested for harmful substances and found to be harmless to human health.

26. **STeP by OEKO-TEX®** Sustainable Textile & Leather Production.

27. **The Higg Index** A suite of tools that enables brands, retailers, and facilities of all sizes—at every stage in their sustainability journey—to measure social and environmental sustainability performance.

The Sustainability Edit

The EDITED **Sustainability Industry Report** annual report breaks down sustainability in fashion and how retailers are evolving their assortments amid the influx of post-pandemic arrivals. With a global customer reach across 40 countries, London-based retail intelligence firm EDITED is used by over 200 leading brands and retailers on six continents. While many retailers have bolstered their sustainability goals to hit targets by 2030 and onward, greater urgency is required. EDITED Retail Intelligence Platform uses real-time global data from 40+ markets tracking the number of styles launched, discounted, and sold out each day, giving visibility of what products are working well, to make informed decisions and adjust assortments.

Contact support@edited.com

In the Round, Denim

The global denim industry is planning its circular future. Industry players have introduced biodegradable stretch jeans, Cradle to Cradle certified platinum denim fabrics, jeans made entirely of recycled content, and jeans that can be traced back to the cotton farm. The Ellen MacArthur Foundation supports circularity guidelines with its Jeans Redesign initiative, and has signed up 60 brands to produce circular jeans this fall.

In the Round, a new report from Rivet, sponsored by eight firms, shares insights from leading denim manufacturers on how they continue to initiate change throughout the industry through investments in new circular technologies.

The downloadable report includes: eight sustainable and stylish brands to watch; a by-the-numbers breakdown of sustainable fashion; case studies from "circular catalysts" within the industry including HNST, Wrangler, Reformation, and others.

The Future of Fashion Resale

The Business of Fashion's *The Future of Fashion Resale* is a definitive guide to fashion resale that covers the evolution of the market, its growth and upside, consumer behaviors, and recommendations for crafting a data-driven resale strategy. Published by BoF Insights Lab, it provides business leaders with proprietary and data-driven research to navigate the fast-changing global fashion industry. The report estimates that the global secondhand fashion market is currently worth $130 billion. Secondhand fashion existed primarily in thrift and vintage stores, but the advent of online resale platforms has led to a steep change in how used items can be bought and sold.

The Business of Fashion Sustainability Index

Business of Fashion's report, "The Business of Fashion Sustainability Index," benchmarks 15 of the industry's biggest companies against ambitious environmental and social goals. The report is downloadable.

The 15 companies assessed in the Index represent the largest publicly listed companies as measured by annual revenue across three verticals: in luxury, in high street, and in sportswear. Not included are companies that operate primarily as retailers, such as department stores or e-commerce platforms. The focus is on companies that own brands with a direct link to apparel and footwear manufacturing. Companies must demonstrate that they are implementing policies and practices across all brands and subsidiaries to meet the criteria in the Index.

The aim is to track progress in transforming the fashion industry ahead of that 2030 milestone.

FDRA Issues Sustainable Guidelines

The Footwear Distributors and Retailers of America (FDRA) issued a Shoe Sustainability Guide focusing on environmentally preferred materials (EPMs) to provide industry leaders with benchmarks and goals to reduce environmental impacts.

SECTION 6

Sustainability: Technology, Inventions, and Resale

Introduction

Environmental impact has become the priority for the fashion industry. Starting at the beginning with the raw materials, to the creations of textiles, through manufacturing and retail presentation, it is a critical international concern. Resale has become a latter-day merchandising phenomenon.

Seeing Green

What's old is new again. Recrafting and repurposing of apparel, accessories, shoes, and household items are the part of burgeoning trend extending from storefront resale boutiques to multimillion dollar industrial-size operations. Items that have assumed new identities—a bag crafted from scrap leather or bottle tops; a dress designed using stock fabric; backpack appropriated from recovered jacket linings—represent the past for a sustainable present and future.

For decades, Americans have had an insatiable appetite for new clothing, spurred on by the fast-fashion industry, which cranks out inexpensive, garments that helped global clothing production double from 50 billion items a year in 2000 to more than 100 billion today. (There are only 7.8 billion humans on the planet.) The environmental toll of this low-price category is steep; they become disposable.

Apparel producers consume 108 million tons of nonrenewable resources every year and emit 1.2 billion tons of greenhouse gases, more than all international flights and maritime shipping trips combined. Meanwhile, a truckload of clothes is either sent to the landfill or incinerated every second.

Numerous startups are innovatively transforming the way clothing is bought and sold, rented or traded. We have space here to mention only a few. Some of these companies, such as CaaStle, are also creating clothing rental services that satisfy people's desire to be in style without having to shop. Others, like thredUp and Trove, are building significant resale marketplaces that extend the life of close to a million pieces of everyday clothes. These variations on a resale theme are challenging the preconception—among shoppers of all ages and genders—that newer is better.

CaaStle

CaaStle is logistics platform integrates with companies' inventory systems and manages the entire rental process on their behalf, from warehousing and cleaning garments to gathering feedback from customers about how an item fits.

In the past year, it partnered with American Eagle to power the first rental service aimed at Gen Z, Scotch & Soda to launch the first men's rental service, Bloomingdale's for the first rental service from a department store, and Banana Republic. (CaaStle also launched Haverdash, its own multibrand rental service for women and the most affordable one on the market, at $59 a month.) CaaStle-powered pop-ups are slated for select Express stores.

thredUp

"People in their twenties and thirties were born into [the sharing economy]," says James Reinhart, thredUp's founder and CEO. "For people in their forties and older, this consumption model requires training."

To reach them, the company set up special secondhand sections in nearly three dozen JCPenneys and worked with Macy's to create secondhand sections in 40 of its department stores. Madewell has thredUp-sourced "archive collections" at several of its stores. thredUp also partnered with companies such as Reformation and Amour Vert to enable fans of those brands to send thredUp old clothes (from any label) in exchange for shopping credit at their stores.

Trove

Trove CEO Andy Ruben says that their company is a resale marketplace that allows clothing labels to create a new revenue stream, get new customers, and capture their fair share of the secondary market. Within six months of Worn Wear's 2017 launch, Patagonia had generated $1 million in sales from the site, which has been profitable ever since.

Trove can purchase, process, price, and photograph secondhand goods before putting them up for sale on each brand's dedicated resale website. Trove even takes care of returns and customer service. It has also attracted new customers, including REI and Eileen Fisher, which has brought in more than $4 million in revenue from its profitable ReNew resale site. Trove has added Arc'teryx and Taylor Stitch to its portfolio, and recently launched a secondhand marketplace for Nordstrom. By having their own resale sites, companies demonstrate their commitment to getting more out of the clothes they've already made.

CHAPTER 6-1

Technology and Inventions

Note: Reports included as of January, 2022

Mylo: A Sustainable Upgrade To Leather

Mylo™ is a leather look-alike created by Bolt Threads, based in Emeryville, California. It has devised a system to reproduce what happens under the forest floor in a controlled indoor environment to Mylo is derived from mycelium, the complex latticework of strong underground fibers, to produce a soft, supple fabric is less harmful to the environment than traditional leather with, the company contends, the look and feel of natural leather.

Figure 6-1.1 Lululemon's prototype Yoga Mat Bag and Barrel Duffel Bag made with Mylo material

Photo courtesy: Bolt Threads

Mycelial cells are combined with sawdust and organic material in an environment with controlled humidity, temperature, and other variables. Sheets of mycelium that become the Mylo material will be used to make footwear, handbags (Figure 6-1.1), wallets, phone cases, and other products for such brands as Adidas, Lululemon, Stella McCartney, and others.

Mylo is an alternative to raising livestock, a resource-intense process of land and water use taking years to raise cattle. The mycelium grown for Mylo can be produced in days, is renewable, and grown by expert mushroom farmers and scientists in indoor vertical facilities in Europe and the United States.

FRAME's (Bio) Degradable Denim Collections

Figure 6-1.2 Frame commissioned Isabel + Helen, a London-based creative company, to build a window for its Madison Avenue, New York store, shown here, as well as SoHo and Dallas stores, and Harrods in London. The sculptures "reflect the cyclical and nearly limitless journey of revolutionary denim," according to the artist

Photo courtesy: Frame

Frame (Figure 6-1.2), a premium denim brand based in Los Angeles, created (Bio) Degradable jeans in collaboration with Candiani Denim, Milan, made from 100 percent biodegradable cotton.

The three (Bio) Degradable denim collections feature fabrics for both menswear and womenswear: Rigid 727, Comfort Stretch 785, and Super Stretch 778 denim, which degrade according to stretch content. While the rigid fabric is made entirely of cotton and is completely biodegradable, the comfort stretch and super stretch fabrics use Roica V550, a yarn that degrades more quickly than normal yarn and leaves no toxic harmful substances.

Candiani's micro plastics-free dyeing method is used so that the jeans are fully biodegradable. Each garment has a QR code for traceability that includes information about the garment's impact and manufacturing.

Ralph Lauren Foundation's Grant to USRCF

The Ralph Lauren Corporate Foundation has made a $5-million-dollar grant to the Soil Health Institute to launch the U.S. Regenerative Cotton Fund (USRCF), a science-based initiative to support long-term, sustainable cotton production in the United States, with the goal of eliminating one million metric tons of carbon dioxide equivalent (CO_2e) from the atmosphere by 2026. Currently, cotton makes up more than 80 percent of Ralph Lauren Corporation's total material use. As part of the company's Global Citizenship & Sustainability goals, it has committed that by 2025, 100 percent of key materials, including cotton, will be sustainably sourced.

The USRCF will work to unite the interests of farmers, partners, and financial supporters around soil health as the foundation for regenerative agriculture. Participating partners include Cotton Incorporated, National Cotton Council, and Field to Market. The USRCF will initially operate in four states—Arkansas, Texas, Mississippi, and Georgia—and plan to expand into Alabama, North Carolina, Missouri, California, and Oklahoma as these nine states represent 85 percent of U.S. cotton production.

Reformation's Sustainable Stretch

Reformation's first activewear collection, crafted with EcoMove and EcoStretch, two fabrics suitable for high-energy and low-impact workouts that use Repreve—a fiber formed from 100 percent recycled plastic bottles—is 100 percent traceable through every part of their supply chain, from raw material to finished goods. Producing the fabric uses 45 percent less energy, 20 percent less water, and 30 percent less GHG emissions than virgin polyester, a common material used in activewear.

Burberry Launched ReBurberry Fabric

To support emerging designers, Burberry launched ReBurberry Fabric, a pilot program in partnership with the British Fashion Council (BFC), which donates leftover materials to students in need across the United Kingdom to ensure they have access to the best-quality fabrics.

Boyish Sets New Targets

Boyish Jeans, a Los Angeles-based denim brand, following United Nations Sustainable Development Goals (SDG), utilizes methods that help reduce its impact on the environment: organic cotton, Tencel, and Tencel x Refibra lyocell. Boyish pledges that all of its products will be made from plant-based fibers by 2023.

In 2020, Boyish planted 14,132 trees and saved more than 3 million days of drinking water, 29,000 miles of emissions, 591 pounds of waste from the landfill, and 187,018 sq.-ft. of pesticide-free land.

Closed: Climate-Neutral Products

Closed, the German denim brand, known for its short and sustainable supply chain and to consumers for its classic on-trend collections, launched 100 percent degradable stretch denim made with the biodegradable stretch yarn Coreva, part of manufactured low-impact dyeing processes and environmentally friendly washing techniques, resulting in saving more than 6.8 million liters of water.

Applying Sustainability Lessons Across Industries

Apparel brand Another Tomorrow lists the materials used in their creations: organic cotton, organic linen, and ethical wool. Each one links to a page that describes that material and its ramifications for sustainability.

Gap Sustainable Collections

Gap's "Generation Good" group made of organic and recycled fabrics has been manufactured using less waste, less water, lower emissions, and better materials, alongside initiatives that support its workers. Gap launched five exclusive denim styles as part of the Ellen MacArthur Foundation's Jeans Redesign challenge.

Sneaker Brand Genesis: Total Sustainability

Genesis, a German sneaker brand that has been sustainable and environmentally friendly from the very beginning, uses upcycled materials, textile innovations made from oyster shells, banana leaves, and pineapple leaves, among others. A portion of profits is donated to charitable causes and environmental organizations, including the Sea Shepherd's Mission, the Surf Rider Foundation, and One Earth-One Ocean.

A Potential Cardboard Replacement

3M developed a type of packaging that it claims can be customized to fit any object under three pounds—which accounts for about 60 percent of all items that are bought online and shipped. The Flex & Seal Shipping Roll, which doesn't require tape or filler, can reduce time spent packing, the amount of packaging materials, and the space needed to ship packages.

The roll is made out of three layers of different 3M-develop plastics: a gray, internal adhesive layer that sticks to itself, a middle cushioning layer to protect items during shipping, and a tougher outside layer that is tear and water resistant. It comes in rolls of assorted sizes, like wrapping paper.

According to 3M, Flex & Seal has an environmental benefit compared with cardboard: shipping companies would be able to fit more of this type of package in a single truck, making the supply chain more efficient and potentially reducing emissions. The U.S. Postal Service handled more than 7.3 billion packages in 2020, a billion more than in 2019.

Gap's Generation Good

Gap launched Generation Good, with garments that address issues related to water usage, sustainable materials, waste, CO_2 emissions, and workers' rights. Spanning women's, men's, kids' and baby, highlights include organic cotton T-shirts with Earth-friendly messages like "There is no Planet B" and "No more waste," and jeans and denim shorts made with recycled polyester and post-consumer recycled cotton.

All items are made using a water-saving wash process that eliminates the need for harmful PP sprays or stonewashing, and include safer dyes and finishing processes. Gap introduced five women's denim styles designed as part of the Ellen MacArthur Foundation's Jeans Redesign program. Items are 100 percent derived from natural fibers, use chemicals that abide by the ZDHC guidelines and include removable hardware for easier recycling at end-of-life. The collection is made of a combination of organic cotton, recycled cotton, and hemp.

Reinventing the Retail Bag

The Consortium to Reinvent the Retail Bag, managed by Closed Loop Partners, launched a series of tests and multi-retailer pilots to advance sustainable alternatives to the single-use plastic bag and accelerate their potential to scale. Running in CVS Health, Target, and Walmart, the pilots refined winning solutions from the consortium's global Beyond the Bag innovation challenge, evaluating multiple factors, ranging from technical feasibility to desirability, in a six-week period in Northern California.

The three founding partners CVS Health, Target, and Walmart, committed $15 million collectively to the program. Winning solutions were submitted by ChicoBag, Fill it Forward, GOATOTE, and 99Bridges. Undergoing testing were multiple reusable bag models, alongside enabling technologies that aim to help serve customers' needs, extend the useful life of retail bags, and provide visibility into the full lifecycle of a bag. Across the select stores, customers signed up to try these new solutions.

"To permanently eliminate the 100 billion single-use plastic bags currently used every year in the United States, we are working collaboratively to build retail solutions that better meet customer needs while lessening the impact on the environment," noted Kate Daly, the managing director of the Center for the Circular Economy at New York-based Closed Loop Partners. "By testing new bag innovations in-store, we will be able to iterate quickly and expand to more communities," said Daly. "Systems change do not happen overnight. These pilots are an essential step to incorporate customer and retailer feedback, improve new solutions, and explore pathways to scale."

Studies show that less than 10 percent of recovered plastic bags are recycled. Discarded plastic bags pollute beaches and waterways worldwide. From the lessons learned from the pilot programs, additional funding will be applied for to finance future product testing and refinements.

Footprint's Anti-Plastic Technology

Footprint is a materials science technology company that develops and manufactures alternative solutions to single-short-term-use plastic. Its sustainable products are designed with the entire product lifecycle in mind, and are from 100 percent bio-based, biodegradable, compostable, and recyclable fibers.

Founded in 2014 by two former Intel engineers, Footprint is head-quartered in Gilbert, Arizona, and employs more than 1,500 people. Footprint Barrier Technology™ was developed to eliminate the need for single-use plastic, based on barrier technologies that protect against oil, water, and oxygen.

Footprint says its plant-based food packaging is biodegradable, yet durable enough to perform like plastic. Its bowls, tray, straws, six-pack rings, and other packaging are being used or tested by McDonald's, Tyson Foods, Healthy Choice, and Molson Coors. The compostable materials can withstand extremes of hot and cold, and Footprint estimates its products have diverted 60 million pounds of plastic from the environment.

FABSCRAP: Addressing Commercial Textile Waste

Fabscrap is a nonprofit organization that works with fashion, interior design, and entertainment industries to recycle and reuse fabric waste. Fabscrap has saved 700,000 pounds of fabric from landfill, the CO_2-reducing equivalent of planting 77,000 trees.

Headquartered in New York City, Fabscrap diverted much unused material as possible from being landfilled or incinerated, while creating an accessible materials resource for creative communities.

The majority of what Fabscrap receives is fabric swatches. These small samples of fabric, most are six-inch squares, are usually stapled, glued, or taped to a card with information about the fabric and the fabric mill that creates it. Designers can receive many hundreds of swatches each season. They keep a few for reference before ordering sample yards but the majority is thrown away. Now they can be directed to Fabscrap. They've secured the support of about 525 companies, including J.Crew, Oscar de la Renta, Marc Jacobs, Macy's, Urban Outfitters, and Nordstrom to participate.

Nordstrom implemented an online fundraising initiative from April 19 to 30, 2021, where customers can add $1 to their Nordstrom.com purchase to support Fabscrap's work and mission. By 2025, Nordstrom aims to contribute $1 million in grants to support industry innovation for textile recycling.

Fabscrap has 6,000 volunteers, mostly based in New York, who sort the swatches for downcycling, recycling, or reuse. Of the fabrics received, 6 percent is 100 percent cotton, polyester is 2 percent, and wool is 1 percent.

Biophilica: Plant-Based Leather Alternative

Biophilica is developing Treekind™, a process that transforms green waste into a plant-based leather alternative that is compostable, recyclable, and estimated carbon neutral. The product is plastic-free (of PU, PVC, and other nonbiodegradable petrochemicals) and nontoxic, making it recyclable as green waste and home compostable.

Based in the United Kingdom, Biophilica states that leather, a $500 billion market, is the world's most environmentally destructive textile. The company says that Treekind uses less than 1 percent of the water in its production. It can be made in a range of colors and textures, suitable for typical leather products including bags, wallets, watch straps, and belts.

Biophilica received funding from Innovate UK, the Government of the Netherlands (RVO), Queen Mary's Social Venture Fund, Central Research Laboratory, Crowdfunder backers, and private sources. The firm is a member of Sustainable Accelerator and Fashion for Good.

CHAPTER 6-2

The Resale Market

A Circular Store: Madewell & thredUp

Figure 6-2.1 Circular Store in Brooklyn, sponsored by Madewell and thredUP

Photo courtesy: thredUP

thredUP, a major online resale platform, and apparel brand Madewell launched "A Circular Store," in Brooklyn, New York, featuring secondhand Madewell pieces sourced from thredUP (Figures 6-2.1 and 6-2.2). Its objective is to educate consumers to make clothes last and why keeping them in use is important. The store is a limited edition extension of the online Madewell Forever denim resale site, and marks the first time

Figure 6-2.2 Circular Store is stocked with secondhand clothes demonstrating how reuse can fight fashion waste and lead to a more circular future

Photo courtesy: thredUP

customers can shop a full assortment of previously owned Madewell, mend and tailor clothes, and pass them on responsibly.

"For too long, the fashion industry has operated with a linear, disposable model. We've designed a store to represent the future of fashion— a circular future in which retailers design for longevity, and consumers shop with resale in mind. Our hope is that visitors will leave inspired and armed with the knowledge they need to take a more sustainable approach to their wardrobes. We believe that working of retail and resale together is a necessary next step in achieving our vision of a circular future for fashion."
— Erin Wallace, VP of Integrated Marketing, thredUP

To meaningfully reduce the impact of fashion on the planet, thredUP and Madewell believe that the future of fashion must shift from a linear model to a more circular one. With the prototype Brooklyn store, consumers can change the way they buy, wear, and care for their clothes to fight fashion waste, building a model of what the future of fashion can look like for consumers and other retailers to follow.

"The fashion industry wasn't built with sustainability in mind, but with the future of our planet at stake, we collectively must do better. At Madewell, we make quality products designed for longevity and are doubling down on solutions that keep clothing in circulation as long as possible and reduce apparel waste. Partnering with thredUP creates a blueprint for other retailers to follow as to integrate circularity into their business model."

— Liz Hershfield, SVP, Head of Sustainability, Madewell

- Prices range from $10–$40 at A Circular Store.
- QR codes at each station offer a deeper dive into how to buy, wear, care, and pass on your clothes for the planet.
- The shop will present educational programming with local designers and sustainable brands, including upcycling and repair workshops with Patagonia's Worn Wear team.
- Clean out to close the loop. An estimated 36 billion apparel items end up in landfills every year. To date, thredUP has processed over 125 million articles of clothing, displacing estimated 2.2 billion pounds of CO_2.

The shop was open from July to November, 2021.

Rotating Set of Styles

As sustainability continues to become a focal point in the fashion industry, views around secondhand clothing have changed. Businesses such as Rent the Runway and The RealReal have seen success from renting and reusing model. URBN, owned by Urban Outfitters, Anthropologie, and Free People, launched their own rental platform called Nuuly.

Banana Republic's Style Passport provides the label with a new sales stream. The brand joins host of others in turning to rental to appeal to new customers, most in partnership with CaaStle.

2020 Was a Big Year for Old Clothes

Lyst's annual *Year in Fashion* report confirmed a rising interest in used clothes. "Vintage fashion" generated more than 35,000 new searches on Lyst, while entries for secondhand-related keywords increased 104 percent. During the spring 2021 collections, more designers said they'd used leftover fabrics from past collections, and in some cases (like Marine Serre), they spliced up vintage garments to create new ones. Coach's spring 2021 collection was styled with items from seasons past to make a statement about longevity, and there were handbags upcycled from archival 70s purses and recycled plastic.

Levi's website, Levi's Secondhand, sells exclusively vintage and secondhand jeans. Gucci launched a major collaboration with The RealReal. Miu will debut a collection of 80 upcycled holiday pieces in its 57th Street Store, each made from vintage items from the 30s to the '70s.

Display Copy magazine features only secondhand and vintage fashion. thredUp predicts the resale market will hit $64 billion by 2024, and that the online secondhand market will grow 69 percent by 2021. Farfetch saw such a positive response to its luxury handbag resale service, Second Life, in the United Kingdom that it launched a United States.

Gem, a search engine for vintage and secondhand fashion, has indexed 30 million items across the Internet. Gem works if the user knows precisely what they are looking for to find vintage or secondhand alternatives to items normally purchased new.

How Sustainable Is Secondhand?

Resale retailer Poshmark, ended its first day of trading in January 2021, with a valuation of $7.4 billion. Poshmark helps protect users from fraud. There are now 30 million active users on the site. It's one of a growing number of online Resale companies that have popped up over the last decade including thredUp, Depop, Rebag, and TheRealReal. The market is worth now $28 billion and is poised to hit $64 billion by 2024, a growth rate that's 25 times faster than the rest of the retail industry.

Resale marketplaces are thriving, but the vast majority of Americans still prefer to buy new products. There's no evidence that people are replacing their new purchases with secondhand ones. They're just buying more of both. The apparel industry has been growing exponentially from 50 billion garments in 2000 to more than 100 billion in 2015. The pandemic pummeled the fashion sector, but it still grew by about 3 percent.

The U.S. secondhand clothing market is projected to more than triple in value in the next 10 years—from $28 billion in 2019 to $80 billion in 2029—in a U.S. market currently worth $379 billion in 2020. In 2019, secondhand clothing expanded 21 times faster than conventional apparel retail did.

Researchers who study clothing consumption and sustainability think the secondhand clothing trend has the potential to reshape the fashion industry and mitigate the industry's detrimental environmental impact on the planet.

The secondhand clothing market is composed of two major categories—thrift stores and resale platforms. It's the latter that has largely fueled the recent boom. Thanks to growing consumer demand and new digital platforms like Tradesy and Poshmark that facilitate peer-to-peer exchange of everyday clothing, the digital resale market is quickly becoming the next big thing in the fashion industry.

Online Thrifting

Consumers want eco-friendly retail practices: 70 percent of all consumers agree that addressing climate change is more important now than ever. Nearly 2.5× more consumers plan to shift their spend to sustainable brands from 18 percent in 2018 to 43 percent in 2019. Eco-brands like Patagonia and Allbirds are churning up an estimated 57 percent more interest on thredUP since COVID-19.

Re-Loved Clothing

Asda's Re-Loved clothing trial followed a sustainable fashion collection in its stores across the United Kingdom as the demand for eco-friendly fashion grows. Asda, which has estimated that £140 million worth of clothing in the United Kingdom goes to landfill each year, has clothing recycling points in almost 500 of its stores.

Durable Goods for Fashion Resale

A year with a pandemic prompted many Americans to realize they have a lot of clothes. It made sense to sell some items.

According to the 2020 Resale Report from online fashion resale marketplace thredUP and Global Data, resale grew 25 times faster than retail in 2019, and 70 percent of surveyed consumers are now open to buying secondhand. Sixty-four million consumers bought secondhand products in 2019.

More than half of all consumers (55 percent) have bought secondhand clothes, according to Cotton Council International (CCI) and Cotton Incorporated 2020 Global Durability Study. The Environmental Protection Agency (EPA) estimates 17 million tons of textile waste were generated in 2018. Of that, 11.3 million tons went to landfills.

Goodwill's Appeal

Nonprofit Goodwill operates 3,000 shops, along with its online store which in early 2021 surpassed $1 billion in sales. Goodwill is part of a network of more than 25,000 resale, consignment and not-for-profit stores in the United States, according to the National Association of Resale and Thrift Shops (NARTS).

Goat: Merging Sneaker Resale and Retail

Goat is an e-commerce destination for young, cool consumers to shop retail and resale at once across luxury, streetwear, and sneakers. Some 80 percent of Goat's members are either Gen Z or millennial. Goat has partnered with 350 brands since launching apparel in 2019.

The Renewal System

The Renewal System takes discarded apparel and textiles and turns them into renewed products or upcycled materials. The company's first factory is located in Cascade Locks, Oregon in 2016, with a second factory opened in Amsterdam in 2019. Their process was developed to bridge gaps, connect systems, and mobilize leadership to make existing linear manufacturing practices circular. It is a collaborative process that relies on progressive brand partners committed to sustainability. Products are sorted, cleaned, and repaired to brand-specific online, store front, or shared market.

Urban Outfitters Launches Online Thrift Store

Urban Outfitters, through its URBN division, launched online resale store Nuuly Thrift, as the company joins the growing secondhand sale trend fueled by younger consumers' concerns over sustainability and repeating outfits.

Urban Outfitters CEO Richard Hayne said, "With the launch of Nuuly Thrift, we're excited for URBN to capitalize on shifting customer behavior and gain market share in the rapidly expanding online resale market." Three-quarters of URBN customers have bought or sold second-hand items in the last year, according to the company.

Users can resell products from any brand, not just URBN brands, and once someone buys an item, the seller can either get money transferred directly to their bank account or redeem the earnings for Nuuly Cash, which is worth 10 percent more on the thrifting platform and with any URBN brand.

Urban Outfitters hopes that the arrangement creates a "cycle of buying and selling within the company's brands." The system also is one way to try to prevent Urban from cannibalizing sales of new items from its other brands by providing the option for the Nuuly Cash to be spent directly on Urban products.

REI: Resale and Rental Grow Customer Base

Outdoor outfitters REI is achieving success with selling its used products online by developing a personalized approach to matching inventory of gear and clothing to individual customers' needs. REI, headquartered near Seattle, is the nation's largest consumer co-op, with a membership of more than 20 million.

REI has 165 locations in 39 states and the District of Columbia. REI is operating a pilot of two standalone used gear pop-up stores located near

Manhattan Beach, California, and Conshohocken, Pennsylvania, stocked with high-quality used outdoor gear and apparel.

"It's not like used businesses or re-commerce businesses are necessarily new," said Ken Voeller, manager of re-commerce and new business development. "I think what's new is, technology is improving to a degree that it starts to make a lot of sense for businesses to offer used products at lower price point categories, and the outdoor industry is certainly ripe for that."

REI doesn't resell everything, though. Voeller said, "The company determines which items to take back based on consumer demand, which means a lot of tents, sleeping bags and other high-demand items for new entrants looking to try out an activity."

Another benefit of offering used gear to customers is encouraging them to come back for full-price products later. "We are noticing that start to happen," Voeller said. "We see our members who are purchasing used items, they'll often turn to 'used' to get into an outdoor activity."

REI limits used gear sales to members at the company's garage sales. As it opens physical locations that sell only used gear, buying remains reserved for members.

REI initiated a trade-in program, giving members more ways to buy and share gently used outdoor gear and apparel and keeping high-quality products rotating through the co-op community at accessible price points. The company reported that its online business was up nearly 100 percent in 2020 compared to 2019.

In many communities where REI has a presence, professionally trained instructors host beginner-to advanced-level classes and workshops on a wide range of activities. REI invests millions annually in hundreds of local and national nonprofits that create access to—and steward—the outdoor places.

Rebag's Resale Kiosk

Rebag, a luxury retailer, has opened a 2,100-sq.-ft. store in Greenwich, Connecticut, with a self-service vending machine.

Rebag's Clair Concierge, a self-service kiosk, allows customers to receive an instant price quote on the item they are selling in three steps via the Clair by Rebag software suite. Launched in 2019, Clair by Rebag includes 7 years' worth of data and millions of image references that instantly determine the resale value of more than 15,000 styles.

Rebag Greenwich will house designer styles from its 20,000-plus inventory, including bags, watches, jewelry, and accessories.

Investing in Resale Platforms

Grailed, the curated menswear resale platform offering labels from Supreme to Saint Laurent, is attracting support from upscale brands and financial sources, led by Goat Group. It is among the bigger players in streetwear resale with a gross merchandise value of $2 billion.

Goat mixes stocked inventory from brands with resold items from 600,000 approved sellers, operating with the look and feel of an e-tailer. Its focus is mixing retail with resale is mostly on sneakers and increasingly on clothing. Grailed is independently run. Eddy Lu, co-founder and CEO of Goat Group, said, "Grailed and Goat share a common approach, based on authenticity, trust, and a highly curated perspective on style."

"From a competitive standpoint, even primary retailers and e-tailers are looking to tap the resale opportunity," says Fabio Colacchio, partner at consultancy Bain & Company. "In China, one of the most dynamic luxury markets, we see a lot of new platforms that are coming up and gaining visibility including Alibaba-owned resale platform Idle Fish."

Rebelstork at The Bay

Canada's The Bay is entering the baby gear resale market through a partnership with Canadian startup Rebelstork Corp. The partnership represents North America's first managed marketplace for the resale of overstock, open box, and quality used baby gear. Rebelstork's platform gives consumers a way to buy and upcycle baby products to others, realize some value from their initial investment, and extend the lifespan of short-term use products.

While Hudson's Bay operates 86 full-line department stores, The Bay operates the retailer's online marketplace. Accepted products will be dated no earlier than 2017 and must be clean, operate well, and be free of stains and fabric tears. Strollers must have working brakes, functioning safety straps, and opens and closes correctly. Items that are older than four years will be donated to charity. The Toronto-based startup now has 12 full-time employees with drop-off depots in Ontario and British Columbia, doorstep pick up in Toronto and Vancouver, and countrywide shipping. Sellers can get up to 80 percent of the sale price.

"Babies are expensive: parents can spend upwards of $10,000–$14,000 on their baby every year and many parents are only beginning to realize the significance that buying second hand or reselling gently used gear can have on the environment and on their finances," Emily Hosie, Rebelstork's founder and CEO, said. "Our mission is to help families declutter, save and make money, and ultimately contribute to the circular economy."

Glossary

B Corporation: A type of certification that measures a company's triple bottom line, looking at workers, customers, suppliers, community, and the environment, and successfully meeting established criteria.

Biodegradable: Biodegradable clothes and dyes break down naturally and decompose after they've been discarded. Linen, hemp, bamboo, and cotton are examples. All materials eventually break down, but for synthetic fabrics, this can take centuries.

Carbon neutrality: Carbon neutrality is a state of net-zero carbon dioxide emissions by its removal in product manufacturing or distribution operations.

Circular fashion: Circularity is about keeping garments in circulation for as long as possible. It takes all parts of the fashion lifecycle into consideration—from design and sourcing to production, transportation, storage, marketing and sale, usage, and end-of-life.

Deadstock fabric: Leftover fabric from fashion houses that are excess stock from overestimation of their needs, samples, or pieces from factory manufacturing. Ethical reuse of deadstock fabrics creates products for resale and saves them from going to landfill.

Eco-friendly/environmentally friendly/environmentally conscious/green: Broad buzzwords directed to bring consumer attention to products promoting sustainability.

Ethical fashion: While often used interchangeably with sustainability, ethical fashion focuses more on what is considered "morally right," involving people, animals, and the planet. This includes safe working conditions and the payment of living wages for workers, how materials are sourced, and their environmental impact.

Fabric made from recycled plastics: The recycling of plastic involves a chemical transformation process that turns it into recycled polyester that can be used to produce apparel and other products.

Fair working conditions: This covers an employee's working environment, including fair remuneration, safe working spaces, capped working hours, paid overtime, and legal rights.

Living wage: A living wage is payment received for a standard work week that covers a decent standard of living for the worker and their family. This includes food, housing, health care, clothing, transportation, utilities, essentials, and emergency savings.

Minimum wage: The lowest amount of compensation that an employer is legally allowed to pay an employee in a particular locale.

Pre-loved/secondhand: A piece of clothing that has previously been owned or worn by someone else; not a new item.

Regenerative: Regenerative agriculture refers to farming practices that rebuild soil organic matter and restore degraded soil biodiversity, essentially improving land used for harvesting crops or other raw material production.

Right to unionize/collective bargaining: Also known as freedom of association, unionizing is a way that employees and employers can reach an agreement on issues affecting the workplace. Employees are allowed to join a union and bargain collectively for fair pay and fair conditions.

Slow fashion: Created in direct opposition to fast fashion, slow fashion champions slower production and a reduction in consumption. It focuses on quality rather than quantity, emphasizing long-lasting, timeless apparel.

Sustainable collection/sustainable line: A range of garments or accessories from a brand that features one, or more, elements of sustainability.

This includes using organic materials, recycled plastic, or environmentally friendly packaging and other elements.

Sustainable fashion: The term is subjective, typically linked to natural, environmental resources. The definition has expanded to include the longevity of social and economic systems as well.

Upcycled: The modification of a product so it is transformed into something new. This is accomplished through altering hemlines, adding new elements, combining multiple items, repairing and more. It promotes circularity as it keeps a product in use for a longer time.

Vegan: Fashion made without animal-derived products, and free from materials such as leather, wool, fur, down, and silk.

Vintage: Generally refers to an item that is at least 20 years old, and has the characteristics of the era from which it was most popular.

Zero waste: Zero waste fashion uses existing materials to their full capacity, including fabric offcuts and scraps to fashion into other items, and offering repair or closed-loop services.

References

Section 1

ALDO. www.aldogroup.com/international-stores: www.prnewswire.com/news-releases/aldo-and-call-it-spring-will-completely-eliminate-single-use-shopping-bags

Amazon. *The Amazon Blog: dayone*; Forbes: "Amazon's Big Opportunity: Transparency is Sustainability," April 02, 2018; Bloomberg Green, "Amazon to Start $2 billion Fund to Back Climate Change," June 23, 2020; Amazon website.

Ecoalf. Ecoalf website.

Everlane. Insights by Stanford Business, February 11, 2020; Fastcompany.com March/April 2018

Gabriela Hearst. Gabriela Hearst website.

IKEA. *Interior Design*, October 23, 2020; Reuters, October 30, 2020.

National Retail Federation. NRF website.

Nestlé. Adapted from, "Climate Change Laggards Put the Planet—and Their Businesses—at Risk;" Nestlé website; Bloomberg Green, Jan. 21, 2021.

Selfridges & Co. Selfridges & Co. websites.

Target. Excerpted from *Target 2019 Corporate Responsibility Report4:* "The Future at Heart: A Message to Our Stakeholders from Brian Cornell, Chairman and CEO, Target Corporation, Minneapolis." *Chain Store Age,* Nov. 18, 2019, *"Target in energy milestone—ahead of schedule."*

Tiffany & Co. Coral reef: Yen-Yi Lee; Tiffany Save The Wild brooches, Courtesy, Tiffany & Co. Tiffany & Co. press releases and website.

UN Alliance for Sustainable Fashion. July 14, 2021.

United Nation Environment. United Nations Environment Programme.

Walmart. *Walmart 2020 Environmental, Social and Governmental Report*; Walmart Sustainable Packaging Playbook.

Section 2

Allbirds. Adapted from Inc.com, Allbirds.com

B. Corp. B Corporation website. Adapted from McMillanDoolittle E-mail, "Using Business as a Source for Good: Banking on B Corps," by Rachel Stern, August 10, 2020.

Baggit. Text, excerpts from *Baggit It All: The inspirational story of an entrepreneur who built a 100-core company with the power of intent and love.* By Nina Lekhi. Jaico Publishing House, Mumbai, 2017.

BestBuy. *Best Buy 2019,* 2020 *and 2021 Best Buy Corporate Responsibility and Sustainability Reports* and Best Buy website.

Cacau Show. SUAFranquia; *Candy Industry*, June, 2019; Cacau Show website.

Eileen Fisher. Eileen Fisher website; *Vogue Runway,* April 22, 2020, by Steff Yotka; *Stores*, Jan, 2019; Eileen Fisher website.

Ellen MacArthur Foundation. Adapted from *ellenmacarthurfoundation.org, sourcingjournal.com.*

Li & Fung. Li & Fung website; *The Robin Report*, August 05, 2019.

ThredUp. Adapted from: nrf.com, fortune.com, retaildive.com; thredUp website.

United By Blue. *United By Blue 2019 Impact Report.*

Section 3

Galeries Lafayette. Adapted from: galerieslafayette.com.

Kering. Source: Kering website: *Kering Sustainability: Biodiversity Strategy;* Kering, logo library

Kingsmen Creative Ltd. Data provided by Kingsmen Creatives Ltd.

Kohl's. Kohl's website documents.

Kroger. Source: *2020 Kroger Environmental, Social and Governance Report.*

Section 3 Introduction. *The Robin Report*, January 13, 2021 "That was the Year that Was…and Wasn't." *The 2021 Sustainability Trends Report*, Rocky Mountain Institute. By Kavita Kumar, *Star Tribune*, August 05, 2021.

Sponsored Education. Kering press release, November 18, 2020. *Fast Company*, July 23, 2021.

Stella McCartney. Sources: Stella McCartney, *ECO IMPACT REPORT 2020.*

Section 4

Closed Loop Partners. Text supplied by Closed Loop Partners. All numbers represent the firm's impact metrics as of the end of 2019, as seen in the firm's 2019 Impact Report.

David Jones. David Jones website.

Fashion for Good. Fashion for Good website.

Harrod's. *Retail Gazette:* Retail Gazette Loves Harrods Fashion Re-Told Charity Pop-up, May 08, 2019; *ES Insider:* Harrods Fashion Re-Told Pop Up is a Charitable Way to Pick Up Vintage Designer Threads This Summer, May 02, 2019; *Campaign:* Harrods Brings Back Fashion Re-Told Charity Pop Up, May 19, 2019.

Shanghai Zhitao Cultural Innovation Co. Data and images supplied by Shanghai Zhitao Cultural Innovation Co., Ltd.

Section 5

5-1 Services. Fashion Revolution, January 27, 2021.
5-2 Books and References. Condé Nast Communications Team, May 20, 2020
5-3 Reports. Adapted from Good Housekeeping Institute. *Sourcing Journal.*

Section 6

Section 6. Introduction. FashionUnited, March, 2021.
6-1 Technology and Inventions. *Sourcing Journal,* March 23, 2021. Sources: FashionUnited, September 09, 2021; Biophilica website.
6-2 The Resale Market. REI Newsroom, October 20, 2020. *Vogue Business,* September 16, 2021.

Glossary

Refinery 29; Condé Nast Communications Team

About the Authors

Ken Nisch, AIA
Chairman, JGA, Inc.
As the Chairman of JGA, Ken Nisch has worked with brands around the world developing their branded consumer retail environments and consumer image and visual strategies, including Whole Foods, Warner Bros., Sundance, El Palacio de Hierro, and Signet. His consumer knowledge and entrepreneurial insights have been applied to the strategic image positioning for many retail operators, manufacturers, and brand marketers in product presentation, travel, wellness and lifestyle markets for more than 40 years.

He was inducted into Shop Association's Hall of Fame and the Retail Design Institute Legion of Honor for his achievements in the field of retail design. He was named as a "Retail Luminary" by *Design: Retail*, and received the Retail Leadership Award at the Asia Retail Congress in Mumbai.

Ken serves on the advisory boards for industry publications and global associations and as a board director to private and public retail companies. He has presented at leading design/retail conferences including the National Retail Federation Big Show, GlobalShop, EuroShop, the International Retail Design Conference, LATAM Retail Show, and Luxury Marketing Council.

He received his degree in Architecture from the University of Cincinnati and is a member of the American Institute of Architects.

Vilma Barr

Collection Editor, Business Expert Press

Vilma Barr's career as a writer chron-
icling the retail industry ranges from
contributing to trade and professional
publications to co-authoring books
on store design. Periodicals published
in the U.S. and overseas that have
carried her features include *Design
Retail, Stores+Shops, Mondo*arc* and
New Zealand Retail. She is also a cor-
respondent for the lighting journal,
ArchitecturalSSL.

She has written, co-authored, or edited 18 books on retailing and the
built environment, such as *Designing to Sell: A Complete Guide to Retail
Store Planning & Design (first and second editions); Stores, Promotional
Strategies for Design and Construction Firms; Building Type Basics for Retail
and Mixed-Use Facilities; The Illustrated Room: 20th Century Interior
Design Rendering:* and *The Reedy Memorial Lecture Series in Photography
at RIT.*

For Business Expert Press, she serves as the contributing Collection
Editor for the Business Career Development group of books. Her responsibilities include developing titles with potential authors, assisting with
content creation, and evaluating proposals and completed manuscripts.

Vilma received a BS in Business Management from Drexel Uni-
versity, Philadelphia, and completed a joint graduate program at the
Massachusetts Institute of Technology in Organizational Studies and
Urban Studies and Planning.

She is a member of the Union League of Philadelphia; Retail Design
Institute (media member); International Association of Lighting Designers (media member); and The Wayne (Pa.) Oratorio Society.

Index

OTHER TITLES IN THE ENVIRONMENTAL AND SOCIAL SUSTAINABILITY FOR BUSINESS ADVANTAGE COLLECTION

Robert Sroufe, Duquesne University, Editor

- *Bringing Sustainability to the Ground Level* by Susan Gilbertz and Damon Hall
- *People, Planet, Profit* by Kit Oung
- *Handbook of Sustainable Development* by Radha R. Sharma
- *Community Engagement and Investment* by Alan S. Gutterman
- *Sustainability Standards and Instruments* by Alan S. Gutterman
- *Sustainability Reporting and Communications* by Alan S. Gutterman
- *Strategic Planning for Sustainability* by Alan S. Gutterman
- *Sustainability Leader in a Green Business Era* by Amr E. Sukkar
- *Managing Sustainability* by John Friedman
- *Human Resource Management for Organizational Sustainability* by Radha R. Sharma

Concise and Applied Business Books

The Collection listed above is one of 30 business subject collections that Business Expert Press has grown to make BEP a premiere publisher of print and digital books. Our concise and applied books are for...

- Professionals and Practitioners
- Faculty who adopt our books for courses
- Librarians who know that BEP's Digital Libraries are a unique way to offer students ebooks to download, not restricted with any digital rights management
- Executive Training Course Leaders
- Business Seminar Organizers

Business Expert Press books are for anyone who needs to dig deeper on business ideas, goals, and solutions to everyday problems. Whether one print book, one ebook, or buying a digital library of 110 ebooks, we remain the affordable and smart way to be business smart. For more information, please visit www.businessexpertpress.com, or contact sales@businessexpertpress.com.